ARCO

Everything you need to score high on

AP
EUROPEAN
HISTORY

Joan U. Levy, Ph.D.
Norman Levy, Ph.D.
Richard Weisberg, M.S.

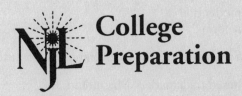

College
Preparation

MACMILLAN • USA

Previous editions of this book were published under the title
AP Exam in European History.

Third Edition

Macmillan General Reference
1633 Broadway
New York, NY 10019-6785

An Arco book. Arco is a registered trademark of Simon & Schuster, Inc.

MACMILLAN is a registered trademark of Macmillan, Inc.

Library of Congress Number: 97-070063

ISBN: 0-02-861716-9

Manufactured in the United States of America

1 2 3 4 5 6 7 8 9 10

To Joshua Seth and Jessica Dawn,
two of the best reasons
for writing this book.

Table of Contents

About the Authors

JOAN U. LEVY, Ph.D.

B.A., City College of New York, M.S. in Guidance and Counseling, Fordham University, Ph.D. in Behavioral Science. Director of NJL College Preparation and Learning Center.

NORMAN LEVY, Ph.D.

B.E., City College of New York, M.S. in Operations Research, New York University, Ph.D. in Educational Administration. Executive Director of NJL College Preparation and Learning Center, a center which instructs students in all subject areas, provides remediation, and does test preparation for college entrance examinations and graduate entrance examinations. In addition, NJL College Preparation works with students in college guidance, college search, and college applications.

Both authors have written the following other works published by Arco:

American College Testing Program (ACT)
CHSPE—California High School Proficiency Examination
College Admissions: A Handbook for Students and Parents
Mechanical Aptitude and Spatial Relations Tests
Preparation for the PSAT/NMSQT—Preliminary Scholastic Aptitude
 Test/National Merit Scholarship Qualifying Test

RICHARD WEISBERG, M.A., M.S.

Assistant Principal, Department of Social Studies, New York City Board of Education. Twenty-four years experience teaching and supervision.

Acknowledgments

A book of this magnitude is not merely the work of the authors. Writers rely heavily on the support and encouragement of colleagues and the input of other professionals and students.

The authors would like to thank the following people: the staff and students of NJL College Preparation who gave impetus to the work; and Linda Bernbach and the Arco editorial staff for their unfailing assistance.

INTRODUCTION

What Is the Advanced Placement (AP)* Program?

The Advanced Placement (AP) program is a way for high school students to study college-level material and receive college credit for their efforts. It is administered by the College Board which contracts with the Educational Testing Service (ETS) for the Advanced Placement examinations. The Advanced Placement Program is a way for stronger students to study courses appropriate to their abilities and interests and be fairly certain that they will not have to repeat these courses on the college level. Students are selected for Advanced Placement courses on the basis of a number of criteria determined by their high school. These criteria may include the following:

- Scholastic record
- Interview and acceptance by the teacher
- Score on nationally normed examinations like PSAT/NMSQT
- Parental approval
- Volunteer record

---

* Advanced Placement Program is a registered trademark of the College Entrance Examination Board

In Which Courses Are Advanced Placement Credits Offered?

The AP program now exists for the following courses:

ART	History	
	Studio	General
		Drawing
COMPUTER SCIENCE	A	
	AB	
ECONOMICS	Microeconomics	
	Macroeconomics	
ENGLISH	Language and Composition	
	Literature and Composition	
GOVERNMENT and POLITICS	Comparative	
	United States	
HISTORY	European	
	United States	
LANGUAGE	French	Language Level 3
		Literature Level 3
	German Language Level 3	
	Latin	Virgil
		Catullus–Horace
	Spanish	Language Level 3
		Literature Level 3
MATHEMATICS	Calculus AB	
	Calculus BC	
MUSIC	Listening and Literature	
	Theory	
SCIENCE	Biology	
	Chemistry	
	Physics	B
		C—Mechanics
		C—Electricity and Magnetism
	Psychology	

In any school year, you may take as many AP exams as you want with certain limitations. You may take one of the following, but not two exams in one subject:

- Computer Science A *or* Computer Science AB
- English Language and Composition *or* English Literature and Compositon
- Calculus AB *or* Calculus BC
- Physics B *or* Physics C
- Studio Art (Drawing Portfolio *or* General Portfolio)

What Is an AP Examination Like?

Each year in early May, AP examinations are given. Most students can take the exams in their own schools.

Each AP examination is a comprehensive evaluation of the subject matter. It may consist of objective questions, essays, data-based questions, and portfolio evaluations. Objective questions require you to choose the correct response from several choices. Free-response questions (including essays and data-based questions) require you to arrange your knowledge and write clear, well-organized answers.

How Are AP Examinations Scored and Reported?

AP examinations are scored on a five-point scale:

Grade	Verbal Equivalent
5	Extremely well-qualified
4	Well-qualified
3	Qualified
2	Possibly qualified
1	No recommendation

Colleges that accept Advanced Placement courses usually accept grades of 3 or better. In order to earn a part score that is equivalent to a total grade of 3, you must answer approximately fifty to sixty percent of the multiple-choice questions correctly.

AP grade reports, together with candidate rosters and interpretive information, are sent to the colleges chosen by the candidates in July. Transcripts can later be sent to other colleges for a $6.00 fee. Grade reports are only sent to colleges you have designated. Grades are also sent to the students and to their high schools. In August, schools receive their AP Teacher Reports comparing their pupils' performance to that of the total candidate group on each examination. If you wish to question your exam results, the multiple-choice section of an exam can be rescored and part scores re-added by hand for a $10 fee for up to one year after the exam administration.

What AP Dates Should I be Aware of?

February	Deadline for finding the local schools that administer AP Examinations
March	Schools hand in Examination and Special Services Order Forms and Fee Reduction Request Forms
April	Intensive review for Exams
Early May Mid-May	Examination Weeks
June	June 15—Deadline for receipt of letters asking for changes in reporting grades to colleges
July	AP Grade Reports are given to selected colleges, to the student and to the high school

What Are the Benefits of the Advanced Placement Program?

The AP program offers a number of benefits to its participant students:

1. It allows high school students to master more challenging coursework in areas of interest and proficiency. It also gives students time to explore college subject areas while still in high school.

2. It permits students to take college-level courses and, if they do well on the AP examination and attend a participating university or college, receive course credit for their work.

3. It provides tuition savings for students. They may receive up to a year of credit for three or more qualifying AP grades.

4. Studies have shown that qualified candidates go on to complete undergraduate programs of real strength, generally achieving records superior to those obtained by students whose basic college courses were taken at the college level.

5. It opens eligibility for honors and other special programs to students who have received AP recognition.

What Are the Fees for AP Examinations?

The current fee for each examination is $62.00. In one year you may take as many AP examinations as you choose with certain limitations. You may take only one examination from each of the following five subject areas:

- Computer Science (A *or* AB)
- English (Language and Composition *or* Literature and Composition)
- Mathematics (Calculus AB *or* Calculus BC)
- Physics (B)
- Studio Art (General *or* Drawing)

You may take either or both examinations from the following four subject areas for one fee:

- Physics C (Mechanics *and/or* Electricity and Magnetism)
- Latin (Virgil *and/or* Catullus – Horace)
- Government and Politics (Comparative *and/or* American)
- Economics (Microeconomics *and/or* Macroeconomics)

You may take either or both examinations from the following five subject areas, but you must pay a separate fee for each:

- Spanish (Language *and/or* Literature)
- French (Language *and/or* Literature)
- History (European *and/or* American)
- Music (Listening and Literature *and/or* Theory)
- Art (History *and/or* Studio Art)

Fees are submitted to the AP Coordinator of the school giving the examination, according to the instructions that accompany the Order Forms.

For students with financial need, a reduced fee of $41.00 per test is available.

Once an examination is begun, you are ineligible for a refund of the $62.00 fee. However, if the examination is not begun, you may request a refund from the AP Coordinator.

Are Special Arrangements Available to Handicapped Students?

If testing modifications are necessary, you should notify the AP Coordinator before February 15 of the school year in which you are taking the exam. Braille or photoenlarged examinations are available to the visually handicapped. Other special testing arrangements are also possible. If the handicap does not require special accommodations, however, it is preferable to test under normal conditions at the regular administration.

How Can the Grades Be Used?

There are a number of different approaches to the AP score, depending on the college that you plan to attend:

- No credit is given.
- No credit is given. Instead, advanced standing is given and you must take a more advanced course in the department.
- Credit is given in the major field of the examination, such as history.
- Credit is given for the course; you must now take a more advanced course in the department.
- Credit is given. You must pay for the credit hours obtained.
- Credit is given for only one introductory course in the major.
- Credit is given. The credits count towards the total needed for graduation.
- Credit is given for three or four AP scores. You now have sophomore standing, skipping freshman year and starting college as a sophomore.

If your AP score is too low to allow college credit, you may wish to take a College-Level Examination Program (CLEP) in European History. This exam, too, can result in college credits.

WHAT TO EXPECT

What Is the Format of the AP European History Exam?

The AP European History examination is a three-hour test broken down as follows:

Type of Question	Number of Questions	Time Allotted
Multiple-choice	80	55 minutes
Free-response	3	130 minutes
Reading time		15 minutes
Document-based essay		45 minutes
Thematic essay		70 minutes

MULTIPLE-CHOICE SECTION

The multiple-choice section consists of 80 questions testing the student's knowledge of European history from the Renaissance to 1970. Approximately half the questions concern the period of 1450 to 1789; the other half address the period from 1789 to 1970. Categories of questions include the following:

Social/economic issues	30–40 percent of the test
Political/diplomatic issues	35–45 percent of the test
Cultural/intellectual issues	20–30 percent of the test

FREE-RESPONSE SECTION

The free-response section starts with a compulsory 15-minute reading period followed by three free-response essays. Part A is a document-based essay question (DBQ), in which you provide an analysis based on your knowledge of European history together with the documents presented. In Part B you must answer two thematic essay questions in 70 minutes. You will choose one essay from two groups of three essays.

How Is the Examination Graded?

Grading of the exam is as follows:

Multiple-choice questions	50 percent of the grade
Document-based essay question	22.5 percent of the grade
Thematic essay questions	27.5 percent of the grade

The AP European History examination is scored on a five-point scale as follows:

5—Extremely well-qualified

4—Well-qualified

3—Qualified

2—Possibly qualified

1—No recommendation

Should I Guess on AP Examination Multiple-choice Questions?

Your score on the multiple-choice sections of AP examinations is based on the number of questions you answer correctly minus a fraction of the number you answer incorrectly. Thus with questions that have five answer choices, one-quarter of a point is subtracted for each incorrect answer. For questions with four answer choices, one-third of a point is subtracted for each incorrect answer.

If you can eliminate one or more of the answer choices, it is desirable to guess. If not, it is better to omit the question.

How Do I Prepare Myself for the Test?

STUDY THE TEXTBOOK!

Notice that we said *study*, not *read*. The two terms are NOT interchangeable. Although it is hoped that the material that you read will enthrall you, it is foolish to conclude that the text will require no more effort than reading an interesting story or watching a good movie. History does not have nice neat plot lines like novels. The factors that influence the events of any era interact in complicated ways. Do not treat the text as a "light read."

Try to focus on the key events or ideas that are emphasized in the chapter assigned. Since key ideas often appear in the title of the chapter or in bold heads within the text, they should not be difficult to find. For example, "The Russian Campaign and Final Defeat" focuses on the invasion of Russia and the consequences of that invasion (for either Napoleon or Hitler).

Another example: " Locke and the Rise of Republicanism," considers Locke's theory of government (Social Contract) and its impact on politics.

Once the key point or points of the chapter are determined, the next step is to put that centerpiece in its proper setting. Train yourself to think about how this particular issue came about and how this key idea or event changed subsequent events. Without seeing an event in context, the fact, no matter how important it may be, is meaningless.

For example, Peter the Great's victory over Charles of Sweden in the Battle of Poltava was important in determining future developments in northeastern European politics. Nevertheless, the fact itself is useless without understanding why Charles was in Russia, why he was a threat, and what his defeat meant to the balance of power in the area.

One way of systematizing the information is to make a kind of flowchart of events and how they relate to each other. An example of how one chart might look for World War I is presented below:

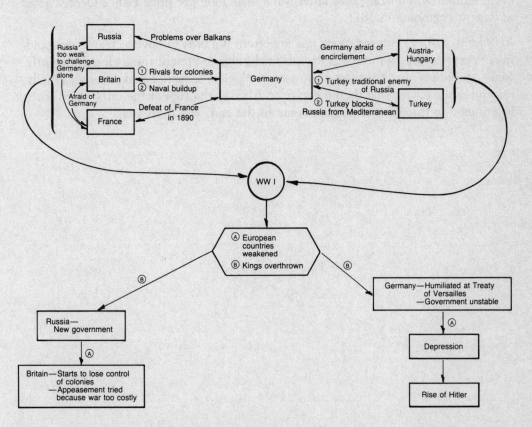

Notice that events and concepts flow both into and out of the key event—World War I.

PAY ATTENTION TO THE LECTURES!

This means not only taking notes in class but also *studying* those notes. An effective way to study is to transfer notes taken in class to a notebook kept at home. Rather than merely copying the notes, however, read them, digest the information, and then write a *condensed* version in your notebook. This takes a little longer, but the time saved on cramming later on will be reduced.

WRITING THE ESSAYS

Writing essays is a key part of the AP exams, and of every AP course, which is consistent with the idea that events or thoughts in isolation are next to useless. As noted on the preceding page, try to think about how the pieces "came together" to cause a particular event, and also what impact this event had on subsequent events. It is extremely difficult to write a solid essay on any moment of historical importance without describing the events that led up to that moment and the consequences that followed. Otherwise, the death of an archduke in a dusty town called Sarajevo in 1914 would be categorized with the passing of insane George III in 1820. The first event ignited World War I; the latter was a mere footnote since Prince George acted as Regent beginning in 1811.

In order to write a coherent essay, it is important not only to have a clear understanding of events and their meanings, but also to be able to present these ideas coherently. Make an outline! For the most part, a chronological sequence makes sense. Finally, remember the advice that the king gave to Alice at the trial of the tarts: Start at the beginning, go through the middle, come to the end, and then stop!

THE ESSAY

Nothing strikes fear in the hearts of most high school students as much as writing an essay, especially one that constitutes a good part of the grade on an important exam. However, essay writing does not have to be frightening nor terribly difficult.

The key to writing a good essay is *organization*. The two essays on the AP European History examination are persuasive essays. They are meant to espouse a point of view and give evidence to support that point of view. Therefore, there are certain techniques in writing the essays.

Steps in Writing a Persuasive Essay

1. PREPARE AN OUTLINE

Some students believe that an outline wastes valuable test time on an AP exam. On the contrary, an outline can actually save you time by organizing your thoughts in an orderly fashion before you begin to write your essay.

The outline functions as a rough guide to your presentation of material. It helps you include relevant material in appropriate places and provide a cogent, well-presented argument. The outline should be organized loosely as follows:

I. **Introduction**

    A. Introduce the topic.

    B. Give a short history, if appropriate.

    C. State the thesis (your point of view in the argument). The thesis is *essential* in a good persuasive essay.

II. **Body**

    A. Provide specific examples to suport the thesis.

    B. Use documentary evidence, if applicable.

    C. Utilize positive as well as negative verification for the argument. Show not only why this thesis is plausible, but why other interpretations are not.

III. **Conclusion**

    A. Summarize the information.

    B. Restate the thesis.

The preceding outline can help in planning the paragraphs, in putting evidence in logical or chronological order, and in mapping out the strategy that will be most convincing.

2. WRITE THE ESSAY

Once the outline is written, the actual essay writing should be fairly straightforward. You should have the informaton and should know where you want to put each piece of supporting evidence. The thesis should be clear and the examples, documentation, and/or arguments should follow in logical order.

Each discrete example belongs in its own paragraph; transitional words—*in addition, another, however, furthermore, moreover, therefore, thus, consequently, hence,* etc.—can be used to make one paragraph flow into the next one.

3. PROOFREAD THE ESSAY

This is a *crucial* step in writing a good essay. Make sure to take the time to read the essay over carefully. Use the following checklist:

—*Is everything spelled correctly?* Nothing looks worse on an essay than misspelled words. If you don't know how a word is spelled, use another in its place!

—*Are the sentences varied in sentence structure?* Try to use simple sentences, compound sentences, complex sentences, questions, and declarative statements. Make the essay interesting to the reader.

—*Is the essay grammatically correct?* Check subject-verb agreement, tense, plurals, etc.

—*Are the essay's arguments well presented?* Are they convincing? Do they support the thesis and argue their case well? Are any essential parts of the argument omitted?

Proofreading need not take a long time but can make the difference between a good essay and a superb one. Don't forget this essential step!

Scoring the Essay

The essay is scored on a 15-point scale as follows:

SCORES

| 1–3 | Demonstrates incompetence | The student does not comprehend the question and addresses the issues in an inapplicable way. |

4–6	Suggests incompetence	The student shows inadequate understanding of the question. Response is minimal.
7–9	Suggests competence	The student understands the question but does not develop it sufficiently.
10–12	Demonstrates competence	The student demonstrates understanding of the question but presents an uneven argument for his point of view.
13–15	Demonstrates superiority	The student fully comprehends the question and delivers apt examples to defend his point of view.

The score for the essay is combined with the scores for the multiple-choice section and the document-based question (DBQ) to produce one score for the exam as a whole.

EIGHT SAMPLE ESSAYS

This chapter contains eight sample essays similar to those found on the Advanced Placement (AP) European History examination. We suggest that you use the topics presented here to write your *own* essays before reading the samples. Remember to outline, write, and proofread! Then read the sample essays and compare yours to the ones given.

Sample Essay 1

Compare and contrast the Russian Revolution of 1905 and the Bolshevik Revolution of 1917.

Revolutions often present an enigma to students of history. They represent a sudden break with authority, tradition, and order that are the framework of human society and perhaps even human nature. The student of history seeks to understand the cause of this phenomena and predict its conclusion and consequences.

In this venture, the historian all too often tends to place too much credit on the ability of a particular individual to control events and outcome. The sinister or benevolent motives of an individual are often offered as the explanation for actions that actually were dictated by larger circumstances.

Actually, many revolutions, when studied in an environment free from emotional rhetoric, can be seen as quite natural progressions within the societies where they occurred. Perhaps the Russian revolutions of 1905 and 1917 provide the best examples of the phenomena of social revolutions.

In 1905, the Romanov regime faced the first serious, organized protest against its rule in a demonstration at the Winter Palace. The Czarist government responded with force and the result was the "Bloody Sunday" massacre. A mere twelve years later, the world was shocked as the once philosophic theories of Karl Marx galvanized the Bolshevik revolution of 1917. Many contemporaries scrambled to explain what they believed was an unforeseeable turn in Russian history.

Actually, both phases of the Russian Revolution can be seen as having begun far in advance of the actual uprisings. By the turn of the twentieth century, Russian society was already developing in at least two very distinct, and contrasting, patterns. Since the 1800s, the upper class had become increasingly westernized and educated, while the peasantry, despite the Edict of Emancipation (1861), had sunk further into poverty, ignorance, and a feudal attachment to land and tradition. The Russian intelligentsia was far removed from the actual lives and loyalties of the Russian people.

Russia had experienced a limited industrial revolution, which was by no means as powerful a social phenomena as it had been in England. Unfortunately, the government had not responded in the same fashion as had the British government. Much of the Russian industrial base was either foreign-owned or in the hands of the Czarist regime itself. In fact, the Russian government, a full twenty years before the actual implementation of "communism" already had the largest state-operated economic system in the world. The results included a very weak middle class, whereas in England the middle class had played the major role in government reform and maintenance of social order. In addition, the government was not financially dependent upon, and therefore not accountable to, the people of Russia. Clearly, unless Russia was to remain feudal and agrarian, conflict was predictable.

The uprising of 1905 was unique in that it was largely lead by "respectable," that is, moderate, forces allied with the middle class. Nevertheless, many of its demands indicated an even deeper urban working class discontent.

The "Constitutional Democratic Party," formed in 1905 after the "Bloody Sunday" massacre, represented mainly the liberal, progressive forces of the Russian middle class who were already active in the "parliamentary politics" of the provincial Zemostrovs. At the same time, the "Social Democratic Labor Party" had already been in existence since 1898 and represented a far more radical threat to the Czar. The failure of the Romanovs to deal with the moderate forces not only led to their later demise but also to the discrediting of the "Kadets."

The uprising of 1905 has always been seen as fundamentally different from that of 1917, which is accurate in many ways. The rebels of 1905 may have been rebellious but they were not "revolutionary." The demands of the protestors on "Bloody Sunday" desired merely factory labor reforms and the removal of inept bureaucrats. Although more "radical" sects were active in the uprising and subsequent strikes, their limited influence was illustrated when the "October Manifesto," with its promise of civil liberties, written constitution, and an elected Duma, appeased enough of the general population to allow not only the elections of 1906 but also the arrest of the more militant Soviets of St. Petersburg.

One major difference between the two "revolutions" is the factionalizing of the opposition to Czarist rule. In 1905, aside from the pro-Czarist nobility and clergy, the opposition was split between the Kadets, representing the bourgeoisie, the Mensheviks, representing the more moderate of the Social Revolutionary Party, and the Bolsheviks, representing the hard-line revolutionary Marxists. The Duma of 1906 was largely the result of the conservative nature of the Russian peasantry, the action of right-wing reactionary groups such as the Black Hundreds and the refusal of either of the Marxist factions to take part in the elections. In the end, the Czarist government had its best opportunity for limited reform rather than total revolution as the moderate Kadets, who were in control of the first Duma, were at least as afraid of the Social Revolutionary Party as they were of the Czarist regime. The dissolution of the first Duma and the constant changing of the electoral rules by the Czar, not only increased the tendency to view elections as tools of deception by the state, but also to discredit "moderates" in general as political opportunists set upon using the peasantry in their own pursuit of power.

Lenin, in his Bolshevik-dominated November Revolution of 1917, had many advantages over his predecessors in 1905. The success of the early attempts at reform under Peter Stolypin (1906–1911) clearly demonstrated the conservative nature of the Russian peasantry and, in Lenin's mind, made them unfit to carry out a "Socialist Revolution." It also made him clearly aware that practical land reform for these people would gain far more support than promises of constitutional rights and elections.

The eventual move by the Mensheviks to participate in the elections to the second Duma allied them with the government. When this Duma was also deprived of power and discredited, it removed yet another source of true opposition. The opposition, especially the most active and militant in the workers' Soviets of Moscow and St. Petersburg, was becoming not only more unified but also more militant.

The onset of World War I initially had the effect of rallying the Russian people around the government, but the ensuing defeats and shortages led to the food riots of March 1917 and the end of the Czarist regime. Lenin gained another advantage from this phase of the revolution, even though he was not involved in it. The Provisional Government was neither as oppressive nor as strong as its predecessor, the Czarist regime. The refusal of the Petrograd Soviet to support the new government illustrated the limited success that could, at this point, be claimed.

For the Bolsheviks, removing the not yet consolidated Provisional Government now became a question and in this effort the desires of the Russian peasantry played a major role. The Provisional Government, under Kerensky, once again called for elections for a Constituent Assembly in order to draw up a consitution. Lenin, however, correctly understood that the mass of the Russian peasants really had no overriding zeal for democracy because they had no experience with this institution. What mattered to the average Russian was food, an end to the war, and economic viability. These ideals (if they can be called that) were realized in Lenin's call for "Peace, Bread, and Land," which made up most of the Bolshevik propaganda effort. For the Provisional Government, the insistence upon continuing the war effort only further associated them with the ideals of the former Czarist regime. This, combined with repressive measures such as those used by General Kornilov against the Soviets, only enhanced the appeal of the Bolsheviks.

Much has been made of Lenin's advocacy of the use of "terrorism" as a political weapon; his dismissal of the ability of the Russian people to take an active part in a socialist revolution; and the fact that the Bolshevik leadership resulted not from a mass swelling of popular support but from maneuvering to take control of the Central Committee. However true these statements are of both Lenin and the Bolsheviks, what can be disputed is just how different these ideals and tactics were from either the Czarist regime or the Provisional government. "Terrorism" had always been a tool of politics used by the Czars as well as by members of the Provisional Government. In many ways, terrorism can be seen as necessary when taking on a government that not only represses open opposition but also has an extensive intelligence network. As far as the ability of the Russian people to undertake democracy and their support for Bolshevism, there is no historic evidence to point towards democratic tendencies within the peasantry. It is very questionable how a "Socialist" could act without the support (or even consent) of the "masses" he represented, but history also shows that in any mass social movement the masses merely follow the actions and desires of the few who lead. Although the revolutions of 1917 clearly represented a drastic change in direction of the Russian Revolution, it would seem that they had much in common with the earlier revolution of 1905 and that both were rather clear continuations and consequences of traditional Russian society.

CRITICAL COMMENTARY

Sample Essay 1

This essay is a very comprehensive treatment of the Russian Revolution in 1905 and the Bolshevik Revolution of 1917. The two revolutions are compared and contrasted thoroughly.

Score: Demonstrates superiority

Sample Essay 2

Why were Portugal and Spain the first nations to create empires overseas?

It has often been said that history does not occur in a vacuum, that the policies, actions, and success or failures of nations are the result of both external and internal factors. Perhaps the clearest illustration of this idea can be seen in the early success of the Spanish and Portuguese in attaining overseas empires.

Although the fifteenth and sixteenth centuries still saw the predominance of feudal "divine right" monarchies in Europe, it must be noted that although in theory they were "absolute monarchs," in reality, the authority of the monarchs was often very limited. In the field of merchant business this was not necessarily detrimental as it afforded much independence of activity within the business community. Even in Spain, where the monarchs of the fifteenth century were inclined to try and dominate the field of commerce and impose strict government regulations and tariffs, the existence of "regionalism" meant that each geographic region of Spain often had its own laws which may or may not have coincided with those of the crown. The net result was that many prohibitive regulations were never enforced.

The inability of the monarchies to enforce their control was sometimes also deliberately allowed to go unremedied by the monarchs as they found themselves increasingly in financial need that could only be met by the growing commercial interests.

The rise and development of the middle class during the Renaissance, and the further development of credit banking institutions (of which the Medicis are but one example) not only provided capital for investment in overseas ventures but also for monarchs whose aggressive policies necessitated standing armies. This, of course, also meant that the middle class gained even further control over the actions of feudal monarchs. Conflicts such as the Hundred Years' War brought two powerful monarchs (England and France) into severe debt but also weakened their ability to play a part in European politics and to remain divorced from the demands of the various groups within their own societies. Although monarchies may have claimed to have the power of God, it was a power rarely heard from for most of the society.

The spread of the Ottoman Empire also helped to further the expansionist tendencies of the Western European nations. They now had to seek alternate routes to the Orient since overland routes were often closed unless treaties were signed as many of the Italian city-states had already done (Ex: the predominance of the Italians in the Levant region).

A further incentive for the nations of Western Europe to expand was that in trade with the Orient, they often had very little to offer and were actually scorned by their Asian partners.

In addition to these European developments, the nations of Spain and Portugal had many internal factors that aided their early ventures in expansionism.

Portugal, especially under monarchs such as Henry the Navigator, actively suppported the exploration that aided the mercantile interests within the country. Combined with their aloofness from much of the warfare which racked the other continental nations, exploration gave Portugal an early lead in expansion.

Spain also enjoyed a successful commercial enterprise which resulted from internal as well as external circumstances. The Moslem and Jewish populations in Spain greatly helped merchant commercial interests by most actively investing in and developing trade. Indeed, the onset of the Inquisition and its persecution of Moslems and Jews cost the Spanish monarchs their most productive segments of society. During the early part of the sixteenth century, when Spain's religious harmony allowed her to avoid the disputes of the continent, she made rapid gains in the New World and accumulations of gold made her one of the wealthiest nations in the world.

It is a great irony that the failure of these Roman Catholic nations to wipe out the pagan Moslems during the Crusades enabled them to expand their own wealth not only through the above mentioned incentives but also through the acquisition of technological advances such as the magnetic compass and ship designs that made long-range navigation and travel possible and economically feasible. In any event, it must be abundantly clear that in spite of the tendencies to divide historic studies into sometimes unrelated segments, the development of society is quite interrelated and dependent.

CRITICAL COMMENTARY

Sample Essay 2

This essay begins very well by putting the essay question into a larger framework. This broader context serves well to answer the question. Specific reasons are given to explain the answer.

Score: Demonstrates superiority

Sample Essay 3

Since the 1880s, what efforts have Europe's rulers made to try and integrate the working class into the larger national society?

The revolutions that shook the European continent from 1848 on served as formal notice to the rulers of the major powers that from this point onwards the interests and even the survival of nations would become more and more connected to the interests of the middle and working classes.

If the conservative elements had been frightened by the liberal nature of the 1848 uprisings in France, Italy, and Prussia, they were even more alarmed by developments during the Paris "Commune" of 1871–1872. Clearly, some accommodations had to be made to the emerging working class if governments were to maintain both social stability and political control. In this effort, the governments of Germany and England served as examples of how reform could be accomplished by both conservative and liberal administrations with no appreciable loss of control by the central government.

Otto von Bismarck, the Chancellor of the German Empire until 1890, was certainly no friend of either nineteenth-century liberalism or democracy and yet he was shrewd enough to appreciate the extent of the changes brought about by the revolutions of the century and the growing importance of the necessity of gaining the acceptance and acquiescence of both the middle class and the working class in an ever more industrial society.

As early as 1871 and 1872, when he first provided that members of the Reichstag be elected by universal male suffrage and then abolished the remaining manorial jurisdiction over the peasantry, Bismarck demonstrated a perception that the concerns of the middle and working classes could be used to gain their support over conservative opposition to his policies. Indeed, many of the social reforms enacted by Bismarck were conducted not in the spirit of the Gladstone reforms of England or even the benevolent despot, but in the pure spirit of "realpolitik," using the desires of one group to play upon the fears of another for the benefit of Bismarck's "monarchy."

Bismarck truly exemplified an industrial Machiavelli. He conducted reforms of the peasant jurisdiction to counter the opposition of the nobility, allied himself with the liberals during his Kulturkampf (Battle for Culture) against the Roman Catholic Church, knowing the liberal dislike for the more conservative Catholic doctrine. Then, in 1879 he established tariffs to protect developing German industry despite liberal opposition. The effect of each of these policies was the furtherance of Bismarck's concept of the German Empire and yet it did have positive immediate results for the development of Germany at least with regards to a productive economy and standing among the other major European powers.

Although the policies of Bismarck have generally been considered regressive in that they did not promote the modern day democratic state, it must be noted that his programs of worker reform, albeit in an effort to undercut the rise of the socialists by stealing their programs, did result in the establishment of workers compensation insurance, sick care, and old age pensions far in advance of any of the other liberal democracies. Perhaps, upon closer inspection, it could be seen that even the "benevolent" reforms of other countries were, more often than not, conducted more as a consequence of the struggle of political survival/power than out of any inherent love for the humanity.

England, during the late nineteenth and early twentieth centuries has been noted by many as the quintessential example of modern liberal democracies.

In fact, the Trades Union Act (1875), the Education Act (1871), and the Secret Ballot Act (1872), by legalizing and establishing workers' union rights, public elementary education, and free elections, are perfect examples of enacting change without destabilizing society. Yet, even these changes must be seen in the context of the growth and needs of an industrial society and the broader context of the nineteenth century as a whole. If society is to be industrial, education at all levels becomes a necessity, not a luxury. In view of the violent rebellions on the European continent, it was clear that it would be far more dangerous to deny the working class the right to organize and vote, especially when considering the past tendencies of revolutionary groups within English society to act in a predictable parliamentary fashion once enfranchised. For example, the results of the Great Reform of 1832 had little effect upon the structure of Parliament although it did lead to further reform. The vast majority of British society had long shown a tendency to trust the inherent justice of their democratic system and to distrust radicalism.

Like many of the policies of Bismarckian Germany, many of the reforms of England during this period were also the consequence of party politics as Liberals sought to ally themselves with socialists against the Conservatives who, in turn, tried to gain the support of the working class by enacting reforms that would otherwise be considered Liberal causes (the Great Reform Bill of 1832 and the Repeal of the Corn Laws are but the earliest examples).

In 1894, Sir William Harcourt introduced the concept of the graduated tax. In 1891, the Liberals first came out in support of the eight hour work-day. In 1897, The Compensation Act brought to England the same workers benefits that Bismarck had already enacted in Germany. Although it is true that these pieces of legislation did represent a fundamental change in social values during victorian England, they also represented the realization among both sections of the political system that accommodation must be made if for no other reason than to undercut the political support of the opposition. Indeed, these sentiments were echoed by Sir William Harcourt himself when he stated, "We're all socialists now."

Much emphasis has been placed in this essay upon the idea that political reform was, and is, used as a tool by competing political institutions, which has social progress only as a by-product. This, however, is perhaps slightly harsh in its outlook as it must be remembered that however limited each individual reform action may seem in today's context, they were often considered quite revolutionary in their own period. Each reform effort also provided the precedent from which later, more far-reaching reforms (such as the Parliament Act of 1911, The Liability Act of 1880), could later be put through. It must also be noted that although the lessons of the revolutions of 1848 to 1871 seem crystal clear now (and perhaps even then), many governments, such as Austria-Hungary and Russia, failed to enact even the most rudimentary reforms mentioned here. Perhaps the main lesson is to analyze each act of government neither in the light of patriotic apologist nor as malevolent skeptic but in the objective light of analyzing the effect and consequence of the individual act itself. In this light, it must be noted and appreciated that the reforms and changes were made as the industrial governments accommodated economic change into the body politic.

CRITICAL COMMENTARY

Sample Essay 3

This essay is very comprehensive in answering the question. Its author offers two detailed examples—the German Empire under Bismarck and England in the late nineteenth and early twentieth century—to show how attempts were made to integrate the working class into larger national society. In addition, the conclusion uses other countries as a counterpoint to Germany and England.

Score: Demonstrates superiority

Sample Essay 4

Discuss the "New Monarchy" of the sixteenth century in England, France, or Spain.

The English monarchy of the sixteenth century developed into an institution that was radically different from the monarchy that had existed before. Even if we overlook the disastrous thirty years of civil war (1455–1485), we can still see fundamental differences between the Tudors and earlier powerful monarchs such as Henry II and Henry V.

First of all, the devastation wrought by the Hundred Years' War, the plague, and the Wars of the Roses left the nobility in a weaker position than ever before. Although Essex proved that a revolt against the Queen was possible, Elizabeth showed decisively that any such revolt was doomed. There would be no threat of a new Runnymede and an expanded Magna Carta to threaten the Tudors.

Rulers in the fourteenth century had involved themselves in the economy to the extent of writing laws setting wages and, of course, collecting taxes, but it was the Tudors who began the practice of chartering companies and regulating businesses through the courts.

An extremely significant change in Tudor times was in church–state relations. Consider first the contrast between the Beckett–Henry II conflict and the battle of wills between Henry VIII and Sir Thomas More. In the first instance, Beckett, though a personal friend of Henry and Chancellor of England, felt compelled to uphold church rights over the rights of the sovereign. Henry II, because of the strength of the church, had Beckett murdered by assassins. The church's opinion was so strong, however, that he had to undergo public penance for his part in the affair.

Thomas More is an interesting contrast because he became more isolated as he clung to church rights. Henry VIII was able to rally public opinion to his side. In the end, Henry VIII was able to try, convict, and execute More with no significant political backlash.

What this event heralded was a change of view of the people. Before, king and church were both equal powers. But in the Tudor era, the crown became "ours," while the church was run by "foreigners." This true national spirit distinguished sixteenth century monarchy from its precursors.

CRITICAL COMMENTARY

Sample Essay 4

This essay addresses the issues well. It gives three significant changes of the "New Monarchy." However, only one of the examples is fully developed, namely, that of church–state relations. The other two examples are only briefly mentioned.

Score: Demonstrates competence

Sample Essay 5

Discuss the concept of "persistence of the old regime" with specific reference to the former Soviet Union.

The Russian Revolution of 1917 produced a number of changes in Russian politics and society. The emperor was overthrown and the Russian Orthodox Church was removed from a position of influence. However, many aspects of foreign and domestic policy hardly changed at all under the Soviets.

First and foremost was the retention of an autocratic system. Whether Lenin had any intention of democratizing Russia in a significant way is unclear. But no Soviet leaders until Gorbachev had made an attempt to decentralize authority. This concentration of power left its mark on Soviet industry. Both in Czarist Russia and in the former Soviet Union, the economy was managed from the capital (which changed to Moscow after the revolution).

Another ghost from the Czarist past that haunted the halls of Soviet power was the "Jewish problem." Though restriction to the Pale (an area in the Ukraine) and state-encouraged programs were no longer the policy of the Soviet government, an unofficial prejudice against Jews did exist, evidenced by the USSR's restrictions on Jewish emigration until the Gorbachev era.

In the sphere of foreign policy, the Soviet Union followed directly in the footsteps of the Czar. One of the areas Russia had to relinquish when it bowed out of World War I was the area encompassing the Baltic states of Lithuania, Latvia, and Estonia. Also, Russia has periodically claimed Finland and was involved in all three partitions of Poland and has fought Poland for centuries. *Taras Bulba*, by Nicolai Gogol, gives a sense of how war with Poland was almost institutionalized. The pull of its traditional role in these areas dragged Stalin to make a pact with Communism's sworn enemy (Hitler) in order to have a free hand to reclaim these lands.

CRITICAL COMMENTARY

Sample Essay 5

This essay gives a number of very good examples of the "persistence of the old regime" in Russia. It deals with internal effects and foreign policy effects. It is concise and answers the question well.

Score: Demonstrates superiority

Sample Essay 6

Evaluate World War I as a "watershed" in politics and society in any two European countries.

World War I altered the political and social order in virtually every country that had an active role in the hostilities. However, Germany and Russia probably suffered the most profound upheavals of any of the nations involved.

Germany in 1914 was a country that suffered from a kind of schizophrenia. It was arguably the most advanced country in the world with respect to industry and science. It had therefore a growing middle class and urban population. However, the nation itself had been forged by the work of the Iron Chancellor, Otto von Bismarck, and he had left his mark upon it.

Bismarck was, first and foremost, a junker. The junkers were noblemen in Prussia. When Bismarck pressed for the creation of the Reich, he envisioned it, for all intents and purposes, as a Greater Prussia. This entailed a strong monarch at the apex with all important posts filled by the aristocracy. (The King of Prussia became the Kaiser, or emperor of the new German empire.) This is why virtually all of the German military leaders up to and through World War I had the aristocratic "von" in front of their names (e.g., von Hindenburg, von Moltke, and von Richthofen). This system of autocracy could last only so long as the monarch was successful. When the Reich collapsed in 1918, there was widespread chaos because this system of autocratic control was discredited. The story of Germany between the wars is the story of a country trying to replace its lost culture. Hitler, in this analysis, could be viewed as the attempt to build a new hierarchy with an industrial base (many of his early supporters were industrialists) in order to resolve the imbalances in the prewar society that were torn down without being properly addressed.

Russia, on the other hand, suffered a collapse not because the system was torn asunder by outside forces, but because it shook itself to death. The inefficiencies of the Czarist regime had caused shortages and military disasters before. In 1905, there were bread riots in the capital that followed on the heels of the humiliating defeat of Russia by Japan. But in 1905, as had been true before, enough was held in reserve to effectively suppress the rioters. The gross incompetence of Nicholas II in commiting his country to a war he was totally unprepared to fight, coupled with the grotesque farce of the emperor being ordered about by his German wife on the whim of Rasputin, served as the final aberrations that the people could no longer tolerate. By following the strict autocratic ideal, the regime undid itself by having the wrong man in power in a dangerous time.

CRITICAL COMMENTARY

Sample Essay 6

This essay starts out very well. The introductory paragraph states the thesis and gives the two required examples. The example of Germany is well developed. It gives a background to Germany before and after the war and explains how World War I was a watershed. Some of the information, however, is extraneous. The example of Russia is less developed. More attention should have been paid to the combination of factors that affected Russia during World War I.

Score: Suggests competence

Sample Essay 7

The Reformation and the Scientific Revolution were contemporary events in Europe. Discuss the relationship between these two events in the following aspects:

A. Their common origins
B. Their influence on economic developments
C. Their creation of political tensions

Both the Scientific Revolution and the Reformation were natural developments of that pivotal era in European history known as the Renaissance, or rebirth. The Renaissance had two major results that provided the Reformation and Scientific Revolution with the intellectual base they required.

First of all, the texts found and distributed vividly illustrated that people could *know* things. Ancient Greek books on nature (Lucretius), architecture (Vitruvius), and other subjects showed that man could puzzle things out. This became the basis of the Reformation—the necessity for a person to read and interpret the Bible for himself. The very existence of science (and, in fact, its name) presupposes that it is possible to know things.

The second gift of the Renaissance was that people discovered that they could know more than their parents and priests. Because of the relatively rapid spread of learning, it became painfully obvious that much that was said by those in authority was wrong. Ultimately, this led Luther to break with a church that refused to accept what his studies of the Bible revealed. Galileo, at the beginning of the Scientific Revoultion, felt confident enough in his powers of observation that he could contradict Aristotle, while Paracelsus overthrew the centuries-old anatomy of Galen.

Needless to say, such questioning of authority and willingness to look for new answers provoked changes in both the economic and political spheres. Economically, the seat of power shifted to those countries that were most willing to adapt new ways of doing things. The English and the Dutch incorporated new discoveries in their trading vessels. The development of steam engines began, and received most of its practical modifications, in

England (though Carnor of France provided the basis of our understanding of how it worked). It seems that for many years the most innovative people in practical areas were those who embraced the Reformation. For example, consider the decline in vigor or French trade after the expulsion of the Huguenots.

This shifting of economic power to the north, and the refusal to meekly submit to authority caused dislocations in the political sphere as well. The religious wars, especially the Thirty Years' War, were struggles that had a foundation in the revolt against authority not supported by reason. The struggle intensified because both sides realized that capital was at stake. Capital became important only when industry became efficient enough to provide a large and dependable return on investment. This efficiency could only be supplied by the development of science.

A movement that had roots back in the days of Nicholas I (1820s), panslavism, saw its ultimate expression in the Iron Curtain. Panslavism in Russian history can be summarized as a kind of Manifest Destiny, whereby all Slavic people will be joined together in brotherhood. The Russian version has the added detail of Russian control. By the end of World War II, all Slavic countries had either a puppet government (e.g., Poland, Czechoslovakia) or a leader helped to power by the Soviets (e.g., Marshal Tito in Yugoslavia).

CRITICAL COMMENTARY

Sample Essay 7

This essay is cogent and addresses the issues very well. It pinpoints the effects of the Reformation and Scientific Revolution both economically and politically and answers the question concisely.

Score: Demonstrates superiority

Sample Essay 8

Discuss the extent that ideology has affected diplomatic relations among European nations during the twentieth century. Be sure to refer to specific agreements and events.

Europe has been a testing ground for political theories for centuries. However, no previous century has seen so many different ideologies compete for ascendancy as the present one. During the twentieth century, there have been powers that have tried communism, constitutional monarchy, absolute monarchy, republicanism, and fascism. What impact has this plethora of beliefs had on international diplomacy? The answer, surprisingly enough, is virtually none!

Consider World War I. The most autocratic ruler of Europe, Nicholas II, went to war ultimately to honor a pact he had made with republican France. Who was his main opponent? Wilhelm II, the second most autocratic ruler in Europe (and also a cousin of Nicholas). Wilhelm's ally was Franz Josef, a monarch who was essentially trapped in the interlocking bureaucracies of the dual monarchy in Austria-Hungary. He was de facto a constitutional ruler, even if he was de jure an absolute monarch. Britain, a consitutional monarchy without a constitution, was an opponent of Austria-Hungary.

The only "natural" opponents were Moslem Turkey against Orthodox Russia. But even here, Turkey allied herself with Christian Germany.

The National Socialist (fascist) regimes of the 1930s were vehemently opposed to the internationalist spirit of communism. This did not, however, prevent the signing of the nonaggression pact of August 26, 1939 between the Soviet Union and Nazi Germany, paving the way for the partition of Poland and the beginning of World War II. One notes that at least two "birds of a feather," Mussolini and Hitler, formed an iron pact, but Spain's fascist leader, Franco, remained neutral.

Until the breakup of the Soviet Union, the Warsaw Pact and NATO dominated the post-war landscape. But considering that Russia traditionally dominated Eastern Europe whenever Austria was weak (for example, in the 1820s to the 1850s during the reign of Nicholas I), it is not difficult to explain the Warsaw Pact as a group of nations locked into an ideology and an alliance by force. Certainly the breakup of the pact revealed these nations had little commitment to communism. NATO, originally formed to check Soviet power, was now evolving into a loosely knit European security pact. Initially it was a grab bag of constitutional monarchies, democracies, and dictatorships, held together by fear of Moscow. Therefore, this "Western Alliance" has changed mainly because the "former Eastern Empire" is no longer a political, economic, or military threat; and not because it has defeated communist ideology. This gives evidence to the thesis that ideology played a relatively small role in European diplomacy in the twentieth century.

CRITICAL COMMENTARY

Sample Essay 8

The essay begins well in a general statement and thesis. The first example is good but could use expansion to prove the author's thesis. The second example is more fully developed and more clear-cut. The third series of examples again could be expanded upon.

Score: Demonstrates competence

THE DOCUMENT-BASED QUESTION (DBQ)

The document-based question (DBQ) tests your ability to create and justify a response to a question using a number of given documents. Each document furnishes information on the subject at hand and may also give perspective on the other documents in that particular series. Each document should be read in context of the series. The documents should be read in the order provided but you may consider them in any order. Most of the documents should be used in the response, although not all are needed. Documents may be appraised as to their reliability as well. The reliability of a document refers to the source's credibility. You should evaluate not only the information presented but also where it comes from and how that impacts on its truthfulness.

The DBQ is meant to assess your ability to interpret and analyze. Therefore, stay away from mere paraphrasing, repetition, or summary of documents and, instead, focus on interpretation, analysis of material, and supporting a conclusion.

The DBQ should be organized as a cogent essay. Therefore, it should have a thesis that is presented in the first paragraph, a body which supports your arguments, and a conclusion that summarizes the evidence presented and restates the thesis.

Primary Source

A primary source is the actual material written in a specific time period. For example, if a speech was made in Parliament by a member of the Whig party, the speech itself would be considered a primary source.

Secondary Sources

Secondary sources are written from an observer's or commentator's point of view. In the example above, an editorial on the speech published by the London *Times* would be a secondary source.

Tertiary Sources

Tertiary sources are once removed from secondary sources. In our example, a discussion of the speech in a history textbook would be considered a tertiary source. In general, textbooks and other historical studies fall into this category.

The good historian must use all three kinds of sources. Certainly, primary sources are first-rate reservoirs of historical information. However, they are not always available. Documents are destroyed, fall prey to the elements, are lost. Secondary sources tell what others thought of historical events and are also important sources of information. Tertiary sources, while the furthest removed from the actual events, use the acumen, the work, and the insight of other historians to help us see events in perspective. Be aware of whether the document you are analyzing is a primary, secondary, or tertiary source.

Documents can also be analyzed as to their method of presentation:

Public Records

These include court decisions, speeches given in legislatures (e.g., Parliament, Congress, the Reichstag), treaties, laws, government agency reports, and official letters.

Public records should be analyzed as to the *content* as well the *context* of the document. Why was it written? When was it written and by whom? Does it represent a special interest group? Which one?

Personal Documents

These include speeches, rough drafts of speeches (sometimes more informative than the actual speech), letters, and diaries.

Analyze the intended audience of the document, its date, and whether it was official or personal.

Printed Matter

These include books, newspapers, magazines, and pamphlets.

Determine the intended audience of the material. What is it trying to illustrate?

Visual Material

These include pictures, photographs, cartoons, diagrams, maps, charts, and graphs.

Assess the content of the material, its date, its title (if any), its intended audience, its emotional impact (if any), and its point of view. Even such "objective" materials as charts and graphs can have points of view, depending on what statistics are presented. You should give a sophisticated interpretation of data, not a mere restatement of the facts.

HOW TO APPROACH THE DBQ

STEP 1 **Read the question.**
Although this may sound trite, and even silly, you are answering a specific essay question. Keep that in mind as you read the documents and plan your response. Do not go off on irrelevant tangents or merely summarize the documents.

STEP 2 **Determine your point of view.**
Many DBQs ask a question that can be answered in more than one way. Decide what your opinion is on the issue and stick to it!

STEP 3 **Marshal the evidence.**
Now that you have your point of view, gather the evidence presented in the documents to bolster your case. You may use some outside information as well, but remember that, first and foremost, this is a *document-based* question.

STEP 4   *Prepare the outline.*
Use the format presented in Chapter 3, "The Essay," to prepare your outline.

STEP 5   *Write the essay.*
Be sure that you have an introduction with your thesis statement, a body with the specific documents utilized to support your thesis, and a strong conclusion.

STEP 6   *Proofread the essay.*
Don't forget this crucial step! It will ensure that you have, indeed, presented your best work.

Outline for the DBQ

Introduction	Paragraph 1	Present introduction to the topic Provide thesis statement
Body	Paragraphs 2–?	Support the thesis Utilize the documents to bolster the arguments
Conclusion	Final Paragraph	Summarize findings Restate the thesis

SCORING THE DBQ

The DBQ is also scored on a 15-point scale as follows:

Scores

1–3	Demonstrates incompetence	The student does not comprehend the question and addresses the issues inappropriately.
4–6	Suggests incompetence	The student shows inadequate understanding of the question. Response is minimal.
7–9	Suggests competence	The student understands the question but does not develop it sufficiently.
10–12	Demonstrates competence	The student demonstrates comprehension of the meaning of the question but presents an uneven argument for his point of view.
13–15	Demonstrates superiority	The student fully comprehends the question and delivers apt examples to defend his point of view.

The score for the DBQ is combined with the scores for the multiple-choice section and the essay to produce one score for the exam as a whole.

SAMPLE DOCUMENT-BASED QUESTIONS AND RESPONSES

Now that you understand the format and techniques of writing the document-based question, we will present two sample DBQs with several responses. We suggest that you utilize this section as follows:

1. Read the DBQ in 15 minutes or less.
2. Prepare your *own* response in 45 minutes or less. Don't forget to outline, write, and proofread!
3. Then read the sample DBQs. Try to assess how your response measures up to those given.

First Sample Document-Based Question

Suggested time—45 minutes

Percent of Section II scoring: 50

Directions: The following question is based on the accompanying documents. (Some of the documents have been edited and/or translated for the purpose of this question.)

The question is designed to test your ability to work with historical source material. Some of the documents are primary sources; others are secondary, but of a period soon after the event in question. Take into account the document's source and the frame of reference of its author. Your essay must integrate your analysis of the documents. You must also refer to historical facts and developments not specifically mentioned in the documents.

Question: Discuss the extent to which the repeal of the Corn Laws (1846) was either a triumph for middle-class commercial interests or a victory for the poor in England.

Historical Background

Passed in 1815 and revised in 1828 and 1842, the Corn Laws prohibited the importation of "corn"—really many types of grain—into Great Britain unless the price at home was above 80 shillings per quarter ton ("per quarter" in the language of the time).

As might be assumed, the landed aristocracy strongly supported the legislation; they were backed in Parliament by the Tory Party. The Anti-Corn Law League, founded in Manchester by Richard Cobden and John Bright in 1838, had the support of the Liberal Party.

In 1846, the Corn Laws were repealed. Robert Peel, leader of the Tories, switched positions and brought with him enough votes to abolish the Corn Laws. Free trade in "corn" signaled a change in commercial legislation in general.

DOCUMENT 1

Sir Robert Peel turns his back on the poor.

Source: Punch, January 18, 1845

DOCUMENT 2

Workingmen's Riots at Ely, Littleport and Downham Market, 7 hanged 1816

Peterloo Massacre (Manchester) 1819

Cato Street Conspiracy 1820

Metropolitan Police Act 1829 creates the first professional police force in Britain

"Burning of Bristol" 1831

"Swing" Riots in the southern counties; 1,976 prisoners, 19 hanged 1830–1831

DOCUMENT 3

You may further examine whether the principle of protection be not carried to an extent injurious alike to the income of the state and the interests of the people. Her Majesty is desirous that you should consider the laws which regulate the trade in corn. It will be for you to determine whether these laws do not aggravate the natural fluctuations of supply, whether they do not embarrass trade, derange the currency, and by their operation diminish the comfort and increase the privations of the great body of the community.

Source: Queen Victoria's speech to Parliament, August 24, 1841

DOCUMENT 4

: 'The Doors of the very lobby of the House are closed against us by order of those in power. It is impossible for us to get in to speak to the members as they pass. The Corn Laws were passed under the protection of the bayonet and its supporters now ensconce themselves under the truncheons of the police. But the time is fast coming when the voice of the people will be heard, and their oppressors will quail before it. Let us give three hearty cheers for the cause of free trade.' The cheers were given with a voice that might be heard within the House. . . .The delegates proceeded up Parliament Street. Just at Privy Gardens they met Sir Robert Peel proceeding in his carriage to the House. He seemed to think at first that they were going to cheer him, but when he heard the angry shouts of 'No Corn Law', 'Down with the monopoly', 'Give bread and labour' he leaned back in his carriage, grave and pale.

Source: John Bright, February, 1846 in *History of the Anti-Corn League, Vol. 1,* 1853

DOCUMENT 5

"When I go down to the manufacturing districts," said Cobden in that same speech, "I know that I shall be returning to a gloomy scene. I know that starvation is stalking through the land, and that men are perishing for want of the merest necessaries of life." And he added, with gathering emphasis, "When I witness this, and recall that there is a law which especially provides for keeping our population in absolute want, I cannot help attributing murder to the legislature of this country; and wherever I stand, whether here or out of doors, I will denounce that system of legislative murder."

"You must untax the people's bread," that was the burden and final call of the speech.

Source: Richard Cobden, Speech in Parliament, 1841 Quoted in Richard Gowing, *Richard Cobden,* London, 1886, pp. 84–85

DOCUMENT 6

Towards the end of 1843 the Council of the League resolved to call upon the supporters of the movement for an additional £100,000 for the expenses of the agitation, and it was not many weeks before the amount was subscribed. One of the objects was to engage Covent Garden Theatre for fifty nights, at a rent of £3,000, for the holding of monster meetings. At one of the general Manchester meetings at this time, some startling figures were quoted as to the machinery and expenditure of the agitation. During a considerable portion of the year, upwards of 300 persons had been employed in printing and making up packets of Free Trade tracts and leaflets for distribution; 500 were employed in distributing them; and tracts to the number of 5,000,000 had been sent to electors, and from 3,000,000 to 4,000,000 to non-electors. Altogether in the year more than 9,000,000 copies of tracts and stamped publications had been distributed in 84 counties and in 187 boroughs.

Source: Richard Gowing, *Richard Cobden,* London, 1886, p. 92

DOCUMENT 7

In the meanwhile Cobden and the League were arousing the country, and the popular excitement was without parallel in the history of the movement. The Executive Council of the League resolved to make a call for subscriptions for a quarter of a million sterling; at a great League meeting in Manchester on the 23rd of December twenty-three persons gave in their names for a thousand pounds each, and within an hour and a half the subscription amounted to £60,000. Within a month the total had run up to £150,000.

Source: Richard Gowing, *Richard Cobden,* London, 1886, p. 98

DOCUMENT 8

The policy of Free Trade was accepted by Parliament, not because a majority of either House was convinced of the soundness of the economic principles, and the wisdom of adopting them, but because there seemed to be no other obvious solution for the difficulties of the moment; the new proposal received an unwilling assent, which was extorted from a Parliament that had received a mandate to maintain the established system.

Source: W. Cunningham, *The Rise and Decline of the Free Trade Movement,* London, 1904, p. 63

DOCUMENT 9

What for Saxon, Frank and Hun,
What hath England's bread-tax done?
Ask the ruin it hath made,
Ask of bread-tax-ruin'd trade;
Ask the struggle and the groan,
For the shadow of a bone,
Like a strife for life, for life,
Hand to hand, and knife to knife.

Hopeless trader, answer me!
What hath bread-tax done for thee?
Ask thy lost and owing debts,
Ask our bankrupt-throng'd Gazettes.
Clothier, proud of Peterloo!
Ironmaster, loyal, too!
What hath bread-tax done for you?
Let the Yankee tariff tell,
None to buy, and all to sell;
Useless buildings, castle strong,
Hundred thousands, worth a song;
Starving workmen, warehouse full,
Saxon web, from Polish wool,

Grown where grew the wanted wheat,
Which we might not buy and eat,
Merchants, bread-tax'd trade won't pay,
Profits lessen every day;
Sell thy stock and realize,
Let thy streeted chimneys rise;
And when bread-tax'd ten are two,
Learn what bread-tax'd rents can do.

What hath bread-tax done for me?
Farmer, what for thine and thee?
Ask of those who toil to live,
And the price they cannot give;
Ask our hearths, our gainless marts,
Ask thy children's broken hearts,
Ask their mother, sad and grey,
Destined yet to parish pay.
Bread-tax'd weaver, all can see
What that tax hath done for thee,
And thy children, vilely led,
Singing hymns for shameful bread,
Till the stores of every street,
Know their little naked feet.

Bread-tax-eating absentee,
What hath bread-tax done for thee?—
Cramm'd thee, from our children's plates,
Made thee all that nature hates,
Fill'd thy skin with untaxed wine,
Fill'd thy breast with hellish schemes,
Fill'd thy head with fatal dreams—
Of potatoes, basely sold
At the price of wheat in gold,
And of Britons sty'd to eat
Wheat-priced roots, instead of wheat.

Man of Consols, hark to me!
What shall bread-tax do for thee?
Rob thee for the dead-alive,
Pawn thy thousands ten for five,
And, ere yet its work be done,
Pawn thy thousands five for one.

What shall bread-tax yet for thee,
Palaced pauper? We shall see
It shall tame thee, and thy heirs,
Beggar them, and beggar theirs,
Melt thy plate, for which we paid,
Buy ye breeches ready made,
Sell my lady's tax-bought gown,
And the lands thou call'st thy own.

Source: Ebenezer Elliott, *Cornlaw Rhymes,*
c. 1846

DOCUMENT 10

"We have been told by the right hon. gentleman that his object is to fix a certain price for corn; and hearing that proposition from a prime minister, and listening to the debates, I have been almost led to believe that we are gone back to the times of the Edwards, when Parliament was engaged in fixing the price of a table-cloth, or a napkin, or a pair of shoes. But is this House a corn-market? Is not your present occupation better fitted for the merchant and the exchange? We do not act in this way with respect to cotton, or iron, or copper, or tin. But how are we to fix the price of corn? . . . I will ask the right hon. Baronet, Is he prepared to carry out this principle in respect to cotton or wool? I pause for a reply." (Sir R. Peel: "I have said that it was impossible to fix the price of food by any legislative enactment.") "Then upon what are we now legislating? I thank the right hon. Baronet for that avowal. Will he oblige me still further by not trying to do it? But supposing he will try, all I ask of him is—and again I shall pause for a reply—will he try to legislate to keep up the price of cottons, woollens, silks, and such like goods? There is no reply. Then we have come to this, that we are not legislating for the universal people. Here is the simple, open avowal, that we are met here to legislate for a class against the people."

Source: Richard Cobden, Speech in Parliament, February 1842

DOCUMENT 11

Sir James Graham had no patience with the delegates or their arguments, and when Mr. Henry Ashworth submitted that it was grossly unjust to restrict the imports of food in order to uphold the rents of farming land, and declared that the effect would be to increase the sense of unfair treatment which was felt by the people, Sir James stopped him with the exclamation, "Why, you are a leveller!" and asked, "Am I to infer that the labouring classes have some claim to the landlords' estates?" Presently Sir James, in reply to the whole case which had been laid before him, asserted that if the Corn Laws were repealed, great disasters would fall upon the country, the land would go out of cultivation; Church and State could not be upheld! all our institutions would be reduced to their primitive elements, and the people whom the Corn Law Repealers were exciting would pull down our houses about our ears. Such was the language of statesmen whom Mr. Cobden was destined to convert to the doctrine of Free Trade in corn in less than seven years.

Source: Richard Gowing, *Richard Cobden,* London, 1886, p. 65

DOCUMENT 12

"The manufacturer turns his back upon the working men and replies to the shopkeeper: 'As to that, you leave it to us! Once rid of the duty on corn we shall import cheaper corn from abroad. Then we shall reduce wages at the very time when they are rising in the countries where we get our corn. Thus, in addition to the advantages which we already enjoy we shall have lower wages and, with all these advantages we shall easily force the Continent to buy of us.'

"The English working men have appreciated to the fullest extent the significance of the struggle between the lords of the land and of capital. They know very well that the price of bread was to be reduced in order to reduce wages, and that the profit of capital would rise by as much as rent fell."

Source: Karl Marx. Speech before the Democratic Club, Brussels, January 9, 1848

DOCUMENT 13

I cannot concur with my hon. friend in speaking of the condition of the working classes, that whatever their condition might have been some few months ago, it is in some respects deteriorated, and that generally speaking the working classes at present are not in so comfortable a state as they were a few months ago. I should deeply regret it, if that were the case. I cannot speak of every district or parish. I know there are great vicissitudes of trade, and consequently of employment for them; but, speaking generally of the working classes, and particularly of the manufacturing classes, I do not believe that there is any deterioration in their condition as compared to that condition some few months ago. On the contrary, I do perceive in the increased consumption of many articles— of coffee, of tea, of sugar, continued even up to the present time, an effective proof that their condition now as compared with their condition some two or three years ago is greatly improved.

What have been the other effects of the operation of the new corn-law of 1842? We were told that the retention of that law would be inconsistent with the prosperity of the manufacturing interest of the country. But has that prediction been verified? Concurrently with that law you have seen a revival of industry, an extension of commerce and a degree of manufacturing activity, which we could hardly have hoped for or contemplated within so short a time. All this has existed concurrently with the new corn-law of 1842. The hon. member for *Stockport (Mr. Cobden)* has admitted these results.

Source: Sir Robert Peel, Speech in Parliament, June 10, 1845

DOCUMENT 14

He [Cobden] insisted that the poor would be benefited even if bread maintained its price; he argued that a very large part of the population were half-starved for want of means of buying bread; he held that the repeal of the Corn Laws would entail, not merely a larger supply of corn, but more regular employment, so that the demand would be increased, because more people would be able to pay for as much food as they needed at the current rates. A large supply would be forthcoming from abroad and from home, but the price need not fall if, as he believed, the people were better able to pay.

Source: W. Cunningham, *The Rise and Decline of the Free Trade Movement*, London, 1904, p. 61

DOCUMENT 15

The principle involved in the resolution is much wider than the resolution itself. 'The hon. and learned gentleman proposes that to-night we should affirm the total and immediate repeal of the Corn-laws; but the great principle is further involved in the resolution, namely, that every duty on every article which savours of protection shall be at once abolished;

But the next consequence that flows from the adoption of this resolution, is the immediate subversion of the whole of the colonial system. The entire colonial system will at once be swept away, unless you will leave the colonial interests to drag on a precarious existence, without letting the capitalist know what is the legislation by which he is to be governed; in fact, it follows, as the necessary consequence of the adoption of this resolution, that the whole colonial system must be at once abolished; that is to say, that this country must not, on a careful revision of the colonial system—must not, after a gradual and well-considered attentive consideration of the abstract principle, but upon a resolution to be affirmed to-night, consent to subvert at once the whole colonial arrangements so recently made. Of course, I apply to the colonists the benefit of the principle we claim for this country. At present, our manufactured goods are admitted into the colonies on a footing more favourable to us than to foreigners. Whether wise or unwise, this is the nature of our colonial connection. This country said to the colonies: "I will be responsible for your security and internal order, and the return I ask for is the favour and privilege of the admission of my manufactures." This is granted; and for this we give the colonies corresponding advantages. This is the system which has endured for years.

Source: Sir Robert Peel, Speech in Parliament, May 9, 1843

DOCUMENT 16

Then, my belief is that, in the present condition of this country, sudden withdrawal of all protection would paralyze commerce, and introduce such general confusion and distress, that so far from the labourers benefiting, they would be involved in the common calamity. The proposal, then, which we have to decide is, whether with respect to the whole of your colonial productions—with respect to the whole of your domestic productions, you shall affirm this resolution, which though it appears to be confined to corn necessarily involves the removal of every protective duty with respect to every product. I believe that nothing but confusion would arise from such a proceeding.

Source: Sir Robert Peel, Speech in Parliament, June 26, 1844

DOCUMENT 17

Do you not admit to me that in the social condition of the millions in the manufacturing districts, who earn their subsistence by the sweat of their brow, the price of wheat is of the first importance, and has become an object of the deepest interest? Have you read the reports on the health of towns? Are you not deeply convinced that some effort ought to be made to improve the social condition of the masses of the population, who earn their subsistence in the manufacturing towns? It seems to me that the first foundation of any such improvement is, that there should be abundance of food. You may talk of improving the habits of the working classes, introducing education amongst them, purifying their dwellings, improving their cottages; but believe me the first step towards improvement of their social condition is an abundance of food.

I think I am not acting as the enemy of that interest, with which my own is so intimately connected, when I recommend this bill to the acceptance of the House. I repeat, that that which I advise is for the true interests of every class. I ask you, do you feel secure? and if you foresee that the present system cannot long be maintained, why will you not take advantage of a favourable time for effecting a change that very soon must come?

Source: Sir Robert Peel, Speech in Parliament, March 27, 1846

First Sample Document-Based Question Analysis

This document-based question asks you to examine not only primary sources, but secondary sources as well. Documents 6, 7, 8, 11, 12, and 14 were all written after the event. A superior essay would note the positions taken by the authors of these secondary works.

In answering this essay you must include certain background information. A discussion of the effects of the Reform Act of 1832 cannot be omitted. The £10 renter received the right to vote; certain manufacturing towns became represented in Parliament for the first time. This shift in voting and representation had definite consequences in the repeal of the Corn Laws.

The Potato Famine in Ireland is another historical event only briefly referred to in the documents. If the decade was known as the Hungry Forties, it was because of the Potato Famine, which occurred in the midst of the debate on the Corn Laws.

John Bright, a leader of the anti-Corn Law League, adhered to a philosophy of liberalism. In the context of the mid-nineteenth century, this meant opposition to government interference in the affairs of men, not only in trade but in laws to improve labor conditions and social welfare. Bright argued that working people would fare better under a laissez-faire system. Free trade was one expression of laissez-faire.

Documents 1, 2, 4, 5, 8, 9, 10, and 17 support the hypothesis that repeal of the Corn Laws was a victory for the worker.

Documents 6, 7, 11, 12, 13, 14, 15, and 16 support the position that the Corn Laws were repealed to help the British manufacturers and merchants. Most insist that this would also help the workers, i.e., more food equals a better life. Karl Marx, on the other hand, viewed this position as another chapter in the exploitation of labor by the bourgeoisie.

First Sample Document-Based Question Response A

The Corn Laws of England represented an attempt to hold off the mad rush of industrialization that has presented Europe (and the world) with the greatest challenge of modern times. The laws, a battlement for the landed aristocracy, became a focal point of the onslaught by the urban population, both merchant and working poor. This essay will attempt to show that the triumph of the forces working against the Corn Laws was victory for both commercial interests and the poor.

The beginning of industrialization can be dated to the steam engine in 1698. From this first use of nonmuscle power came the notion that machines can be used to multiply the productivity of people to an almost unlimited extent. The new machines were different from the old ones in that the person who used the machine operated the tool instead of guiding it. The worker now turned switches that performed tasks in a way that was beyond his comprehension, unlike the simple plows and other tools from earlier times.

This profound change precipitated the development of the factory. One result of the growth of factories from the mid-eighteenth century on was the concentration of wealth in the hands of those who owned, as Karl Marx called it, "the means of production." This ability to concentrate wealth required, of course, that there be a market for the goods.

One way of creating a market for the goods was to force people to buy them. This was the main justification for the colonial system of Great Britain. Sir Robert Peel, in Documents 15 and 16, pointed out that repealing laws that favored certain groups (i.e., manufacturers) over others (i.e., colonials) would wreck the industrial base of the country.

The only other markets for industrial goods are domestic (as opposed to colonial) and foreign. As the Depression of the 1930s showed, a domestic market will not support growth in industry unless it has the free capital to spend on the goods. Moreover, as United States relations with Japan have increasingly shown, foreign markets are not sympathetic to countries that have set up high tariffs or otherwise limit trade.

From the preceding discussion, it appears nonsensical to create laws that artificially inflate the price of a staple. First of all, measures that inflate prices reduce the domestic market for industrial goods by forcing people to allocate a disproportionate amount of money to necessities. Second, restricting trade alienates markets. Yet, as Documents 1, 4, 5, and 14 testify, the working class was indeed forced to spend its meager funds on food. Also, as the references to Huns, Poles, and Yankees in the rhymes (Document 9) point out, the Corn Laws affected the trading relations of Britain with the world.

Queen Victoria (Document 3) felt called upon to request that Parliament look into the impact of these laws on both people and industry. That the poor felt unusually hard pressed is suggested by the rioting presented in Document 2, and the fact that anti-Corn Law groups were able to collect so much support in people as well as in moneys (Documents 6 and 7). The money raised implies that the merchants realized their plight was tied up with the poor. That this thought was current, if not vocalized, is revealed in Sir Robert Peel's argument that industry was not hurt by the Corn Laws (Document 13).

Why were these laws passed, then? Consider that the first Corn Law was passed in 1815, the same year as the Congress of Vienna. The spirit of that Congress, set up to undo the French Revolution, and the spirit of the Corn Laws were the same. This was the Old Order's last attempt to turn back the clock, strikingly proved by the nature of the arguments used in the debate on repeal. In Document 11, Sir James Graham decries the attempt to overturn the social order (use of the epithet "leveller"). In Document 10, Cobden clearly calls the Baronet on the point that the law is set up to benefit "a class against a people." Peel, in his switch to the repeal side, admits that the debate has an "us against them" air (Document 17).

The result of the repeal of the Corn Laws in 1846 allowed Britain freer trade which, in turn, allowed her to be the preeminent commercial power until World War I. Clearly, this was a victory for the merchant class. But, contrary to Karl Marx (Document 12), the people were also given relief. As evidence of this, consider that England was the only industrial power in Europe that did not have a revolution in the fateful year of 1848.

CRITICAL COMMENTARY

This essay is certainly interesting. Its author knows his history and has a larger sense of context—as evidenced by his examples of the Great Depression and U.S.–Japanese trade relations. His introduction is well done. It is terse, to the point, and states the author's thesis, namely that the repeal of the Corn Laws was a victory for both commercial interests and the poor. Paragraphs 2 and 3 give background to the problems. They are not essential but give the reader additional historical information. The remaining paragraphs in the body use the documents presented to provide evidence of the author's thesis. The conclusion summarizes his findings and restates the thesis in an eloquent manner.

Score: Demonstrates superiority

First Sample
Document-Based Question
Response B

The incident of the Corn Laws which occurred in England during the first half of the eighteenth century clearly represented the age-old struggle between the rich and the poor, between those controlling the government and those subject to it. Ultimately, the Corn Laws were repealed, representing a victory for England's middle-class merchants and the poor. However, this victory did not put an end to all of England's problems.

The poor conditions suffered by the majority of England's population in the early 1800s is clearly illustrated in Documents 3, 5, and 9. Queen Victoria herself attributed these problems largely to the Corn Laws and made clear the need for their repeal. Document 1 depicts the struggle between the rich and the poor, making obvious the gap that separated the "haves" and the "have-nots." The Corn Laws only encouraged that gap.

The Corn Laws also destroyed any hope of a peaceful society. Document 2 lists the riots, massacres, and violence resulting from the resentment of the Corn Laws. The cost of protesting and fighting the Corn Laws was immense and yet another problem, as seen in Documents 6 and 7.

In Documents 4 and 8, the reluctance of Parliament to repeal the Corn Laws is evident. This only gives credence to the idea that the victory of the lower classes would only create greater resentment on the part of the rich towards the poor. However, many legislators did join the anti-Corn Law cause after some time, giving the lower classes a greater say in government (Document 11).

With the repeal of the Corn Laws, manufacturing, commerce, and industry all experienced a revival (Document 13). However, Document 18 shows how trade flourished while the Corn Laws were in existence. Furthermore, Document 17 depicts poor social conditions well after the Corn Laws had been abolished. Finally, even in 1842 Parliament was still a government of the rich and for the rich (Document 10).

The repeal of the Corn Laws was certainly a victory for the middle and lower classes, but that victory was limited. Probably the greatest victory was the removal of the government's economic restrictions and the beginning of free trade. In the short run, social conditions also improved and the power of the people in Parliament undoubtedly increased. Unfortunately, the age-old struggle between the upper classes and the lower classes continued. In addition, social conditions deteriorated quickly. However, it is clear that for England to have survived, the Corn Laws had to be repealed. More good than damage was done.

CRITICAL COMMENTARY

This essay starts off well. Its thesis is clearly stated in the first paragraph. Paragraphs 2, 3, and 4 develop the thesis. Paragraph 5, however, is an anomaly; the student seems to argue *against* his thesis. Therefore, this paragraph should have been cut. (NOTE: A careful outline will expose problems like this *before* you write your essay.) The concluding paragraph summarizes the arguments and restates the thesis.

Score: Demonstrates competence

Second Sample Document-Based Question

Suggested time: 45 minutes

Percent of Section II Scoring: 50

Directions: *The following question is based on the accompanying documents. (Some of the documents have been edited and/or translated for the purpose of this question.)*

The question is designed to test your ability to work with historical source material. Some of the documents are primary sources; others are secondary, but of a period soon after the event in question. Take into account the document's source and the frame of reference of its author. Your essay must integrate your analysis of the documents. You must also refer to historical facts and developments not specifically mentioned in the documents.

Question: Analyze the Conference of Berlin of 1884–1885 as a turning point in the history of European imperialism in Africa and/or a piece in Bismarck's European diplomatic jigsaw puzzle. Were the origins of the Berlin West African Conference in Europe or in the Congo?

Historical Background

The British and Portuguese had been negotiating for several years and were near signing an agreement effectively turning Portugal's possessions in the Congo area over to the British.

At the same time, King Leopold of Belgium, the French government under Jules Ferry, and even Bismarck of Germany were becoming increasingly interested in African colonies. Some historians have characterized the period as reminiscent of a "gold rush mentality." A highly competitive and dangerous situation was developing. A conference among interested powers was called to deal with these problems.

The French and German governments sent the following invitation to the world's Great Powers:

> The expansion of the commerce of western Africa has suggested to the governments of France and Germany the idea that it would be to the common interest of the nations engaged in this to regulate in the spirit of accord the mutual conditions which assure development and prevent conflicts . . . . To attain this end the government of Germany in accord with the government of the Republic of France proposes that representatives of the different powers interested in the continent of Africa meet in conference at Berlin during the course of the month to reach an entente on the principles which have been announced.

DOCUMENT 1

"What I wish to establish is a sort of equilibrium on the seas . . . . I do not want war with England, but I want her to understand that if the navies of the other nations unite they will counterbalance her on the oceans . . . . A Franco-German Alliance is not an impossibility."

Source: Chancellor von Bismarck, letter to Baron de Courcel, French Ambassador in Berlin, September 21, 1884

DOCUMENT 2

The following countries were represented at the Conference:

Austria-Hungary, Belgium, Denmark, France, Germany, Great Britain, Holland, Italy, Norway, Portugal, Spain, Sweden, Turkey, the United States of America.

Observers from The International Association of the Congo also attended.

DOCUMENT 3

"At every point at which Germany had endeavored to found a colony, England had closed in, making new acquisitions, so as to restrict Germany's power of expansion."

Source: Statement made in a private conversation between Chancellor von Bismarck and Sir Edward Malet, the British Ambassador at Berlin, January 24, 1885

DOCUMENT 4

Source: Baron de Courcel, French Ambassador in Berlin, letter to Bismarck, September 29, 1884: [translated and edited]

"... The Government of the Republic of France is in accord with the German Imperial Government that it considers it desirable that the principles adopted by the Congress of Vienna to guarantee freedom of navigation on several waterways, later applied to the Danube, should be equally applied by the interested parties under international guarantees, to the Congo and the Niger.

We also think that in order to assure the regular development of European commerce in Africa and to prevent regrettable 'contests' on the subject of territorial possessions between the different nations, it would be useful to arrive at an accord on the formalities to observe for new occupations on the African coast to be considered effective."

Source: Le Figaro, October 14, 1884

DOCUMENT 5

THE WEST AFRICAN CONFERENCE AND THE NIGER

It is currently stated that at the approaching West African Conference the discussion will not be confined to the Congo but will include the Niger, by which I presume is meant the Lower Niger. The astonishment of all who have for over 40 years looked on the Lower Niger as a British river is heightened by the statement in a well-informed Parisian journal that France has expressly excluded from discussion the Senegal and Gaboon [sic] rivers....

I am not advocating any national or international legislation restricting freedom of commerce. The great rivers of Africa, including the Senegal and the Gaboon, should be left free to all who choose to enter them. The day has gone by when exclusive privileges to trade could be granted to an association, however open its share-list may be to the world. I am replying only to arguments which have been urged by those who, from the association of ideas, view with a prejudiced eye the natural monopoly which has grown up on the Niger, and which will assuredly, after much ruin and disappointment, arrive on the Congo.

The claim, however, that the Lower Niger regions are British does not rest alone on grounds of discovery, nor of (practically) sole commercial occupation, nor of parliamentary subsidies, nor of the sacrifice of so many British lives before experience had taught a partial solution of the climatic problem, nor of the very large amount of British capital lost up to 1879 in forming the complicated but stable local organization which now exists, and in building up a widespread system of treaties with the native chiefs. It is based rather on the protection consistently afforded by the British Government, and by it alone, ever since the opening of these regions to trade. British gunboats have there maintained order as well as in the numerous mouths on the delta of the Niger. The British Consul has been regarded as sole arbiter of disputes, not only between Europeans and the natives, but among the indigenous tribes themselves, and has, by treaties, by presents, and by consistent and conciliatory representations abated the scourge of Africa—slave raids and slave caravans . . . .

Can such a record be shown by any other nation on any African river? Can actual occupation be here denied to a country whose merchants have nearly 100 stations spread over the greater part of the navigable waters? Is the Lower Niger basin to be unnecessarily dragged into a conference on the Congo question? Is it to be withdrawn from the protection of Great Britain to be treated as a no man's land and to be internationalised, while France expressly excludes from discussion both the Senegal river—thus closing against Europe the vast basin of the Upper Niger—and the Gaboon River—thus stopping the natural road to Central Africa north of the Congo?

All African rivers should be free to all traders, subject, of course, to the natural law which no legislation can over-ride the law of free competition, where the weaker goes to the wall. International commissions may regulate the traffic of a river as on the Danube . . . . To keep the Niger open to the world no international commission is needed. . . .

Source: London Times, October 15, 1884

DOCUMENT 6

It is a question of international law to establish. Up to now, England has not adhered to the principle that has been stated as follows:

In order to be effective, occupation must not simply be written on paper but must exist in fact and continuously.

Up to now, England and Portugal are the only two powers that have raised objections to Bismarck's foreign policy. The battle for sharing the world has entered a dangerous phase. For half a century England has not tolerated any encroachments by any other power. Her ill humor has been manifest at every expansion of France's colonial dominion.

Mr. Ferry has seized on this opportunity to make common cause with the greatest number of powers on the question of Africa's future.

Source: Le Figaro, October 10, 1884

DOCUMENT 7

There is still a great deal of discussion in Paris about the Conference of Berlin, but it is going too far to state that President Ferry has meekly played Germany's game and got nothing in return for France.

A second conference is needed not just on solutions to the colonial questions, but on relations between European powers.

Source: Gazette Allemande, Vienna,
October 16, 1884

DOCUMENT 8

. . . At this moment there are more common interests between Germany and us than there are between Germany and England. Should we repel or accept Germany's appeal? It is a question . . . which depends completely on England's attitude toward us and toward Europe in general. At present we are persuaded that England is the only country with which we could have an alliance. But if England—which could have helped us in China but didn't—continues to have an anti-European attitude in Africa, how can we but side with those European powers that have been menaced by the blows we have felt first. . . .

It would not be weakness or humiliating on our part to make common cause with the Germans. What would be the worst thing would be to accept, and then reject, Germany's advances. There are sure to be violent attacks on such an acceptance in the press, but we cannot let Germany believe that France is incapable of withstanding the pressures of blind patriotism.

Source: Gabriel Charmes, *Journal des Debats*,
Paris, October, 1884

DOCUMENT 9

The colonial expansion of certain powers has been a continual subject of disquiet. We have seen in less than four years England take over Egypt, the Red Sea, Suez, one-third of Zululand, Betckuanland, all of Southern Africa from the Orange River to Cuneme. Each has consolidated its African possessions around Sierra Leone.

It permitted German occupation of Cameroon, but only with compensation in the Niger Delta. She has also established a new East India Company in North Borneo and has proclaimed a British protectorate over the east half of New Guinea. All this in less than four years. . . .

It is because of this insatiable need of Britain to expand that the Conference's real mission is to stop it, to establish laws on occupation of countries not yet occupied. In a word, the Berlin conference has proclaimed the internationalization of certain territories and countries. They are not to become the possessions of one country but to remain open to all. For us, France needs to see this principle applied in Egypt, which could become an insurmountable barrier between the mother country and her colonies.

Source: Le Figaro, October 13, 1884

DOCUMENT 10

"The resolutions . . . secure to the trade of all nations free access to the interior of the African Continent . . . . You have sought for the means to withdraw a great part of the African Continent from the vicissitudes of general politics, and confine the rivalry of nations to the peaceful competition of trade and industry."

Source: Chancellor Bismarck, speech to the delegates just before signing the agreements they negotiated

DOCUMENT 11

ARTICLE 5

No Power which exercises or shall exercise sovereign rights in the above-mentioned regions shall be allowed to grant therein a monopoly or favour of any kind in matters of trade.

ARTICLE 13

The navigation of the Congo, without excepting any of its branches or outlets, is, and shall remain, free for the merchant-ships of all nations equally. . . .

ARTICLE 17

There is instituted an International Commission, charged with the execution of the provisions of the present Act of Navigation.

The Signatory Powers of this Act, as well as those who may subsequently adhere to it, may always be represented on the said Commission, each by one Delegate. But no Delegate shall have more than one vote at his disposal, even in the case of his representing several Governments.

ARTICLE 26

The navigation of the Niger, without excepting any of its branches and outlets, is and shall remain entirely free for the merchant-ships of all nations equally. . . .

ARTICLE 30

Great Britain undertakes to protect foreign merchants and all the trading nationalities on all those portions of the Niger which are or may be under her sovereignty or protection as if they were her own subjects, provided always that such merchants conform to the rules which are or shall be made in virtue of the foregoing.

ARTICLE 34

Any Power which henceforth takes possession of a tract of land on the coasts of the African Continent outside of its present possessions, or which, being hitherto without such possessions, shall acquire them, as well as the power which assumes a Protectorate there, shall accompany the respective act with a notification thereof, addressed to the other Signatory Powers of the present Act, in order to enable them, if need be, to make good any claims of their own.

ARTICLE 35

The Signatory powers of the present Act recognize the obligations to insure the establishment of authority in the regions occupied by them on the coasts of the African Continent sufficient to protect existing rights, and, as the case may be, freedom of trade and of transit under the conditions agreed upon.

Source: General Act of the Conference of Berlin, 1885

DOCUMENT 12

"All industrial countries under the necessity of finding markets are expanding in Africa and Asia. It is not true that France is weakening her resources in going also. She is strong now and that is why she can go and take her place again as a great power. . . .

In the name of an exalted and short-sighted chauvinism, ought we to drive French politics into an impasse, and with eyes fixed on the blue line of the Vosges, let everything alone, let everything become pledged and determined about us, without us?"

Source: Jules Ferry, *Tonkin et la Mère-Patrie: Témoignes et Documents*, Paris, 1890, pp. 48–51

DOCUMENT 13

"The treatment which England has inflicted on us for several months makes rapprochement necessary for us under pain of the most absolute and dangerous isolation. Germany on her side desires and seeks it. But what are her motives? There are two; the hope of making us forget Alsace and the desire that we detach ourselves definitely and irremediably from England."

Source: Baron de Courcel, *Le Figaro*, October 14, 1884

DOCUMENT 14

BISMARCK: I want to reach a point where you will pardon Sedan as you have pardoned Waterloo.

COURCEL: I never speak to you of Alsace, but from your side, if you sincerely desire an entente on this point, beware of turning the knife in our wound, for the French nation will not be able to control its feelings.

Source: Private Conversation between Bismarck and Courcel, December 1884

DOCUMENT 15

"Today . . . the semi-official newspapers, *The Temps* in particular, publish articles designed to reassure those alarmed at the prospect of France becoming a star in the Germanic constellation. One sentence will give an idea of the singular tone of *The Temps*:

'Prince Bismarck, after deliberately isolating France, to prevent her from prosecuting redress of the wrongs inflicted on her, has conceived the ambition of making her forget her grievances.'

Who would have expected such an euphemism from *The Temps*—the description of the war of 1870, and its consequences as 'wrongs inflicted on France.' Colder water could scarcely be poured on the heated brain of French patriots. Yet *The Temps* is quite right in saying that a Government should not resentfully refuse the co-operation of any Power because of having an old score to settle with it.

In this case, however, it must be borne in mind that, in the eyes of Prince Bismarck, as of all the strange Frenchmen encouraging the advances between the two countries, the sacrifice of the good understanding with England was to be the result, if not the condition. It is only on condition of being cool towards England that the Franco-German concert is feasible, and people are entitled and bound to ask if this price, already paid in part, does not far outweigh the advantage to be reaped from an understanding with Germany in Africa, when that understanding cannot be established in Europe.

Source: London Times, October 15, 1885

Second Sample
Document-Based Question
Analysis

This document-based question asks you to examine two separate, although somewhat related, developments in nineteenth century European history; the diplomatic history of the period and the history of western imperialism in Africa. In answering this document-based question, you should discuss each theme separately at first and then try to link them together.

At the end of the Franco-Prussian War of 1870–1871, France was forced to sign the very harsh Treaty of Frankfurt. It created a France in which nationalists called for revenge and a Germany that sought to prevent France from feeling strong enough to start such a war. The diplomatic history of the period, sometimes referred to as "Bismarck's system," involved a shifting arrangement of alliances and alignments. Despite what might look like friendliness towards France, he never lost sight of the main point—France always presented a danger. Bismarck sought to attract allies to Germany and to keep France isolated.

By means of the Three Emperors' League (1872), Bismarck allied Austria and Russia to Germany. Bismarck's actions at the Congress of Berlin (1878), however, were viewed in Russia as anti-Russian, and Russia became an uncertain ally. A secret defensive alliance was struck between Austria and Germany (against Russia) in 1879; when Italy joined the two allies three years later, the Triple Alliance was formed. Although Bismarck was able to revive a shaky Alliance of the Three Emperors (1881–1887), it lapsed after six years. (A substitute Reinsurance Treaty between Russia and Germany was supposed to have replaced it.) With the presumed loss of Russian support after 1879, Bismarck needed even more to keep France isolated, especially from Britain. Apparently friendly moves towards France were actually moves to keep Britain and France apart.

Documents 1, 7, 8, 12, 13, 14, and 15 refer to relations between France and Germany. The "hole in the Vosges" or "the blue line of the Vosges" refers to the territory of Alsace-Lorraine which France was forced to cede to Germany in the Treaty of Frankfurt.

Bismarck had consistently stated that Germany was a satisfied country and did not seek colonies overseas. There were, however, several factors that made such a nonimperialist policy difficult, if not impossible to maintain. Germany, during the 1850s and 1860s industrialized more rapidly than any country in Europe. From the mid 1870s on German industrialists sought protection from foreign competition (high tariffs) and a colonial policy which would enable them to have a guaranteed market for their products.

Public opinion in Germany at the time was increasingly strong in favor of acquiring colonies. A German Colonial Association was formed in 1882; one claim it made was that German missionaries in Africa were unprotected. The recent British moves in Egypt and in West Africa seemed to indicate that very shortly there would be no places that had not been, at least on a map, already taken.

Documents 3, 4, 5, 6, 9, 10, 11, and 12 refer to colonization in Africa.

Both themes find a point of convergence in the increased tension that was engendered between Germany and Britain. In both its colonial and diplomatic policies, Germany found itself opposing British plans in Africa. In addition, the same forces in Germany that pushed for an overseas empire, strongly advocated an expanded fleet to patrol and protect that empire. Naval rivalry between the two nations also had consequences in 1914.

Second Sample
Document-Based Question
Response A

The Conference of Berlin of 1884–1885 clearly originated in Europe. The conference was developed to solve European conflict and deal with European power. Africa was the object of European imperialism at the time but was not the cause. It was the actions of the European nations themselves that made the conference necessary.

The changes and provisions proposed by the conference did indeed mark a turning point in European imperialism and in European relations. A few of the major attitudes of the General Act of the Conference of Berlin, outlined in Document 11, opened Africa to all European nations. It provided for free trade and free navigation while simultaneously putting an end to earlier Acts of Navigation. It also restricted imperialism and the power that came with it. Not only do these drastic changes support the fact that this conference would have a major impact on Europe but the list of nations attending (Document 2) illustrates the conference's importance.

Both Documents 1 and 6 express the prospect of a new alliance between France and other powers, specifically Germany. They also suggest the end to an alliance with Great Britain. However, France is unsure of what to do and, in Documents 7 and 8, simply resolves to act in its own best interests. However, France is unsure of exactly where those interests lie. On the one hand, Britain's growing power in recent years, evident in Document 9, could cause France to remain friendly with England. On the other hand, that power could cause France to join Germany in its crusade against England. However, France's conflicts with Germany in the past create a reluctance on France's part to become a part of Germany's plans (Documents 14 and 15). Unfortunately, France became a pawn in conflict with itself and was caught in the middle of the growing conflict between Germany and England.

The Conference of Berlin could be described as it is by Bismarck in Documents 1 and 10 as a means to control the balance of power and a resolve to compete only on an economic level with an equal chance to everyone. However, this could have simply been a ruse to disguise Germany's real desire to increase its own power and, at the same time, to take England's power away.

Documents 3, 6, 8, and 13 also depict the resentment developing towards England in both Germany and France. England had been expanding both its power and its territory as it prevented Germany from doing the same. England also treated France poorly thus isolating itself from both countries. However, England shows how it is clearly the target at the Conference of Berlin in Document 5. England notes that its possessions are to be included in the Conference while France's territory will remain undisputed. Thus since it was singled out, England had no choice but to oppose Germany and its Conference.

The original intentions of the Conference of Berlin were clearly lost. The Conference worked only to encourage conflicts among England, France, and Germany and left only resentment rather than peaceful cooperation and agreement. Imperialism meant competition and a struggle for power. Trying to put an end to that struggle only fueled the fire.

CRITICAL COMMENTARY

This is a well-organized and well-presented essay. The introductory paragraph clearly presents its author's thesis. The body of the DBQ (paragraphs 2–5) provides evidence to support the author's point of view. He uses the documents to support his generalizations. The conclusion summarizes the information given; however, it could have been more specific. The student answers the questions of the origins of the Berlin West African Conference but does not tell us whether the Conference was a turning point in European imperialism in Africa and/or a piece in Bismarck's European diplomatic jigsaw puzzle.

Score: Demonstrates competence.

Second Sample Document-Based Question Response B

The Congo Conference of 1884, sponsored by Bismarck of Germany, was an attempt to patch together a system that would keep the powers of Europe from tearing each other apart. The actual interest of Germany or even France in Africa was, at best, minimal.

Germany had few colonies in Africa except for part of the Congo, Cameroon, and Togo. As a central European power, Germany could not afford to expend much effort on developing far-flung colonies. In fact, during this period Germany lost the Caroline Islands to Spain. Because of this geo-political reality, Germany's interest in Africa hinged on keeping trade lines open and, most important of all, whatever could be done to shift European alliances in her favor.

France's main colonial interest was in Indochina, where she was to remain until the 1950s (until the defeat at Dienbienphu). Document 12 mentions this interest in Asia. But, at this time, France was caught between feelings of vengeance after her crushing defeat in the Franco-Prussian War of 1870 and the knowledge that the only way to "get even" lay in helping Britain, whose naval supremacy severely limited French ability to expand. That this limitation was keenly felt is noted in Documents 6 and 8. Document 4 points out concerns for preventing "conflicts," and considering that Britain was the preeminent colonial power, the "conflicts" would most likely be with Britain who, after all, had blocked Germany too (Document 3).

Bismarck, in appraising the current European status quo, knew that Germany could not allow herself to be surrounded by enemies. This had been his guiding principle in setting up the Alliance of the Three Emperors, the last such treaty being in 1881. But Russia was an unreliable ally, especially since she could never really forget the humiliation of being left in the lurch by Prussia and young King Wilhelm in the Crimean War.

Bismarck desperately wanted a more stable alliance than what he had with Russia. This was made even more urgent as Russia and France flirted with each other and because Britain expressed disapproval of a too close Russian alliance. Bismarck needed either to outflank France by getting Britain as an ally or otherwise break the circle by neutralizing France. That neutralization required either a direct alliance with Germany or active enmity between Britain and France.

That Bismarck tried and failed to gain Britain as an ally is clear. Despite the bluster in Document 1, Bismarck was very careful to keep from antagonizing Britain. The conciliatory words in Document 10 underlie the fact that the pact put a seal on British ownership of large portions of Africa. But the British policy of "splendid isolation" (as typified in England's questioning the need for a conference in Document 5) prevented that course from becoming profitable.

While still keeping the British option open, Bismarck next turned to the possibility of either attracting France to Germany (Document 14) or detaching France from Britain by playing on the fear that Britain acts against the interests of the rest of Europe (Documents 9, 13, 15). While he garnered some slight French sympathy (Document 7), especially in inciting France's appropriation of Tunis in 1882, he could not overcome what was seen as the theft of Alsace–Lorraine in the French mind. The second path became closed as Germany's growing industrial might make her a far more immediate threat to Europe than Britain's far-flung colonies.

CRITICAL COMMENTARY

This is a well-written and knowledgeable essay. The author states his thesis in the first paragraph and uses both the documents and his knowledge of history to prove his point. He does not, however, restate his thesis in the conclusion nor does he summarize his findings.

Score: Demonstrates competence

THE REVIEW OF EUROPEAN HISTORY

This chapter provides a review of the major time periods in European history that are covered on the Advanced Placement examination. The time periods are divided as follows:

A. The Renaissance
B. The Reformation
C. The Age of Exploration
D. The Scientific Revolution
E. The Rise of Nation-states
F. Absolute Monarchies: France, Russia, Austria, and Prussia
G. The Enlightenment
H. The French Revolution
I. The Napoleonic Era (1799-1815)
J. The Industrial Revolution
K. Reaction, Romanticism, and Revolution (1815-1867)
L. Nationalism
M. Nineteenth Century Social and Political Change (Democratic Reforms)
N. The Age of Imperialism
O. The Fin De Siècle: Modernization or Decadence?
P. World War I
Q. The Russian Revolution
R. Totalitarian Societies
S. World War II
T. The Cold War (World War II-1968)
U. The End of Imperialism: Africa and Asia
V. The Changing World: Technology and Society
W. The Demise of the Soviet Union

A Review of European History from the Renaissance to the Present

Each history review is divided into five sections:

1. Chronology

This section organizes the unit in correct time sequence. The AP European History exam often asks the students to put events, e.g., the early Reformation, into their proper, chronological order. Many of the terms and concepts of the era are introduced in the chronology.

2. Major Terms and Concepts

This section is a list of important names, places, ideas, and events that fall within the time frame of the unit.

3. Major Themes and Questions

In this part, several large questions of analysis are posed that suggest some of the major issues of the unit.

4. Sample Outline

This section is an outline of an answer to a question of analysis. Some are designed to answer very large questions; others deal with much narrower aspects of the period involved.

5. Short Reading List

This part includes major works of interpretation, some classic sources, e.g., Burke's *Reflections on the French Revolution* and Paine's *The Rights of Man*. It also may list a few works of fiction which give a sense of the period (or at least the author's notion of what the period was like). You may need to be familiar with generally recognized literature in the field.

None of these review chapters is designed to replace a text of European history. They are based on learning theory which stresses reinforcement of previously learned material. They cannot be used without reference to your own AP course. They do, however, recall and suggest information useful for the examination.

Unit Review A
The Renaissance

CHRONOLOGY

1434 Cosimo de' Medici establishes his family's dominance in Florence

1438 Pragmatic Sanction of Bourges establishes the French Catholic Church's independence from Rome

1453 Ottoman Turks capture Constantinople; end of the Byzantine Empire

1456 Johannes Gutenberg prints the Mazarin Bible

1469 Marriage of Isabella of Castile and Ferdinand of Aragon

1471–1484 Pope Sixtus IV builds the Vatican Library

1492 Completion of the *Reconquista*; expulsion of the Jews from Spain

1494 Invasion of Italy by Charles VIII; Medici family is expelled from Florence (until 1512)

1509 Erasmus publishes *In Praise of Folly*

1516 Concordat of Bologna between Pope Leo X and King Francis I rescinds the Pragmatic Sanction of Bourges; Thomas More publishes *Utopia*

1517 Machiavelli completes *The Prince*

1518 Castiglione completes *The Book of the Courtier*

1527 The Sack of Rome by Holy Roman Emperor, Charles V

1534–1541 Michelangelo at work on *The Last Judgment*

1603 Shakespeare's *Hamlet*

MAJOR TERMS AND CONCEPTS

Alexander VI (1431–1503)
Dante Alighieri (1265–1321)
Giovanni Boccaccio (1313–1375)
Sandro Botticelli (1444–1510)
Filippo Brunelleschi (1377–1446)
Michelangelo Buonarroti (1475–1564)
Baldassare Castiglione, *The Book of the Courtier* (1478–1529)
Benvenuto Cellini (1500–1571)
Leonardo da Vinci (1452–1519)
Miguel de Cervantes (1547–1616)
Lorenzo de' Medici, "The Magnificent" (1449–1492)
Pico della Mirandola (1463–1494)
Donatello (1386–1466)
Erasmus (1466–1536)
Jacob Fugger (1459–1525)
Lorenzo Ghiberti (1378–1455)
Giotto (1266–1337)
Francesco Guicciardini (1483–1540)
Hans Holbein the Younger (1497–1543)
humanism

individualism
Julius II (1443–1513)
Leo X (1475–1521)
Niccolò Machiavelli, *The Prince* (1469–1527)
Masaccio (1401–1428)
Montaigne (1533–1592)
Sir Thomas More (1478–1535)
"new monarchs"
Pazzi conspiracy
Petrarch
Quattrocento
François Rabelais (1490–1553)
"Renaissance Man"
revival of antiquity
Raphael Santi (1483–1520)
Fra Girolamo Savonarola (1452–1498)
secularism
Caterina Sforza (1463–1509)
Lorenzo Valla (1405–1457)
Giorgio Vasari (1511–1574)
vernacular

MAJOR THEMES AND QUESTIONS

1. Compare and contrast the Renaissance in Italy and in northern Europe.
2. Why was Italy the birthplace of the Renaissance?
3. How does Renaissance humanism reflect a change from medieval thought?
4. Explain the Renaissance as an urban phenomenon.
5. Describe the ideal Renaissance individual. Illustrate the ideal Renaissance individual, choosing the biography of Leon Batista Alberti, Isabella d'Este, Lorenzo de' Medici or Leonardo da Vinci.
6. How did the philosophies of the Renaissance change people's attitudes towards the Church?
7. Describe changes in painting, poetry, architecture, and sculpture that arose during the Renaissance. How did these cultural achievements reflect the values of Renaissance society?
8. Describe the position of women during the Italian Renaissance.

SAMPLE OUTLINE

Topic: *The Renaissance was a period of increased secularism.*

I. Defining Secularism

A. The secular attitude emphasizes the "here and now" rather than the "other world" of heaven. This belief was expressed perfectly in Lorenzo de' Medici's poem:

> How beautiful is youth
> How fast it flies away
> Youths and maids—enjoy today
> Of tomorrow, nothing is certain

B. Emphasis is placed more on material rewards than on spiritual happiness.

C. The world is usually explained in terms of discoverable causes. The Bible is superseded as the ultimate authority.

II. Characteristics of Secularism in Italy

A. Commercial interests of the rising bourgeoisie occupied an increasing portion of their time and energy.

B. Wealthy Italians were able to enjoy a relatively splendid lifestyle.
  1. They became patrons of the arts. Michelangelo's creation of the Medici tomb is just one example. Portrait painting was a new art form introduced.
  2. Luxuries—jewels and fine clothing—were increasingly displayed by the well-to-do.
  3. Family histories and poems extolling lineal virtues were commissioned to bring them fame and glory.
  4. Castiglione's *Book of the Courtier* taught "proper" etiquette for the perfect gentleman.

C. The materialist lifestyle became an increasingly frequent subject of literature.
   1. Lorenzo Valla's *On Pleasure* praised sensual experiences.
   2. Boccaccio's *Decameron* is a set of tales picturing a lusty and lustful society.

D. The secular attitude entered the Church.
   1. Pope Julius II, referred to as Mars since he personally led troops into battle against the French, used Michelangelo and other artists to help beautify the city of Rome.
   2. Innocent VIII and Alexander VI were, perhaps, the two most scandalous popes.
   3. Leo X, son of Lorenzo de' Medici, is reported to have said, "God has given us the Papacy. Now let us enjoy it."

E. A critical attitude sought to inquire into the nature of things and to explain them "realistically."
   1. The scholar Lorenzo Valla proved the Donation of Constantine, a document which since the fifth century had traditionally been used by the Catholic Church to legitimize papal rule in central Italy, to be a forgery. According to this document, when Constantine founded his new capital Constantinople in Byzantium, he relinquished the secular government of Rome to Pope Sylvester.
   2. Machiavelli's *The Prince* examined what he considered to be the true nature of power. In Machiavelli's work, the emphasis of "divine right" as the justification for leadership gave way to a more pragmatic explanation. According to Machiavelli, as long as a leader could enforce his decisions by whatever means necessary, his success in and of itself was justification. The legitimacy of any government, therefore, was determined by its success and survival.

F. The prominence of the secular outlook, however, should not be exaggerated.
   1. It was largely confined to the well-to-do.
   2. Most people remained deeply faithful and committed to the Church. Religious issues were still important enough to cause bitter disputes.

SHORT READING LIST

Volume I of *The New Cambridge Modern History* deals with the Renaissance.

M. P. Gilmore, *The World of Humanism,* is still valuable despite its nearly thirty years in print.

L. Martines, *Power and Imagination: City-States in Renaissance Italy,* is a more recent (1980) broad survey of the period.

Henry Lucas, *The Renaissance and the Reformation,* although an older work, is a very good general introduction to the period.

W. K. Ferguson, *The Renaissance in Historical Thought,* is a classic example of historiography, placing the "idea" of the Renaissance against the background of different historical periods.

J. Huizinga's books *The Waning of the Middle Ages* and *Erasmus of Rotterdam* deal with the Renaissance in the North of Europe.

I. Maclean, *The Renaissance Notion of Women* (1980), is a recent addition to the field.

G. Vasari, *Lives Of The Artists,* remains a classic.

C. M. Ady's *Lorenzo de' Medici Renaissance Italy* is a short biography that considers Lorenzo the most representative figure of Renaissance Italy.

F. Schevill, *History of Florence,* is more than a half century old but in many ways not surpassed.

B. Berenson, *Italian Painters of the Renaissance,* is a classic interpretation.

J. Burckhardt, *The Civilization of the Renaissance in Italy,* is both a fact-filled survey and a seminal work of interpretation.

J. A. Symonds, *The Age of the Despots* and *The Revival of Learning,* are two volumes of his three-volume, mid-nineteenth century study, *The Renaissance in Italy.*

George Eliot's *Romola* is an exceptional work of fiction set in Florence at the time of Savonarola. It is based on meticulous research by the author and presents a novelist's recreation of the life of the times.

Unit Review B
The Reformation

CHRONOLOGY

1517 Martin Luther's 95 *Theses* are posted on the door of the Court Church in Wittenberg.

1518 Luther refuses to recant his assertions.

1519 Luther debates theologian John Eck on the issue of the authority of the Pope and church councils.

1520 Luther is excommunicated by Pope Leo X.

1521 Luther is declared an outlaw by Charles V and the Diet of Worms.

1524 Peasants' rebellion in Germany is stirred by Luther's writings though condemned by Luther personally.

1527 Henry VIII of England petitions Pope Clement VII for a divorce from Catherine of Aragon.

1529 German Lutheran princes protest imperial decrees against their faith (hence the origin of the term "Protestant").

1530 Archbishop of Canterbury Thomas Cranmer annuls the marriage of Henry VIII and Catherine of Aragon.

1531 Ulrich Zwingli killed.

1534 The Act of Supremacy completes the English reformation.

1534–1535 The Anabaptist movement, led by John of Leyden, takes control of the German town of Munster in an attempt to make it a "City of God."

1536 John Calvin's *Institutes* are published in Geneva.

1539 British Parliament passes the *Six Articles* reaffirming many of the sacraments of the Catholic Church.

1540 The Jesuit Order is founded by the Roman Catholic Church to counter the spread of Protestantism.

1541 Calvin constructs a government based on the subordination of the state to the church and becomes "ruler" over the city of Geneva until his death in 1564.

1545 The Council of Trent is called by Pope Paul III. It reaffirms the seven sacraments.

1547 The *Six Articles* are repealed by Parliament.

1549 The British Parliament passes acts adopting the Anglican mass and prayer book as the implements of the new state religion.

1550 John Knox establishes Presbyterianism in Scotland.

1551 Thomas Cranmer publishes *42 Articles of Religion*.

1553 Michael Servetus, one of the founders of Unitarianism, is burned at the stake by orders of John Calvin.

1562 Conflicts between Huguenots and Catholic nobles lead to civil wars in France that end in the Treaty of Nantes (1598).

1563 British Parliament adapts thirty-nine of Cranmer's *42 Articles of Religion*. The Elizabethan prayerbook is developed.

MAJOR TERMS AND CONCEPTS

Act of Supremacy
Anabaptists
Anglicanism
Antinomian
Robert Browne (1550–1633)
Brownists
John Calvin (1509–1564)
Calvinism
consubstantiation
Council of Trent
covenant
Thomas Cranmer (1489–1556),
  42 Articles of Religion
Diet of Worms
Johann Eck (1486–1543)
Edict of Nantes
Edict of Worms
excommunication
High Church Anglicanism
Huguenots
John Huss (1369–1415)
Ignatius de Loyola (1491–1556),
  Spiritual Exercises
indulgences
The Institutes

Jesuits
John of Leyden (1509–1536)
John Knox (1513–1572)
Low Church Anglicanism, *The Index*
Martin Luther (1483–1546), *Appeal to the*
  Christian Nobility of the German Nation
Pope Clement VII (1475–1534)
Pope Leo X (1475–1521)
Pope Paul III (1468–1549)
Pope Pius V (1504–1572)
predestination
Presbyterianism
salvation
Michael Servetus (1511–1553)
seven sacraments
The Six Articles
synod
Johann Tetzel (1465–1519)
transubstantiation
The Twelve Articles
Unitarianism
Thomas Wolsey (1475–1530)
John Wycliffe (1329–1384)
Ulrich Zwingli (1484–1531)

MAJOR THEMES AND QUESTIONS

1. To what extent were Luther's 95 Theses a political as well as a dogmatic protest against the Roman Catholic Church?
2. In what ways did Lutheranism differ from Calvinism?
3. In what ways did Calvin's beliefs differ from those of Zwingli?
4. Discuss the political significance of Calvinist and Lutheran doctrine.
5. In what ways was the Anabaptist movement an extension of the Lutheran and Calvinist reformation?
6. What caused the spread of Lutheranism throughout the German states among the nobility and the common people?
7. What reasons might explain the failure of Protestantism to spread to the French nobility to the degree that it did in the German states?
8. Was the Reformation in England more of a political or dogmatic reformation? Explain and prove.
9. Why did Protestantism and Anglicanism fail to gain the popular support in Ireland that they did throughout the rest of the British Isles?
10. To what extent did the Council of Trent address the issues in Luther's 95 Theses?
11. What impact did the spread of Protestantism have upon the political balance of power in Europe from 1520 to 1603?

SAMPLE OUTLINE

Topic: *To what extent could the Reformaton be viewed as a further progression in the rise of an educated middle class?*

I. The development of the middle class

A. The Hanseatic League not only began the trend towards economic unity in the German states but also financed many of the German feudal princes. There was growing unity among middle class merchants from different states.

B. In both France, under Louis XI, and England, under the Tudor monarchs, the bourgeoisie were relied upon for finances.

C. Development of credit and institutionalized banking during the Hundred Years' War brought recognition and power to families such as the Medici, the Bardi, and the Peruzzi.

D. In Italy especially, it was the wealthy merchant and banking families that not only patronized the arts but also populated the universities. Education, in the Renaissance sense, including math, science, literature, and rhetoric, was available even to the middle classes.

E. Catholic doctrine regarding interest and fair price (also known as "just price") ran counter to the needs of a capitalist class. Conversely, Calvinist and Puritan ideals saw hard work and wealth as a sign of God's favor and as a form of tribute towards the Lord. In addition, the elimination of many of the religious holidays complemented the requirements of a business class.

F. Middle class materialism paralleled, in economic terms, the Renaissance ideal of humanism. Similarly, both displayed distrust of traditional Catholic superstitions. Both also stressed achievement in this world over the expectation of reward in heaven.

II. The Reformation and the catholic church

A. Indulgences and tithes used to finance the building of cathedrals burdened the poor and middle class and increased the tendency to view Rome as a foreign power.

B. Papal involvement in a series of political power conflicts with European monarchs (for example, Henry IV, Holy Roman Emperor vs. Gregory VII; The Crusades; papal involvement in the Lombard League; the Babylonian Captivity in Avignon) combined with the tendency of the papacy to be a politically appointed seat (for example, the Borgia family control of the papacy) resulted in a loss of prestige and hence much of the temporal mystique once afforded the clergy.

C. In countries such as Germany and England where a developed and thriving middle class existed, and where the government lacked any central control (as in German states), or where the government was congenial to the needs of the middle class (as the Tudors had been though usually in order to play the middle class against the nobility), Protestantism thrived.

D. Protestantism and Lutheranism offered monetary reward to feudal leaders since it did not accept ecclesiastic immunity from taxation. Conversion, or threat of conversion was also used as a political weapon to gain favors from the popes or to counter alliances (German princes saw Lutheranism as a way to counter the Hapsburg power. Henry VIII, even after his split with Rome, constantly reversed himself and "his" church when political pragmatism dictated an alliance with Rome.).

E. In the more extreme Protestant faiths such as Presbyterianism, a synod or council of elders regulated the actions of the clergy and also claimed the right to question the king as, according to feudal tradition, he was answerable to God. Many of these councils were populated by the middle class and lesser nobility.

SHORT READING LIST

J. Atkinson, *Martin Luther and the Birth of Protestantism*, is a scholarly biography of the reformer.

Roland Bainton, *Here I Stand: A Life of Martin Luther* (1950) and *The Reformation of the Sixteenth Century* (1952), are dramatic yet scholarly accounts of the period.

Robert Bolt, *A Man For All Seasons* (1962), is a fictionalized account of Thomas More's role in the English Reformation.

G. R. Elton, *Reform and Reformation: England, 1509–1588* (1977). Elton asks: How did the religious movement influence political changes?

John T. McNeill, *The History and Character of Calvinism* (1954), is an informative study of the Reformation Leader.

W. E. Monter, *Calvin's Geneva* (1967), is a social history of Reformation Geneva.

George Mosse, *The Reformation* (1969), is a short and fairly routine account.

S. Ozment, *When Fathers Ruled: Family Life in Reformation Europe* (1983), is a very recent approach to Reformation Studies.

Bernard Reardon, *Religious Thought in the Reformation* (1981) and L. W. Spitz, *The Protestant Reformation* (1985). Both include much recent research.

Unit Review C
The Age of Exploration

CHRONOLOGY

1393–1450 Prince Henry the Navigator of Portugal.

1445 The Portuguese conquer Cape Verde, Africa.

1472 Portuguese reach the "bulge" of West Africa.

1474 Toscanelli, Italian map maker, publishes a map reintroducing the ancient Greek concept of a spherical world.

1488 Bartholomew Diaz reaches the Cape of Good Hope.

1492 Christopher Columbus sails for India.

1493 Pope Alexander VI grants all territory south and west, in the Atlantic, between the Azores and Cape Verdi to Spain.

1494 Treaty of Tordesilla moves the Papal demarcation line of 1493 west to give Brazil to Portugal.

1497 Vasco da Gama reaches the Indian coast.

1497–1498 John and Sebastian Cabot explore Nova Scotia, Newfoundland and the coast of eastern America.

1500 Pedro Cabral reaches Brazil.

1513 Vasco Nuñez de Balboa reaches the Pacific from the Isthmus of Panama.

1519–1522 Ferdinand Magellan circumnavigates the world.

1519 Hernando Cortes conquers the Aztecs of Mexico.

1524 Giovanni da Verrazano explores the coast of North America.

1531–1533 Francisco Pizarro conquers the Incas of Peru.

1534–1541 Jacques Cartier explores the St. Lawrence River, Canada.

1542 Spain outlaws enslavement of the natives in South America.

1542–1543 The Portuguese land in Japan.

1557 The Portuguese establish trade bases in Macao.

1583 Sir Humphrey Gilbert claims Newfoundland for England.

1584 Sir Walter Raleigh attempts English colonial settlement at Roanoke Island, North Carolina.

MAJOR TERMS AND CONCEPTS

Alphonso d'Albuquerque (1453–1515)
Audencias
the Aztecs
Vasco Nuñez de Balboa (1475–1517)
Martin Behaim (1459–1507)
John (1425–1500) and Sebastian (1474–1557) Cabot
Pedro Cabral (1467–1520)
Jacques Cartier (1491–1557)
Bartholomew de las Casas (1474–1566)
Christopher Columbus (1451–1506)
Conquistadores
Hernando Cortés (1485–1547)
Bartholomew Diaz (1450–1500)
Sir Francis Drake (1540–1596)
Encomienda
King Ferdinand (1452–1516) and Queen Isabella (1451–1504)

Sir Martin Frobisher (1535–1594)
Vasco da Gama (1469–1525)
Sir John Hawkyns (1532–1595)
Prince Henry the Navigator (1394–1460)
the Incas
Isthmus of Panama
Ferdinand Magellan (1480–1521)
the Mestizos
Northwest Passage
Francisco Pizarro (1478–1541)
Pope Alexander VI (1431–1503)
Sir Walter Raleigh (1552–1618)
Roanoke Settlement
Evangelista Toscanelli (1608–1647)
Treaty of Tordesillas
Giovanni da Verrazano (1480–1527)

MAJOR THEMES AND QUESTIONS

1. In what ways was the Age of Exploration an extension of the Renaissance?
2. What relationship, if any, exists between the Age of Exploration and the Crusades?
3. What factors (social, political, geographic) enabled Portugal to take the early lead in exploration?
4. Discuss the major factors that influenced the original Papal demarcation line of 1493 and its revision in 1494.
5. Discuss the reasons and political factors which caused England and France to delay in joining the exploration of new territories.
6. Discuss the following: Portuguese and Spanish exploration brought with it Catholic missionaries bent upon conversion. Though they achieved much success in Central and South America, they failed, by comparison, in Asia.
7. What social/political effects did European exploration have upon the societies conquered?
8. What factors caused Portugal, and later Spain, to relinquish their lead in empire building?
9. Discuss the following: The Age of Exploration was both the cause and the effect of the rise of the European middle class.
10. In what ways did Spanish colonial conquest differ from that of Portugal?

SAMPLE OUTLINE

Topic: *What factors in European society gave rise to the Age of Exploration?*

I. Science and technology

A. The development of the magnetic compass made long-distance, accurate travel possible. By the mid-fifteenth century, this device was in common usage.

B. Shipbuilding in western Europe, perhaps drawing from the Moorish designs, had begun to develop ships that were longer and narrower and therefore better able to resist the swells of the deeper ocean waters.

C. The development of the telescope during the Renaissance brought better knowledge of the stars and, in turn, led to more accurate maps. Combined with more widespread use of movable type printing presses, maps made the dissemination of data easier and more accessible.

D. In addition to the tangible advances brought about by the Renaissance and the interchange of ideas with the Moslem world, the Renaissance mentality instilled a more investigative spirit in men that impelled them to prove or disprove many of the traditional theories.

II. Politics and economics

A. The Ottoman conquest in the Mediterranean cut off many of the traditional overland trade routes with the Near East.

B. Alliances between the Italian traders and the Ottoman Turks meant that merchants from the western European nations, if they wished to avoid compromising their profit margins, had to find other routes of trade.

C. The advances made by the banking and credit institutions meant that there was a larger available pool of capital for investment. Earlier reports of the treasures of the New World lured many of the banking families to invest in these ventures.

D. English and French preoccupation with their on-again, off-again Hundred Years' War and continental supremacy allowed Portugal and later Spain to take the initiative in exploration. The relative bankruptcy of the English and French monarchies at the conclusion of their wars also meant that investors and traders would look to other nations for potential investment. In both France and England, the middle class made significant gains against the feudal monarchs and it was their interests that guided later overseas adventures.

E. The failure of the Crusades to convert the pagans of the Islamic world led many within the Christian kingdoms to spread their faith by other means. Rome also saw overseas expansion as a means to gain converts (and, of course, income).

F. Rome also was able to use the new interest in overseas conquest as a means to gain political power against the European monarchs by acting as a mediator in territorial disputes (examples are the Papal demarcation line, 1493 and its revision in 1494).

SHORT READING LIST

Carlo Cipolla, *Guns, Sails and Empires: Technological Innovation and the Early Phases of European Expansion, 1400–1700* (1965), is mainly concerned with the effects of technology on the spread of empire.

John H. Elliot, *Imperial Spain, 1469–1716* (1964), is a mercantilist view of empire.

——, *The Old World and the New: 1492–1650* (1970), is a study that includes much intellectual history.

William McNeill, *Plaques and People* (1976). McNeill presents a novel hypothesis to explain how a few Spaniards were able to conquer the New World.

Samuel Elliot Morrison, *Admiral of the Ocean Sea: A Life of Christopher Columbus* (1946)

——, *The Northern Voyages*. Morrison follows Columbus' route. There is no better biography of the explorer.

J. H. Parry, *The Establishment of the European Hegemony*, combines careful scholarship with a clear writing style.

Hugh Trevor-Roper, ed., *The Age of Expansion: Europe and The World, 1559–1660* (1968), is a comparative study that traces the influence of the major imperialist nations on the rest of the world.

Unit Review D
The Scientific Revolution

CHRONOLOGY

1543 Publication of *On The Revolution of the Heavenly Spheres* by Nicolaus Copernicus; publication of *Humani Corporis Fabrica* by Andreas Vesalius.

1590 The first microscope is made by Zacharias Jansen.

1603 Galileo invents the alcohol thermometer; the Accademia dei Lincei, a scientific society, is organized in Rome.

1605 Publication of *The Advancement of Learning* by Sir Francis Bacon.

1608 The telescope is invented.

1610 Publication of *Starry Messenger* by Galileo.

1611 Publication of John Donne's *An Anatomie of the World* in which he criticizes the new science.

1616 The Roman Catholic Church bans Copernicus' ideas.

1620 Publication of *Novum Organum* by Sir Francis Bacon.

1628 Publication of William Harvey's theory of blood circulation.

1632 Publication of *Dialogue Concerning the Two World Systems* by Galileo.

1633 Trial of Galileo.

1637 Publication of René Descarte's *Discourse on Method*.

1642 Birth of Isaac Newton.

1654 Otto von Guericke demonstrates atmospheric pressure.

1655 Evangelista Torricelli constructs the first mercury barometer.

1656 Christian Huygens builds the first pendulum clock.

1660 Otto von Guericke constructs the first rotating electric generator.

1661 Publication of Robert Boyle's *The Sceptical Chymist*.

1662 Founding of the Royal Society For The Improvement of Natural Knowledge (London).

1665 Publication of Robert Hooke's *Micrographia* describing plant cells.

1666 Founding of the Academy of Sciences in France.

1682 Edmund Halley observes a "new" comet.

1687 Publication of *Principia* of Isaac Newton.

MAJOR TERMS AND CONCEPTS

Aristotelian world view
Francis Bacon (1561–1626)
Tycho Brahe (1546–1601)
Robert Boyle (1627–1691)
Anders Celsius (1701–1744)
Nicolaus Copernicus (1473–1543), *Heliocentric Theory*
René Descartes (1596–1650)
deductive reasoning
Discourse on Method
Empiricism
Gabriel Fahrenheit (1686–1736)
Four elements
Galileo Galilei (1564–1642), *Two New Sciences, Siderus Nuncius, Dialogue on the Two Chief Systems of the World*
Gresham College
William Harvey (1578–1657)
Christian Huygens (1629–1695)
inductive reasoning
Zacharias Jansen
Johannes Kepler (1571–1630)
Gottfried Leibniz (1646–1716)

Carl Linnaeus (1707–1778)
Medieval universities—philosophy and science
Natural laws
Isaac Newton (1642–1727), *Principia*
Paracelsus (1493–1541)
Blaise Pascal (1623–1662)
Pope Urban VII vs. Galileo
Ptolemy's system (Alexandria-second century A.D.), Geocentric Theory
quintessence
Responses of Luther and Calvin to Copernicus' views
On the Revolutions of the Heavenly Spheres
The Royal Society of London
Development of science and mathematics as an aid to navigation (of merchant fleets and the Royal Navies of Portugal and England)
Barometer, Microscope, Pendulum Clock, Telescope, Thermometer
Evangelista Torricelli (1608–1647)
Uraniborg
Anton van Leeuwenhoek (1632–1723)
Andreas Vesalius (1514–1564)

MAJOR THEMES AND QUESTIONS

1. Why did the Church view the ideas of Copernicus and Galileo as a threat?
2. Describe the scientific achievements of the sixteenth and seventeenth centuries.
3. How did the new scientific method differ from medieval attempts to discover truth? In what ways did medieval universities also contribute to the development of science as an independent field of study?
4. The Scientific Revolution began at about the same time as the Reformation and Counter-Reformation. How can the two developments be thought of as related?
5. How does the scientific method combine Francis Bacon's inductive reasoning with René Descarte's deductive reasoning?
6. How did the scientific view of evidence and discovery affect other branches of human endeavor, e.g., political theory and history?
7. "If I have seen farther than others, it is because I have stood on the shoulders of giants." How did Newton synthesize scientific thought?
8. How did the Renaissance interest in antiquity (e.g., Greek science) stimulate scientific investigation during the sixteenth century? What role did patronage play in support of science?
9. What effect, if any, did the Scientific Revolution have on the everyday lives of ordinary people?
10. To what extent was the Scientific Revolution a result of economic, social, and political events rather than a result of the efforts of scientists independent of external factors?

SAMPLE OUTLINE

Topic: *In what ways was the Scientific Revolution revolutionary?*

I. Defining the Scientific Revolution

A. Since the development was gradual, spreading over 150 years, can the Scientific Revolution truly be considered "revolutionary" (c. 1540–1700)?

B. Scholars began to view the world differently; Aristotle (commonly referred to as "the philosopher") and the Bible were challenged as the standards of knowledge.

C. New instruments of measurement and observation made more careful recording of data possible. Practical benefits (technology) of what was an essentially intellectual revolution were very limited before the nineteenth century.

II. Challenges to ancient ideas

A. The Copernican Revolution overturns the Ptolemaic System.
   1. Tycho Brahe: observation.
   2. Johnannes Kepler: Three Laws of Planetary Motion.
   3. Galileo Galilei: the experimental method.

B. The Newtonian Synthesis: Universal Gravitation, a "natural law".

C. Advances in medical knowledge.
   1. Anatomical studies after Leonardo (autopsies and dissections): Versalius.
   2. Paracelsus.
   3. William Harvey: circulation of blood; challenge to Galen's description of blue and red veins.

III. Inductive v. deductive reasoning

A. Inductive reasoning is associated with Francis Bacon. This method is sometimes known as empiricism.

B. Deductive reasoning is associated with René Descartes.

IV. The Scientific Revolution was not so "revolutionary"

A. Old ideas and superstitions persisted.
   1. Astrology and witchcraft (about 7,000 people in Europe, mostly women, were condemned as witches during the years of the Scientific Revolution).
   2. Medical practices such as leeching and bloodletting flourished.

B. The great majority of people were not affected by the work of physicists and mathematicians. Despite Bacon's belief that there would be practical results from modern science, these results only appeared in the following centuries.

SHORT READING LIST

Herbert Butterfield, *The Origins of Modern Science* (1951), is an older but classic work.

Hugh Kearney, *Science and Changes: 1500–1700* (1971).

T. Kuhn, *The Copernican Revolution* (1957), is still the standard work.

Abraham Wolf, *A History of Science, Technology, and Philosophy in the 16th and 17th Centuries* (1968). This book has been considered "the standard survey."

Unit Review E
The Rise of Nation-states

CHRONOLOGY

The Dutch Republic and the Hapsburgs of Spain

1556–1598 Reign of Phillip II of Spain.

1556–1564 Reign of Ferdinand I, Holy Roman Emperor.

1558 Elizabeth I of England ascends to the throne.

1564–1576 Reign of Maximillian II, Holy Roman Emperor.

1567 William I, Prince of Orange, converts back to the Lutheran faith.

1568 Revolt breaks out in the Netherlands against Spanish rule. The rebellion is lead by William of Orange.

1571 The Battle of Lepanto.

William of Orange becomes a Calvinist.

1576 The 17 Northern Provinces sign the Pacification of Ghent to unite so as to drive out the Spanish from the Netherlands.

1576–1612 Reign of Rudolf II, Holy Roman Emperor.

1580 Phillip II makes an attempt to claim the Portuguese throne.

1584 William of Orange is assassinated.

1588 Spanish Armada, under Phillip II, is defeated by the English navy.

1598 Phillip II of Spain dies.

1603 Elizabeth I dies and James VI of Scotland becomes James I of England.

1604 Anglo-Spanish naval war, begun in 1588, ends.

1618 Fear of persecution and dissatisfaction amongst the Bohemian nobility leads to the Defenestration of Prague.

Truce between Spain and the 17 Northern Provinces ends and religious wars renew. The Thirty Years' War begins.

1619–1637 Reign of Ferdinand II, Holy Roman Emperor.

1625–1626 Albrecht von Wallenstein, a Bohemian Protestant noble, assumes command of the Imperial Catholic forces (after converting) and defeats the rebels.

1630 Gustavus Adolphus, Swedish king and leader of the Northern Provinces, lands in Germany and defeats the Imperial forces at Breitenfeld.

1632 Swedish forces defeat Spain at Lutzen. Gustavus Adolphus killed.

1634 Wallenstein is murdered by his own troops after being declared guilty of treason by Ferdinand II.

Imperial forces defeat Swedes at Nordlingen.

1643 Battle of Rocroi; the Duke of Enghein defeats the Imperial forces. Peace negotiations begin.

1648 The Treaty of Westphalia is signed to end the Thirty Years' War.

1654–1660 Reign of Charles X of Sweden.

1659 The Treaty of Pyrenees is signed, bringing a final end to the claims from the Thirty Years' War.

1660 Signing of the Treaties of Oliva and Copenhagen expand Swedish territory.

1697–1718 Reign of Charles XII of Sweden.

1700–1721 The Great Northern War.

1700 Battle of Narva. Charles XII of Sweden defeats Peter "the Great" of Russia.

1709 Battle of Poltava. Russian troops under Peter the Great defeat Swedish forces.

1720–1721 The signing of the Treaties of Stockholm and Nystadt ends Swedish expansionism.

Tudor and Stuart England

1455 Wars of the Roses, between the House of Lancaster and the House of York, begins in England.

1485 Henry Tudor, of the House of Lancaster, defeats Richard III (brother of Edward IV) of the House of York and ends the Wars of the Roses.

1485–1509 Reign of Henry VII.

1509 Henry VIII assumes the throne of England.

1515 Thomas Wolsey is named Archbishop of Canterbury by Henry VIII.

1527 Archbishop Wolsey petitions Pope Clement VII for an annulment of Henry's marriage to Catherine of Aragon.

1529 Archbishop Wolsey is dismissed by Henry VIII.

1529 Parliament is summoned to session by Henry VIII to formalize the establishment of the Catholic Church of England.

1547 Edward VI assumes the throne of England.

1553 Mary Tudor (Bloody Mary) succeeds Edward VI.

1558–1603 Reign of Elizabeth I of England.

1603 James VI of Scotland (son of Mary Stuart, Queen of Scots, and cousin of Elizabeth I) becomes James I of England.

1625–1649 Reign of Charles I of England.

1628 Charles I accepts Petition of Right prohibiting taxation without consent, arbitrary arrest, quartering the troops in private houses, and arbitrary declaration of martial law.

1629 Charles dissolves Parliament after it passes legislation against his wishes and objections.

1633 William Laud made Archbishop of Canterbury.

1637 Charles forces a new, more Anglican, prayerbook upon Scots Presbyterians. The Solemn League and Covenant is formed to resist.

1640 Charles reconvenes Parliament to raise money to put down the Scots rebels. Parliament uses the opportunity to abolish Star Chamber and the Court of High Commission.

1645 Oliver Cromwell and his New Model Army defeat Royalist forces at Naseby. Charles is forced to surrender and later is executed.

Cromwell purges Parliament of all opposition. The Rump Parliament convenes.

1653 Cromwell and his troops oust the Rump Parliament. The Barebones Parliament is formed (and dissolved in five months time).

1658 The death of Oliver Cromwell.

1660 The Restoration; Charles II, son of the executed Charles I, becomes king of England.

Declaration of Breda issued.

1673 Parliament passes the Test Act requiring an Anglican communion for all government officeholders.

1681 Members of Parliament attempt to exclude James II from the throne on the basis of the Test Act.

1685 James II becomes king of England.

1688 During the Glorious Revolution, James II is ousted by Parliament in favor of William of Orange and Mary (James's daughter by a previous, Protestant, marriage).

1689 A Bill of Rights is passed by Parliament to prevent the constitutional violations experienced under the Stuarts.

1690 William of Orange defeats James II at the Battle of the Boyne in County Derry, Ireland.

1701 The Act of Settlement is passed by Parliament excluding the Stuart line from the throne in favor of Sophia of Hanover.

France Under Henry IV and Louis XIV

1589–1510 Reign of Henry of Navarre (Henry IV) of France.

1610–1643 Reign of Louis XIII and Cardinal Richelieu.

1643 Anne of Austria becomes Regent of France for the five-year old Louis XIV.

Cardinal Mazarin becomes her advisor and de facto ruler of France.

1661 Louis XIV assumes control of the throne of France.

1667 Louis sends armies into Spanish Netherlands.

1685 Louis revokes the Edict of Nantes.

1686 War of the League of Augsburg begins.

1697 War of the League of Augsburg ends.

1701 War of the Spanish Succession begins.

1713 The Treaty of Utrecht ends the War of the Spanish Succession.

The Wars of Religion in Central Europe

1555 Calvin sends pastors from Germany into France to convert the populace.

1560–1561 The French monarchy, under leadership of Catherine de' Medici, attempts to convene the Estates General in order to unite the nation. Estates meets but only serves to underscore the weakness of the position of the crown.

1562 The Wars of Religion break out in France between Catholic and Huguenot nobles.

1588 Henry III, last son of Henry II, assassinates the Duke of Guise and allies himself with Henry of Navarre, the Bourbon Huguenot leader.

1589 Henry III is assassinated, Henry of Navarre becomes Henry IV of France. French kingdom is both religiously and regionally divided.

MAJOR TERMS AND CONCEPTS

Act of Settlement
Gustavus Adolphus (1594–1632)
Anne of Austria (1601–1666)
Barebones Parliament
Battle of the Boyne
Bill of Rights
Charles I (1600–1649)
Charles II (1630–1685)
Charles X (1622–1660)
Charles XII (1682–1718)
Oliver Cromwell (1599–1658)
Declaration of Breda
Defenestration of Prague
Edict of Restitution
Edward VI (1537–1553)
Elector of Brandenburg
Elizabeth I (1533–1603)
Ferdinand I (1503–1584)
Francis, Duke of Guise (1519–1563)
Frederick V (1596–1632)
The Glorious Revolution
Great Northern War
Henry of Navarre (1553–1610)
Henry Tudor (1457–1509)
Henry VIII (1491–1547)
Holy Roman Empire
House of Lancaster
Hussites
James I (1566–1625)
James II (1633–1701)
William Laud (1573–1645)
League of Augsburg
Battle of Lepanto
Louis XIII (1601–1643)
Mary I (1516–1558)

Mary, Queen of Scots (1542–1587)
Maximillian II (1527–1576)
Cardinal Mazarin (1602–1661)
Catherine de' Medici
Narva, Battle of
Naseby
Pacification of Ghent
Peter the Great (1672–1725)
Petition of Right
Phillip II
The Restoration
Cardinal Richelieu (1585–1642)
Rump Parliament
Solemn League and Covenant
Sophia of Hanover (1630–1714)
Spanish Armada
The Test Act
Thirty Years' War
Thomas Wolsey (1475–1530)
Treaty of Copenhagen
Treaty of Nystadt
Treaty of Oliva
Battle of Poltava
Treaty of Pyrenees
Treaty of Stockholm
Treaty of Utrecht
Treaty of Westphalia
Gustavus Vasa (1496–1560)
Albrecht von Wallenstein (1583–1634)
War of the Austrian Succession
Wars of the Roses
War of the Spanish Succession
William I (1533–1584)
William II of Orange (1626–1650)

MAJOR THEMES AND QUESTIONS

1. Discuss the role of religion in the Thirty Years' War. Was religious belief the cause or merely a rallying point for underlying political disputes? Compare this situation with the role played by religion in modern-day conflicts such as Northern Ireland, the Middle East, and the role of the Catholic Church in Eastern Europe.

2. What effect did the Thirty Years' War have upon the balance of power in Europe socially, politically, and economically?

3. Compare and contrast the Treaty of Westphalia (1648) with the Peace of Augsburg (1555). Discuss its effects upon the middle class and also upon the status of the Hapsburg empire.

4. What effect, if any, did the Thirty Years' War have upon the future unification of Germany? Explain and discuss.

5. To what extent could the overthrow of the Stuart monarchy be considered a triumph of the middle class in England?

6. Discuss the role of religion in the downfall of the Stuarts. Was it the immediate cause or merely an overt symptom of deeper conflicts?

7. Did the Cromwellian revolution and subsequent Glorious Revolution result in any greater democratization of English society?

8. To what extent were the Wars of Religion in France the result of an already ineffective and decentralized monarchy? What was the actual role played by religious differences within French society?

9. Compare and contrast the handling of religious conflicts between the Stuart monarchs of England and the French monarchy under Louis XIII? To what do you attribute these differences in policy and what were the ultimate effects of each upon their societies?

10. What effect did the Thirty Years' War have upon the reign of Louis XIII and his advisor, Richelieu? What effect did the decisions made by this administration have upon the future of the French state?

11. What steps did Louis XIV take to create a more efficient and centralized state? In what ways did he succeed in both increasing the authority of the crown and also in assuring its eventual overthrow in the French Revolution?

SAMPLE OUTLINE

Topic: *To what extent did religion dictate the alliances and policies of seventeenth-century Europe?*

I. Spain and the Hapsburgs

A. The revolt of the Netherlands, although it had religious overtones and alliances, was essentially a revolt against Spanish rule, not against religious doctrine.

B. The religious record of men such as William, Prince of Orange, would suggest that although religious practice and political alliances were frequently united, they could both be switched according to the current political climate.

C. William had trouble getting the Catholic and Protestant nobles to cooperate against the Spanish, but the Pacification of Ghent (1576) illustrates political pragmatism ultimately triumphing over religious zeal.

D. The rebellion among the Bohemian nobility, culminating in the Defenestration of Prague and the Thirty Years' War, certainly had a lot to do with religious differences between the Catholic Hapsburgs and the Protestant Electors (three of the seven were Protestant, and Bohemia held the crucial fourth vote, which could elect a Protestant, non-Hapsburg, emperor). It is, however, debatable whether religious zeal or merely a competition for power between the Hapsburg emperor and the German nobility was the true motivating factor.

E. The alliances in the Thirty Years' War would indicate that religion could and would be relegated to a secondary role behind political survival. This is clearly illustrated behind the convenient conversion of Albrecht von Wallenstein to Catholicism and his being chosen to fight against his former Lutheran "brothers" on behalf of the Catholic Ferdinand II. His later assassination by Ferdinand further exemplifies the thin attachment of religious sentiment to political alliance.

II. France under the Bourbon Monarchs

A. The Wars of Religion in France were only in part due to actual religious conflicts. The bankruptcy of the Bourbon monarchs after the Hapsburg-Valois wars increased the tax burden which led to conflict between the middle class and the nobility.

B. The convening of the Estates General (1560 and 1561) saw the Estates members push for political reform and the crown for more revenues thus illustrating the heart of the conflict.

C. The actual fighting during the Wars of Religion saw the nobles try to assert control over various provinces and the middle class try to free themselves from the authority of royal officials.

D. Ultimately, Henry III would ally himself with a Huguenot leader, Henry of Navarre, and assassinate a Catholic, the Duke of Guise, in order to retain political control.

E. Henry IV would later convert to Catholicism and yet maintain the Protestant Duke of Sully as his advisor. Although Protestant opposition did force him to issue the Edict of Nantes (1598), the nobility and bureaucracy were bought, bribed, and beaten rather than converted.

F. Under Louis XIII and Richelieu, France still faced religious conflict but even the Catholic Cardinal did not lobby for the outlawing of the Huguenots and dealt with the conflict as a series of separate individual rebellions. Louis and Richelieu also saw no problem with allying themselves against the Catholic Hapsburgs at various times during the Thirty Years' War.

III. England under the Stuarts and Cromwell

A. The conflict between James I and the English nobility had its religious roots in the differences between the more Catholic order of the High Anglican Church and the more Puritan nobility as well as perceived leniency of the king towards Catholics.

B. The attraction of a more Catholic doctrine to the Stuarts could also very well be explained by the compatibility of Catholicism (in structure and doctrine) with absolute monarchy. The Stuarts believed far more in absolute monarchy than in either Roman Catholicism or Protestantism, as James was born a Catholic, raised a Presbyterian, and crowned an Anglican.

C. The Petition of Right in 1628 illustrates that political power conflicts between noble and monarch were at least as important to the Protestant nobles as religious freedom.

D. The defeat of Charles I by the Protestant, Oliver Cromwell, could very well be seen as a triumph of Puritanism over Catholicism and surely Cromwell himself probably believed in the "holiness" of his cause. However, Cromwell's later attack against his own "brethren" in 1645 (the Rump Parliament) and 1653 (the Barebones Parliament) illustrates the shaky nature of religious ties when political goals are seen.

E. The policies pursued by Cromwell also serve to illustrate the political nature of this religious conflict. For example, the abolition of the House of Lords was a political action.

F. Although the defeat of the Catholic James II by the Protestant William of Orange at the Battle of the Boyne (1690) is still heralded by some as a victory of Protestantism over Catholicism, it must be remembered that William's campaign was financed in part and supported by the pope.

SHORT READING LIST

M. Ashley, *England in the Seventeenth Century* (1980), a recent study including new social history.

Fernand Braudel, *The Structures of Everyday Life* (1981)

R. S. Dunn, *The Age of Religious Wars, 1559–1715* (2nd edition, 1979), is a good synopsis for the young college student.

Pearl Hogrefe, *Tudor Women: Commoners and Queens* (1975), is a study of social classes. The questions of gender and class are discussed.

Hajo Holborn, *History of Modern Germany* revised edition (1982), is an updated edition of a classic work.

Elizabeth Jenkins, *Elizabeth the Great* (1958), is an older biography that covers a great deal of ground.

J. P. Kenyon, *Stuart England* (1978), covers the rise and fall of the Stuart monarchy.

Garrett Mattingly, *The Armada* (1959). Old, but still exciting. Did Protestant England defeat Catholic Spain, thereby opening the world to capitalism?

Susan Morgenstein and Ruth S. Levine, *The Jews in the Age of Rembrandt* (1982). A valuable monograph.

J. L. Motley, *The Rise of the Dutch Republic* (1898). A classic.

J. E. Neale, *Queen Elizabeth I* (1957). A good beginning.

G. Parker, *Europe In Crisis, 1598–1618* (1980)

Simon Schama, *The Embarrassment of Riches: An Interpretation of Dutch Culture in the Golden Age* (1987)

———, "Rembrandt and Women," *Bulletin of the American Academy of Arts and Sciences*, #38 (April, 1985)

Lacey Baldwin Smith, *Henry VIII: The Mask of Royalty* (1973), emphasizes political history and examines Henry VIII as a strong monarch.

Unit Review F
Absolute Monarchies: France, Russia, Austria, and Prussia

CHRONOLOGY

1618 Brandenburg and Prussia are united; beginning of the Thirty Years' War.

1624 Richelieu becomes chief minister of France.

1638 Birth of the future Louis XIV.

1640 Frederick William, the Great Elector, comes to throne of Brandenburg-Prussia.

1642 Death of Richelieu; Mazarin becomes chief minister.

1643 Louis XIV becomes king at age five; Anne of Austria is Regent.

1649 Russian Code of Laws makes it illegal for a peasant to leave the land on which he works; the previous nine-year limit during which a noble could recover his serf was eliminated.

1653 Hereditary subjugation of serfs is established in Prussia.

1661 Beginning of Louis XIV's personal rule; death of Mazarin.

1667 During the War of Devolution, Louis XIV attempts to seize the Spanish Netherlands.

1668 English, Dutch, and Swedes ally against Louis XIV.

1670 Treaty of Dover signed in secret between Louis XIV and Charles II of England.

1678 Peace of Nijmegen gives Franche-Comte to France.

1682 Peter becomes Czar at age ten, but shares the throne with Ivan and Sophie, his half-brother and half-sister.

1683 Turkish invasion in the east; the siege of Vienna.

1685 Revocation of the Edict of Nantes.

1694 Establishment of the Bank of England.

1696 The death of Ivan makes Peter Czar in his own right.

1697 Peter begins his tour of western Europe.

1698 Revolt of the Streltsy. Peter crushes the revolt and executes 1,700 rebels.

1700 Beginning of the Great Northern War; Russia against Sweden and her allies.

1701 Opening of the first Russian School of Mathematics and Navigation.

1703 Start of building of St. Petersburg.

1708 Russian nobility is forced to move to St. Petersburg.

1709 Battle of Poltava.

1713 The Treaty of Utrecht ends the War of the Spanish Succession; the Pragmatic Sanction is issued by Charles VI (Hapsburg).

1715 Death of Louis XIV, whose 72-year reign is the longest in European history.

1721 End of the Great Northern War.

1725 Peter sends Vitus Bering to find a new route to America; death of Peter the Great.

MAJOR TERMS AND CONCEPTS

balance of trade
Battle of Blenheim (1704)
Jacques Bossuet (1627–1704)
boyars
Brandenburg
Charles II (1661–1700)
Charles XII (1682–1718)
Jean-Baptiste Colbert (1619–1683)
Diplomatic Revolution
Pierre Corneille (1606–1684)
effects of revocation of the Edict of Nantes
Frederick William, the Great Elector (1620–1688)
Frederick I (1657–1713)
Frederick William I ("The Sergeant King" or "The Soldiers' King") (1688–1740)
Frederick II, the Great (1712–1786)
French Classicism
French colonies
the Fronde
Great Northern War
Hohenzollern family
Holy Synod
Huguenots
Junkers
Prince Kaunitz-Reitberg (1711–1794)
League of Augsburg
"L'etat c'est moi." ("I am the State.")
Louis XIV (1638–1715)
Jean Baptiste Lully (1632–1687)
Maria Theresa (1717–1780)
Marquise de Maintenon (1635–1719)
Marquis de Louvois (1641–1691)

Cardinal Mazarin (1602–1661)
mercantilism
Molière (1622–1673)
Le Notre
Peace of Paris (1763)
Peter I, the Great (1672–1725)
Peter's relationship with the Russian Orthodox Church
Battle of Poltava (1709)
Nicholas Poussin (1593–1665)
potatoes
Pragmatic Sanction
Jean Baptiste Racine (1639–1699)
robot
Romanov dynasty
the Russian Calendar as a symbol of "modernization"
serfdom in Russia and in eastern Europe
Seven Years' War
Silesia
"Sparta of the North"
St. Petersburg, the "Window on the Sea"
State bureaucracies—tax collection, tax farming
Treaty of Aix-la-Chapelle (1748)
Treaty of Nijmegen (1678)
Treaty of Utrecht (1713)
War of the Austrian Succession
War of Devolution
War of the Spanish Succession
Le Vau
Versailles

MAJOR THEMES AND QUESTIONS

1. Is there a difference between divine right monarchy and absolute monarchy? Explain.
2. What techniques did absolute monarchs use to increase their power?
3. What conception of the state does the expression "I am the State" reveal? Is centralization a necessary component of absolutism? Was the development of France's transportation network more of a political or more of an economic maneuver?
4. Can an absolute monarchy coexist with laissez-faire capitalism or is mercantilism a necessary economic expression of absolutism?
5. Discuss the foreign policies of the absolute monarchs.

6. Compare and contrast the ideologies of Louis XIV, Charles I, and Peter the Great. How successful was each in creating or expanding the role of monarchy in his own nation? Why were the English less willing to accept absolutism than were (at least apparently) the French or the Russians? How were the Dutch able to resist absolute rule? Why did absolutism in Eastern Europe turn out to be more durable than in western Europe?

7. What was the role of the army in the creation of the Prussian state? How did the Hohenzollern family make use of the army for its own purposes?

8. Discuss the religious policies of the absolute monarchs. Were the economic effects of the Revocation of the Edict of Nantes severe (older view) or minor (more recent view)?

9. What was the relationship of absolute monarchy to the culture of the period (art, architecture, music, literature)?

10. Compare Louis XIV's wars with the War of the Austrian Succession.

SAMPLE OUTLINE

Topic: *The Major Wars of Louis XIV:*
Why was France unable to dominate Europe militarily?

I. Underlying causes of Louis' Wars

A. Rivalry with England and Holland; Louis desired to eliminate them as possible commercial competitors.

B. Rivalry with the Hapsburgs; Louis saw this dynasty as his major competition for the leadership of Europe.

C. Desire to expand France's territory to what Louis considered its "natural frontiers," the Rhine River, the Alps, and the Pyrenees.

D. A belief that war and glory were connected; a king needed to be a war leader and Louis believed he could be "above" all the other rulers of Europe through victory in war against them.

II. The War of Devolution, 1667–1668

A. Against the Dutch; immediate cause was Louis' claim that his wife, Maria Theresa, was the rightful heir (as eldest daughter of Philip IV of Spain) to the Spanish Netherlands (Belgium).

B. Although Louis was successful at first, a combination of Holland, Sweden, and England finally was able to force Louis to relinquish most of his conquests. By the Treaty of Aix-La-Chapelle, France acquired Lille and Tournai, two important commercial towns.

III. The Dutch War, 1672–1678

A. Separate, although related, to the War of Devolution; Louis personally led the invasion into Holland.

B. Louis' army was again successful at first (the Dutch escaped defeat by opening the dikes and flooding the countryside), but a coalition made up of the

Dutch, Brandenburg, the Spanish and Austrian Hapsburgs, and Denmark formed against him.

C. By the Treaty of Nijmegen France got parts of Alsace, Artois, and the Franche-Comte.

D. 1678 may be thought of as the acme of Louis' military power, although in the early 1680s Louis did seize Strasbourg and other territory in Lorraine.

IV. The War of the League of Augsburg, 1688–1697

A. The League of Augsburg was made up of the following:

1. Leopold, emperor of Austria (Hapsburg).
2. The King of Spain (Hapsburg).
3. The King of Sweden.
4. The Electors of Bavaria, Saxony, and the Palatinate.
5. The Dutch Republic.
6. After 1689, William of Orange as King of England.

B. Louis started the war by attacking German cities along the Rhine River.

C. The war dragged on for eleven years without any decisive victories or defeats.

D. By the Treaty of Ryswick, territories were returned to the status quo ante.

V. The War of the Spanish Succession, 1701–1714

A. Charles II of Spain was without an heir. Both Louis and Leopold claimed the throne as grandsons of Spanish kings (they were also brothers-in-law, each married to a granddaughter of Philip III).

B. In a treaty of 1698, France and Austria agreed to divide Charles' possessions between them. When Charles died in 1700, however, he left all his lands (worldwide) to Philip of Anjou, the 17-year old grandson of Louis XIV.

C. Louis abrogated the treaty with Leopold and accepted Charles' will. Philip became ruler of Spain in name; Louis became ruler of Spain in fact. Louis declared, "The Pyrenees no longer exist."

D. Behind the dynastic conflict was a more serious fear of French domination in Europe as well as commercial domination of France and Spain in the Western Hemisphere and Asia.

E. The Grand Alliance of England, Holland, Prussia, and Austria was formed against France. Spain and Bavaria were allied to France.

F. Louis' army had some initial successes against the Austrians, but from the very early years the war went badly for France.

1. The Battle of Gibraltar was a combined fleet of English and Dutch ships that captured the Rock of Gibraltar, an important strategic assest.
2. At the Battle of Blenheim, the English Duke of Marlborough (John Churchill) and the Italian Eugene of Savoy won "a glorious victory" against the French at Blenheim plain along the Danube River.
3. At the Battle of Ramillies in Brabant, Marlborough won another important victory.

G. Louis tried several times to withdraw from the war, but because he insisted that Philip be permitted to keep the Spanish throne, he was not permitted to do so before 1713. By the Treaties of Utrecht (1713) and Rastatt (1714):

1. England kept Gilbraltar and received Minorca, Nova Scotia, Newfoundland, and the Hudson Bay Territory.
2. England also gained the right to send a ship per year to the Spanish colonies as well as control of the slave trade from Africa.
3. The Dutch gained some land as a barrier against French invasion and a trade monopoly along the Scheldt River.
4. Austria received the Spanish Netherlands, Milan, Naples, and Sardinia.
5. The Elector of Brandenburg was allowed to style himself "King of Prussia." The Duke of Savoy became the "King of Savoy." The two kings were granted small concessions of territory.
6. France was permitted to keep Alsace; the Bourbons remained on the throne of Spain.

VI. Results of War

A. The treasury of France was drained. France had been the wealthiest country in Europe; Louis left it bankrupt largely as a result of his war policy.

B. The loss of life was tremendous; about 20 percent of French subjects died as a result of Louis' warfare. There were starvation and peasant revolts in France.

C. Trade was disrupted; the tax system was in ruins.

D. The eighteenth century inherited a legacy of warfare. The principle of the balance of power was maintained.

SHORT READING LIST

H. Rosenberg, *Bureaucracy, Aristocracy, and Autocracy: The Prussian Experience, 1660–1815* (1966), examines the growth of the Prussian state against a background of social history.

R. Pipes, *Russia Under the Old Regime* (1974), is an excellent general survey.

R. Ergang, *The Potsdam Fuhrer: Frederick William I. Father of Prussian Militarism* (1972), is a classic biography.

Max Beloff, *The Age of Absolutism 1660–1815* (1962), tries to explain the creation of the absolutist state as a reaction to demographic and social changes.

William Church, *Louis XIV in Historical Thought* (1976), reviews the most important literature on Louis XIV.

W. H. Lewis, *The Splendid Century: Life in the France of Louis XIV* (1957)

Sidney Fay and Klaus Epstein, *The Rise of Brandenburg-Prussia To 1786* (1981), takes the story of Prussia through the reign of Frederick the Great.

Robert K. Massie, *Peter the Great: His Life and World* (1980), is a Pulitzer Prize-winning biography.

Raymond Birn, *Crisis, Absolutism, Revolution: Europe, 1648–1789/91* (1977). Birn believes that ideas have a direct influence on political events.

Unit Review G
The Enlightenment

CHRONOLOGY

1642 Isaac Newton born.

1674 Jethro Tull, English agricultural inventor, is born.

1687 Newton publishes *Mathematical Principles of Natural Philosophy*.

1690 John Locke publishes *An Essay Concerning Human Understanding* attacking the Cartesians and applying Newtonian concepts to philosophy.

1694 François Arouet, better known as Voltaire, born.

The Bank of England is formed.

1707 Carl Linnaeus, Swedish scientist and originator of species classification, born.

1711 Charles VI, Hapsburg Holy Roman Emperor, ascends to the throne.

1712 Jean Jacques Rousseau is born.

1713 The War of the Spanish Succession ends.

1714 Bernard de Mandeville publishes *The Fable of the Wicked Bee*, which put forward the idea that self-interest would benefit society as a whole.

1717 The Abbot of Saint-Pierre publishes *Project for Perpetual Peace*, arguing for a general council of nations and a world court for arbitration of conflicts.

1728 James Cook, explorer of the Pacific region from the Arctic to the Antarctic, born.

1733 Voltaire publishes *Letters on the English*.

1740 Maria Theresa succeeds Charles VI to the throne of the Holy Roman Empire.

The War of the Austrian Succession begins.

1741 David Hume is born.

1743 Antoine Lavoisier, "father of modern chemistry" born.

1744 The first detailed and geographically accurate maps of France are published.

1745 Henry IV and the Duke of Sully publish their *Grand Design*, for world peace.

1748 The Baron de Montesquieu publishes *The Spirit of Laws* borrowing Locke's concept of universal laws.

1749 Edward Jenner, developer of small pox vaccination, born.

1751–1772 *Encyclopedia*, edited mainly by Denis Diderot, published in order to classify and organize general information. It is 28 volumes in all.

1754 Rousseau publishes *Discourse on the Origin of Inequality*.

1756 Marquis de Mirabeau publishes *The Friend of Man* stressing the importance of agriculture to the health of the state and land as the ultimate source of wealth. Nature is equated with economics.

1760 The Industrial Revolution begins in England.

1766 Chemists are able to break down the components of air.

1768–1771 *Encyclopedia Britannica* published.

1776 American *Declaration of Independence* puts forth the concept of natural and "unalienable rights" of man.

1776 Adam Smith publishes *An Inquiry into the Nature and Causes of the Wealth of Nations*.

1780 Joseph II succeeds Maria Theresa as the Emperor of the Holy Roman Empire.

1789 French *Declaration of the Rights of Man* is published.

MAJOR TERMS AND CONCEPTS

A Discourse on the Origin of Inequality

François Marie Arouet (Voltaire) (1694–1778)
 Candide

François Boucher (1703–1770)

capitalism

Captain James Cook (1728–1779)

cosmopolitanism

deductive reasoning

Deism

René Descartes (1596–1650)

"Enlightened Despot"

Enlightenment

"General Will"

William Hogarth (1697–1764)

humanitarianism

inductive reasoning

Joint Stock Companies

John Law (1671–1729)

John Locke (1632–1704), *Essay Concerning Human Understanding*

Letters on the English

Carl Linnaeus (1707–1778)

"Natural History"

Natural Rights of Man

Sir Isaac Newton (1642–1727), *Mathematical Principles of Natural Philosophy*

physiocrats

Alexander Pope (1688–1744)

Rococo

Jean Jacques Rousseau (1712–1778)

Adam Smith (1723–1790), *An Inquiry Into the Nature and Causes of the Wealth of Nations*

The Social Contract

The Spirit of Laws

Jethro Tull (1674–1741)

MAJOR THEMES AND QUESTIONS

1. Compare and contrast the works of Sir Isaac Newton, René Descartes, and Galileo.

2. In what ways did the expansion of the natural sciences during the Age of Enlightenment affect the intellectual and political culture of the period?

3. Choose two of the following figures from the Age of Enlightenment:
     Carl Linnaeus
     George, Count of Buffon
     Antoine Lavoisier
     Edward Jenner
     Captain James Cook
   For each individual chosen, discuss the importance of his work not only upon his direct field of study, but also upon the fields of economics, politics, or religion.

4. To what extent did the philosophic writings of men such as John Locke, Voltaire, and Jean Jacques Rousseau reflect their social status within their respective societies? Discuss and explain.

5. What impact, if any, did the philosophers and scientists of the Age of Enlightenment have upon the religious ideology of the times?

6. To what extent could the writings of Adam Smith be viewed as an extension of the ideas developed by Locke, Voltaire, or Newton?

7. What were the essential concepts of humanitarianism and cosmopolitanism and to what degree did they reflect the philosophic and scientific developments of the period?

8. How did the concept of the Natural Laws of Man reflect the growing conflict between the emerging middle class and the aristocracy?

9. Discuss the ways in which the writings of the philosophers and scientists of the period affected the political actions and policies of the European monarchs.

10. In what ways did the popular art from the Age of Enlightenment reflect the change in popular philosophic ideologies?

SAMPLE OUTLINE

Topic: *To what extent could the Age of Enlightenment be viewed as a "Second Renaissance"?*

I. Description of each period

A. The original Renaissance.
   1. Rediscovery of the "ancient" works and concepts from Greek and Roman society.
   2. Growth of a more materialistic and rational approach to the legitimacy of governments, the functioning of the universe (e.g., Galileo's refutation of the geocentric theory of the movement of the universe was again popularized), and the development of society in general.
   3. Skeptical inquiry about the universe.

B. The Age of Enlightenment.
   1. A questioning of the logic as well as the morals of religious doctrine.
   2. A revival of the interest in science and technology and its relationship to society.
   3. The connection is made between the physical sciences and the political world; there is a trend to link political philosophies with scientific theories (e.g., Social Darwinism and Darwinian Theory of Evolution).

II. Philosophic and political comparison of writers

A. John Locke's *Essay Concerning Human Understanding* and Machiavelli's *The Prince* both take an extremely pessimistic view of human nature. Both philosophers emphasized the baser impulses of human beings and the tendency of these impulses to dominate most decisions. Neither writer had any great faith in the concept of the inherent "goodness" of mankind.

B. On the other hand, writers such as Rousseau and Sir Thomas More took an extremely optimistic view of human nature and tendencies, demonstrating the conflicting ideologies that existed in their respective periods.

C. In both societies, skepticism of traditional customs was exemplified by men such as Erasmus and Voltaire. This shift in ideology reflected not only the disenchantment with a very temporal and political church but also the conflict between an aristocratic feudal society and a developing merchant class.

III. Theological comparison

A. During the Renaissance, theologians such as St. Thomas Aquinas responded to the rising tendency towards logical explanations of the universe by proposing five logical steps in reasoning to explain the belief in the existence of God. Similarly, the Deists and writers such as Voltaire combated the religious skepticism of their time by arguing on behalf of the existence of a God (although not necessarily along the guidelines of the Roman Catholic Church).

  B. Compare the ideas of David Hume regarding the validity in the belief of miracles with the earlier works of Erasmus on the validity of religious doctrine in general.

  C. In both periods, the discovery of new scientific principles and rediscovery of works from earlier societies conflicted with traditional religious teachings. These works fed the philosophic political battles and forced the Roman Catholic Church to revise its practices; for example; More's *Utopia* and the writings of St. Thomas Aquinas on the logical existence of God, and the works of Alexander Pope and Voltaire on the development of religion.

IV. Social and economic comparison

  A. The development of trade economies during the Renaissance led to a weakening of the feudal monarchies and a more cosmopolitan outlook of the world. During the Age of Enlightenment, industrial capitalism led to the revision of government policies away from traditional mercantilism and towards more free and open policies in those governments with a developed middle class.

  B. The refutation of traditional ideas, of which the Roman Catholic religion was merely one of the most widespread, reflected the changing economic, and therefore sociopolitical status quo. For many in the intellectual community, who were middle class in background, the philosophies espoused broadly justified their existence.

SHORT READING LIST

Carl Becker, *The Heavenly City of the Eighteenth Century Philosophies* (1932)

Isaiah Berlin, *The Age of Enlightenment* (1956). A general overview.

Raymond Birn, *Crisis, Absolutism, Revolution: Europe, 1648–1789/91* (1977)

J. B. Bury, *The Idea of Progress* (1932). Has been substantially revised.

Peter Gay, *Voltaire's Politics* (1959)

——*The Enlightenment: The Rise of Modern Paganism* (1966). An interesting interpretation of the Enlightenment.

P. Hazard, *The European Mind, 1680–1715* (1963)

Leonard Krieger, *Kings and Philosophers, 1689–1789* (1970)

Carolyn Lougee, *Le Paradis des Femmes: Women, Salons, and Social Stratification in Seventeenth-Century France* (1976)

Frank Manuel, editor, *The Enlightenment* (1951). An older but still useful review.

David Ogg, *Europe in the Seventeenth Century* (1962). General test-like survey.

R. O. Rockwood, editor, *Carl Becker's Heavenly City Revisited* (1958)

R. T. Vann, editor, *Century of Genius: European Thought, 1600–1700* (1967)

Unit Review H
The French Revolution

CHRONOLOGY

1789 May 5: The Estates-General are summoned by Louis XVI for their first meeting in 175 years.

June 17: The Estates-General becomes the National Assembly.

June 20–27: The Tennis Court Oath; Louis agrees to the demand for a new constitution.

July 14: Storming of the Bastille.

July–August. The Great Fear in the countryside.

August 4: Abolition of feudal privileges.

August 26: Publication of *The Declaration of the Rights of Man*.

October 5: Women's march on Versailles; the Royal Family is forced to return to Paris.

November: Confiscation of Church property by the National Assembly.

1790 February 13: Suppression of religious orders and monasteries.

July 12: *Civil Constitution of the Clergy.*

1791 June 21: Royal Family tries to escape in the "Flight To Varennes."

June: Declaration of Pillinitz; Austria and Prussia express their "willingness" to intervene in France.

October 21: The Legislative Assembly convenes; Girondins in control, but Jacobins make their presence felt.

1792 April 20: France declares war on Austria and Prussia.

August 10: Attack on the Tuilieries.

September 2–6: The September Massacres.

September 20: The National Convention; Jacobins in charge; the Battle of Valmy.

September 21: Abolition of the monarchy; France becomes a republic.

October 25: All emigrés are banished for life.

1793 January 21: Execution of Louis XVI.

February 1: France and Britain are at war; the First Coalition against France.

March 11: Counterrevolution erupts in the Vendée.

April 6: Formation of the Committee of Public Safety.

June 2: Overthrow of the Girondins.

July 13: Assassination of Marat by Charlotte Corday.

July 28: Robespierre on the Committee of Public Safety.

September: Price controls by the Committee of Public Safety; only "the bread of equality" permitted.

October 5: The Revolutionary Calendar is published.

October 16: Execution of Marie Antoinette.

1794 March 24: Execution of the *Enragés* and the *Hebertistes*.

April 5–6: Execution of Danton and Desmoulins.

June 8: Festival of the Supreme Being.

July 27: Execution of Robespierre; beginning of Thermidorean Reaction.

December 8: Girondins reenter the Convention.

1795 February 21: Restoration of freedom of worship.

October 5: Napoleon breaks up the attack on the Convention by reactionary forces.

October 26: Amnesty for political detainees.

November 3: Directory takes control (until 1799); suppression of the sans-culottes.

1799 Napoleon's coup d'etat.

MAJOR TERMS AND CONCEPTS

Jean Le Rond D'Alembert (1717–1783)
Aliens Bill
Ami du Peuple
assignats
August decrees
"Gracchus" Babeuf (1760–1797)
Joseph Bara
Bastille
Battle of Jemappes
Beaumarchais (1732–1799)
bonnet rouge
bourgeoisie
Brittany
Brumaire
Edmund Burke (1729–1797)
cahiers de doléances
Ça Ira
Revolutionary Calendar
Thomas Carlyle (1795–1881)
Carmagnole
Catholic Church
centralization
citizen
Committee of Public Safety
Conciergerie
Confessions of Rousseau
Conspiracy of Equals
Consulate
Convention (National Convention)
Charlotte Corday (1768–1793)
Georges Danton (1759–1794)
Jacques-Louis David (1748–1825)
Declaration of the Rights of Man and of the Citizen
Camille Desmoulins (1760–1794)
Directory
83 Departments
emigrés
Encyclopédie
Estates-General
equality
Festival of the Supreme Being

Fête de la Fédération
First Coalition
fraternity
gabelle
Girondins
Great Fear
guillotine
Jacques René Hébert (1755–1794)
Hébertistes
intendants
Jacobins
Law of Suspects
lettres de cachet
levée en masse
liberty
liberty trees
Louis XVI (1754–1793)
Louvre Palace
Jean-Paul Marat (1743–1793)
Marie Antoinette (1755–1793)
La Marseillaise
Comte de Mirabeau (1749–1791)
Baron de Montesquieu (1689–1755)
modernization of the economy
Joseph (1740–1810) and Jacques (1745–1799) Montgolfier
the Mountain
National Assembly
Jacques Necker (1732–1804)
Thomas Paine (1737–1809)
Price-fixing: control of the economy by the Committee of Public Safety
Maximilien de Robespierre (1758–1794)
Jacques Roux
Louis Saint-Just (1767–1794)
sans-culottes
September Massacres
What Is the Third Estate?, Abbe Sieyes
Albert Soboul
Social Contract, Rousseau
Society of Republican Women

Madame de Staël (1766–1817)
Swiss guards
Tennis Court Oath
the Terror
Thermidore
Third Estate
The Old Regime and the Revolution, de Tocqueville

Tuileries
Battle of Valmy
Varennes
Vendée
Versailles
Elisabeth Vigée-Le Brun (1755–1842)
Mary Wollstonecraft (1759–1797)

MAJOR THEMES AND QUESTIONS

1. What grievances did the bourgeoisie, the sans culottes, and the peasants have against the Old Regime?
2. How did the Revolution contribute to French nationalism?
3. Contrast the National Assembly and the National Convention.
4. Compare the French Revolution to the Russian Revolution.
5. Contrast the views of Edmund Burke and Thomas Paine on the French Revolution. Choose two more modern historians (e.g., Soboul and Furet) and show how their views of the causes and events of the revolution differ.
6. Discuss the role of women during the French Revolution.
7. Did the French Revolution retard economic development in France?
8. During the eighteenth century, conditions in Eastern Europe were far worse for most people than they were in France during the same period. Yet a revolution broke out in France and not in Eastern Europe. How do you account for this?
9. At the very moment feudal privileges were being abolished in France, Leopold II was reestablishing serfdom in Austria. How can these movements in opposite directions be accounted for?
10. Describe the opposition, French and non-French, to the French Revolution. How did the Revolutionary government deal with enemies?
11. "The French Revolution, in both its causes and its course, can no longer be thought of as simply a struggle between the bourgeoisie and the nobility. It was a much more complicated event than that." Discuss the validity of this statement citing relevant historiographical studies.
12. "Robespierre symbolized all that was good and all that was tragic in the French Revolution." Evaluate this statement.

SAMPLE OUTLINE

Topic: *How did the French Revolution embody the ideas of the Enlightenment?*

I. Scientific and rational thought led to desire for political reform

    A. Progress in all fields, including government, was seen as necessary and possible.

    B. Political science could be based on natural laws. The economy, too, was made more "rational" through the ending of internal barriers to trade.

II. Phase One. The Period of Montesquieu: Pre-1789—The Monarchy

A. In *The Spirit of the Laws* (1753), Montesquieu argued for a constitutional monarchy and a liberal government.

B. Division of powers among the nobles, the monarchy, and the representatives of the cities to replace the Old Regime.

C. Mirabeau agreed with the idea of a separation of powers between the king and the legislature, although he disagreed with the idea of power being retained by the nobles.

D. *The Declaration of the Rights of Man* called for freedom of expression, representative government, and equality before the law.

III. Phase Two. The Period of Rousseau: September 1792–November 1799—The Republic

A. *The Social Contract* expresses the following republican views:

1. Popular Sovereignty—To have freedom, the people must control their own government.
2. Christianity should be replaced by a civil religion.
3. Force might legitimately be used to bring about freedom; a strong government might be needed to express the "general will."

B. These ideas were adopted not only by the Republic, but also by the Committee of Public Safety.

IV. Phase Three. The Period of Voltaire: 1799–1815—Napoleon

A. Voltaire had argued for "enlightened absolutism."

1. An efficient, organized state was the best design to bring about "progress."
2. A centralized state was not necessarily a threat to freedom; in fact it might increase freedom by reducing the power of the Church and the Parlements.

B. Napoleon was attracted to Voltaire's updating of the "philosopher-king" concept.

1. Napoleon believed he was bringing "scientific" government to France and to Europe.
2. Napoleon's use of the plebiscite had not been contemplated by Voltaire, nor would have Napoleon's military campaigns been approved of by Voltaire.

V. The Revolution cannot be considered simply as the playing out of different philosophies: Serious economic, political, and social problems caused the fall of the Old Regime. But the ideas and the discourse of the Revolution can be found in the thoughts of the people cited in the preceding.

SHORT READING LIST

Richard Andrews, *Paris of the Great Revolution.* Andrews is one of the historians who challenges Soboul's *Sans-Culottes.*

Keith Baker, *Inventing the French Revolution.* A very recent interpretation which reemphasizes the political origins (superstructure) over the social origins (base) of the Revolution.

Edmund Burke, *Reflections on the Revolution In France.* An early critic of the Revolution arguing that the Terror was an intrinsic part of it, not an aberrant phase.

Thomas Carlyle, *The French Revolution* (1857). A classic 19th century study.

Richard Cobb and Colin Jones, *The French Revolution, Voices From a Momentous Epoch 1789–1795.* Source readings from the period.

Alfred Cobban, *Social Interpretation of the French Revolution* (1968). A seminal work which challenged the classic interpretation of the Revolution as the "blocked bourgeoisie's" confrontation with the aristocracy.

Robert Darnton, *The Literary Underground of the Old Regime* (1982). Darnton is a leading "cultural" historian. Here he analyzes the question of literacy as a factor in the revolutionary movement. Rousseau, the Encyclopedists, broadsides—what else was being read?

Williams Doyle, *The Oxford History of the French Revolution*
——, *The Origins of the French Revolution.* Doyle presents not only the events but also the major interpretations and arguments over the French Revolution.

Francois Furet, *Marx and the French Revolution Interpreting the French Revolution* (1978).
—— and Mona Azouf, (editors), *A Critical Dictionary of the French Revolution* (1989). Furet's views concerning the French Revolution have become a subject of debate themselves. These and his other works are challenging studies.

Hugh Gough, *The Newspaper Press in the French Revolution.* This work complements that of Robert Darnton.

Ruth Graham, "Loaves and Liberty, Women in the French Revolution," in *Becoming Visible: Women in European History,* by Bridenthal and Koonz (1979). How did French women participate in the Revolution? Only actively or in many silent ways?

P. M. Jones, *The Peasantry in the French Revolution,* (1988). How did the Revolution in the countryside differ from the Revolution in Paris and Lyon? How did the countryside influence the urban movements?

Linda Kelly, *Women of the French Revolution.* Did women gain or lose as a result of the Revolution? Was gender as important a concept as class in the revolutionary period? These are some questions discussed.

Emmet Kennedy, A *Cultural History of the French Revolution.* A new look at what happened at the end of the Old Regime.

Georges Lefebvre, *The Coming of the French Revolution* (1947); *The Peasants of the Nord During the French Revolution; The Great Fear of 1789: Rural Panic in Revolutionary France* (1973). These are important studies that emphasize the social origins and the role of the lower class in the Revolution.

D. Levy and H. Applewhite, *Women in Revolutionary Paris* (1979). Professors Levy and Applewhite try to examine the lives of Parisian women using their own words.

Dorinda Outram, *The Body and the French Revolution, Sex, Class and Political Culture.* This is a specialized study but shows how research continues using new methods of attacking old fields.

George Rude, *The Crowd in the French Revolution* (1986). Definitely a classic. The 1986 edition is the most recent.

Simon Schama, *Citizens, A Chronicle of the French Revolution* (1989). A detailed study by a critic.

Albert Soboul, *The Sans-Culottes: The Popular Movement and Revolutionary Government, 1793–1794* (1968). Who were the sans-culottes? How did they affect the course of the Revolution? Were they merely the tools of the bourgeoisie? This is the English translation of a much longer French work. It has not been left unchallenged.

Alexis de Tocqueville, *The Old Regime and the French Revolution*. Although not the earliest study of the Revolution, many of the questions de Tocqueville posed have continued to frame the debate.

Unit Review I
The Napoleonic Era (1799–1815)

CHRONOLOGY

1795 October: Napoleon defends the National Convention from attack by Royalists; he is noticed by the Abbé Sieyès.

1796–1797 Napoleon is appointed commander of French forces fighting Austria and the Kingdom of Sardinia; victory in Milan.

1799 November 9: Napoleon's coup d'etat overthrows the Directory.

December: Plebiscite in which the French approve the new Constitution.

1800 February 13: Ogranization of the Bank of France.

June 14: Battle of Marengo (Austria).

December 24: Attempted assassination in the Rue Saint-Nicaise.

1801 February: France defeats Austria; the Treaty of Luneville gives France Italian and German territory.

July 15: Concordat with Pope Pius VII signed (officially proclaimed April 18, 1802).

1802 March 25: Treaty of Amiens with the British. Plebiscite makes Napoleon consul for life with 3.5 million yes votes to 8,300 no votes, which are questionable figures. There were probably many falsifications.

May 19: Creation of the Legion of Honor.

September: Annexation of Piedmont.

1803 April 12: Law prohibiting workers coalitions.

1804 March 21: Monarchist "plot;" execution of the Duke of Enghien.

December 2: Napoleon crowns himself emperor.

1805 March 9: Organization of the "Press Bureau" for publications and plays.

October: Battle of Trafalgar (Britain and Spain). Battle of Ulm (Austria).

December: Battle of Austerlitz (Russia and Austria).

1806 January 31: End of the Republican Calendar.

April 4: Introduction of the Imperial Catechism.

May 10: Founding of the University of France.

September 26: Opening of the Industrial Exhibition.

November 21: Berlin Decree.

Battle of Jena (Prussia).

1807 Battle of Friedland.

Treaty of Tilsit.

March 2: Decree on the Civil Status of the Jews.

1810 February 17: Annexation of Rome; Napoleon's son, born March 20, 1811, to be king of Rome.

March: Marriage to Marie Louise of Austria.

December 13: Annexation of Holland, Hamburg, and Bremen.

1812 March 11–May 8: Food riots leading to price controls of grain.

June 24: Invasion of Russia; Battle of Borodino.

Winter: Retreat from Moscow; destruction of the Grand Army.

1813 October: Battle of Nations, also called the Battle of Leipzig, where Napoleon is defeated by the Grand Alliance.

1814 March: Quadruple Alliance enters France.

April 6–May 4: Napoleon is exiled to Elba; Louis XVIII is restored to the throne.

1815 February–June 18: Napoleon's escape
from Elba; the 100 Days; the final defeat
at Waterloo.

MAJOR TERMS AND CONCEPTS

Alexander I (1775–1825)
Amnesty/Notables
Battle of Austerlitz
Battle of Waterloo; Blücher and Wellington
Bank of France
Berlin Decree
Caroline Bonaparte (1782–1839)
Jerome Bonaparte (1784–1860)
Joseph Bonaparte (1768–1844)
Borodino, Battle of
Careers Open to Talents
Concordat
Confederation of the Rhine
Congress of Vienna
Consulate
Continental System
Egyptian Campaign
First Consul
The First Empire
Duke of Enghien/Monarchists
Joseph Fouché (1763–1820)
The Grand Army
The Grand Empire
guerrilla warfare
La Harpe
Holy Roman Empire, Dissolution of the
Battle of Jena
Legion of Honor
Louis XVIII (1755–1824)
Marie Louise (1791–1847)

Clemens von Metternich (1773–1859)
Napoleon I (1769–1821)
Napoleonic Code
Napoleon and the Jews
Napoleon and the Polish landlords
Napoleon's reforms in education
Battle of Nations
Nieman River
Battle of Nile
The 100 Days
Peace Interim, 1802
Peninsular War
Plebiscite
Public works under Napoleon
Battle of the Pyramids
Quadruple Alliance
Rosetta Stone
Saint Helena
Second Coalition (Austria, Russia, Great Britain)
Talleyrand (1754–1838)
Third Coalition (Austria, Russia, Great Britain, Sweden)
Trafalgar
Treaty of Amiens (1802)
Treaty of Luneville (1801)
Treaty of Paris: May 30, 1814 [the "first" treaty]
Treaty of Tilsit

MAJOR THEMES AND QUESTIONS

1. What were the main goals of Napoleon's domestic policy? Evaluate his success or failure in achieving these goals. Were his goals unrealistic?
2. To what extent did Napoleon continue the ideals of the Revolution? What impact did Napoleon's reforms have on the subsequent history of France?
3. "In exchange for equality and fraternity, order, and unity, Napoleon deprived the French of their liberty." Discuss this statement.

4. Evaluate Napoleon's foreign policy. Was Napoleon a French nationalist or a Europeanist? What role did the continental system play?

5. How can Napoleon be considered both as an enlightened despot of the eighteenth century and the personification of forces that were to show themselves in the nineteenth century. Refer also to Germany, Italy, and Spain.

6. The real victor of the Napoleonic era was: France, Great Britain, Austria, and Germany. Choose one and explain your choice.

SAMPLE OUTLINE

Topic: *How did Napoleon deal with opposition to his regime?*

I. What opposition was there?

A. The Right was seen to be a greater threat than the Left.
1. The Church.
2. The émigres.
3. Counterrevolutionaries in the west of France.

B. The Plebiscite of 1802 seems to indicate that there was no viable opposition. This has been shown not to be the case (Louis Bergeron, *France Under Napoleon*).

II. Appeasement of the Left

A. July 14 (Bastille Day) was retained as a national holiday.

B. The Extremists deported in 1795 were allowed back into France.

III. Appeasement of the Right during the early years

A. The celebration of January 21, the anniversary of the execution of Louis XVI, was suppressed.

B. Priests were allowed to take an oath of loyalty to the Constitution to be eligible to perform Mass.

C. Church services were reopened on Sundays.

D. Concordat with the Papacy.

IV. A sterner treatment of the Right after the Battle of Marengo

A. Rebuff of approaches by the Count of Lille (future Louis XVIII).

B. Execution of the Duke of Enghien after a monarchist plot.

C. Napoleon crowns himself emperor in the presence of the Pope.

V. A sterner treatment of the Left after the assassination plot of the Rue Saint-Nicaise

A. Deportation of 130 Jacobins.

B. Arrests and removal of officers suspected to have republican sympathies.

C. Purging of twenty Tribunes who expressed some opposition.

D. Supression of the classes in political science at the Institute, a possible source of independent thought.

VI. Popular protest expressed itself in several forms

A. Grain Riots.
B. Military disobedience.
C. Banditry.

VII. Napoleon's biggest weapon was his military success, more than his secret police (led by Joseph Fouché) or his censorship of the press. When he failed to win in battle, he lost his support.

SHORT READING LIST

H. Balzac; many of his novels deal with the Napoleonic period. A *Murky Business*, for example, is one of the first "whodunits" and set in France in the early 1800s.

Louis Bergeron, *France Under Napoleon* (1981), mixes institutional and social history.

Richard Cobb, *The Police and the People: French Popular Protest, 1789–1820* (1970).

P. Geyl, *Napoleon, For and Against* (1949). Although somewhat dated, this book summarizes just about everything written about Napoleon up to that date.

R. Jones, *Napoleon: Man and Myth* (1977), is a more recent treatment.

Felix Markham, *Napoleon*.

Stendhal's works, such as *The Charterhouse of Parma*, are also set in the Napoleonic period.

Tolstoy's *War and Peace* dramatizes the invasion of Russia.

Unit Review J
The Industrial Revolution

CHRONOLOGY

1702 Thomas Newcomen builds the steam engine used to pump water out of coal mines.

1730 Josiah Wedgewood, developer of Wedgewood china, which was flamed in a steam powered kiln, born.

1733 John Kay invents the flying shuttle.

1740 Henry Cort, inventor of the puddling process and rolling mill for iron manufacture, born.

1756 John McAdam, developer of the first drained and rolled highway, born.

1761 The first load of coal is delivered to Manchester from the canal built by the Duke of Bridgewater.

1767 James Hargreaves invents spinning-jenny.

1768 Richard Arkwright invents the water frame.

1769 James Watt invents and patents the first efficient steam engine.

1771 Robert Owen, one of the early utopian socialists, born in Scotland.

1772 Charles Fourier, French socialist philosopher, born.

1779 Samuel Crompton combines the concepts of the spinning-jenny and the water frame into the mule.

1781 George Stephenson, the developer of the first efficient locomotive, is born.

1784 Edmund Cartwright invents a loom that is powered by horses, water, or steam.

1785 James Rumsey powers the first steamship up the Potomac River.

1790 Steam power used to operate the mule.

1792 Eli Whitney invents the cotton gin.

1799 The Combination Acts are passed by Parliament and labor unions are banned by law.

1803 The first steam wagon appears on the streets of London.

1807 Robert Fulton drives the steamboat *Clermont* up the Hudson from New York to Albany.

1812 The steam wagon is adapted for use on rails.

1815 The Congress of Vienna is held to hold back the advance of liberalism.

1820 Ampère sends a message across the Atlantic by wire.

1825 The Bubble Act is repealed by Parliament and joint stock companies are again legalized.

1829 The locomotive becomes widely used in England.

1832 The first of many Parliamentary reform bills, designed to enfranchise more of the middle class, is passed.

1833 A Factory Act is passed in England prohibiting the employment of children under nine.

1834 The Poor Law is passed to centralize government control for poverty relief in English industrial towns.

1837 The first fully operative telegraph is developed.

The Chartist Movement is born and the London Workingman's Association draws up *A People's Charter*.

The Anti-Corn Law league is born.

1838 The first steamship crosses the Atlantic Ocean.

1839 The Charter Petition is introduced into the House of Commons for the first time and is defeated 235 to 46.

1846 The Corn Laws are repealed by Parliament.

1847 Karl Marx and Friederich Engels join the Communist League in Paris.

1848 Karl Marx and Friederich Engels publish their *Communist Manifesto*.

1849 The last of the Navigation Acts are repealed.

1851 England is connected to the European continent by wire.

1856 Lowes Act passes in Parliament and the concept of limited liability becomes law.

1866 The United States and Europe are connected by telegraph wire.

1867 The Reform Bill of 1867 becomes law in England and the franchise is increased by 124 percent.

1872 The Secret Ballot Act becomes law in England.

1880 Elementary school attendance becomes compulsory in England.

1891 School fees are abolished in England for elementary school.

MAJOR TERMS AND CONCEPTS

Sir Richard Arkwright (1732–1792)
Bubble Act
Jeremy Bentham (1748–1832)
Duke of Bridgewater (1736–1803)
Edmund Cartwright (1743–1823)
Chartism
Charter Petition, 1839
Combination Acts
Communist Manifesto
Corn Laws
Henry Cort (1740–1800)
cotton gin
Benjamin Disraeli (1804–1881)
Friederich Engels (1820–1895)
Factory Act
flying shuttle
Charles Fourier (1772–1837)
Earl Grey (1764–1845)
James Hargreaves (d. 1778)
Industrialization
John Kay (1704–1764)
laissez-faire capitalism

Lowes Act
Karl Marx (1818–1883)
John McAdam (1756–1836)
Thomas Newcomen (1663–1729)
Robert Owen (1771–1858)
Lord Palmerston (1784–1865)
Sir Robert Peel (1788–1850)
A People's Charter
Phalansteries
Poor Law, 1834
Reform Bill, 1832
Reform Bill, 1867
James Rumsey (1743–1792)
Scientific Socialism
Secret Ballot Act
spinning-jenny
Tory
Utopian Socialism
water frame
James Watt (1736–1819)
Whig
Eli Whitney (1765–1825)

MAJOR THEMES AND QUESTIONS

1. Identify three major inventors from the Industrial Revolution and discuss their works and the effects their inventions had upon the development of industrialization.

2. What was the significance of the Reform Bill of 1832? To what extent was the Duke of Wellington justified in his comment: "The revolution is made"?

3. Explain and discuss the relationships among the Combination Act, the Bubble Act, and the Lowes Act. In what ways were they vital to the future development of industrialization?

4. What were the immediate social effects of industrialization upon British society? To what extent did conditions improve over earlier feudal periods?

5. In what ways did the Chartists differ from the Socialists and in what ways did the success of the former effect the future of the latter?

6. To what extent did the theories espoused by economists such as David Ricardo and Thomas Malthus reflect the spirit of laissez-faire capitalism?

7. In what ways did scientific socialists such as Karl Marx differ from utopian socialists such as Robert Owen?

8. Why was England able to avoid much of the revolutionary activity that shook the European continent during the 1840s?

9. Discuss and explain the relationship of liberalism like that espoused by John Stuart Mill to the growth of industrial capitalism.

10. Use your knowledge of Parliamentary legislation in nineteenth-century England to discuss and evaluate the validity of the following statement from a Parliamentary committee of 1851:

   "The course of modern legislation seems to have been gradually to remove restrictions on the power which everyone has in the disposal of his property, and to remove those fetters on commercial freedom which long prevailed in this country."

SAMPLE OUTLINE

Topic: *What factors enabled England to take the lead in industrialization?*

I. Requirements for an industrial society

A. Land and geography.

B. Labor supply.

C. Available capital for investment.

D. Management.

E. Stable government, friendly to enterprise.

II. England's geographic advantage

A. Her island isolation offered protection and separation from many of the continental wars that forced monarchies like France and Spain into bankruptcy.

B. Wales and Northern England had abundant supplies of coal and iron to develop heavy industry and to power both heavy and light manufacture independent of foreign assistance.

C. England's water network offered both many sources of alternate power for factories and a navigable transport route for trade and communication. The development of canals, such as those by the Duke of Bridgewater, throughout England completed the basic needs of related industries (i.e., the railroad, steel, and coal industries which were complementary and interdependent).

D. Since the sixteenth century, England had developed her navy and her ports which not only afforded her protection against foreign invasion but also aided her later commercial empire.

III. Labor supply

A. Unlike nineteenth-century Russia, England had long since abolished serfdom. People were free to move about in search of land or other forms of employment. Also, the traditional feudal attachment to land had been reduced, thereby creating an atmosphere more conducive to long-term urban development.

B. The improvements in agricultural techniques not only meant that England could produce enough food to feed an urban, industrial population, but this could also be accomplished with fewer laborers than ever before. There was an ever ready labor pool for industry to draw upon.

IV. Capital

A. England's ability to avoid many of the costly continental wars meant that she entered the nineteenth century with a financially stable government that could help business develop.

B. British merchants and gentry had prospered during the continental wars, creating a class that could invest their surplus capital in other ventures.

C. The establishment of the Bank of England and insurance companies such as Lloyd's of London provided businessmen with institutions to support growth and development.

V. Management

A. Any industrial society must possess an educated class that can bring together the necessary elements of production.

B. English society was sufficiently fluid to allow young men from the gentry to undertake careers in business. The concept of primogeniture created a degree of mobility between the aristocracy and the upper middle class. This relative lack of stratification also allowed members of the middle class to aspire to rising into the nobility from the wealth created in business.

VI. Government

A. England's long history of a limited monarchy meant that feudalism, though not dead, was not in a position to stifle the growth and expansion of the middle class as in French and Russian societies.

B. The gradual but constant rise of the House of Commons as an instrument of the middle class not only provided a means for the middle class to gain government cooperation but also meant that this group remained firmly behind the establishment, unlike many of the other continental nations where the middle class often led the revolutionary movements.

C. Parliamentary legislation, such as the repeal of the Bubble Act, legalizing joint stock companies, the Lowes Act, allowing for limited liability, and repeal of the Navigation Act and the Corn Laws, not only created an atmosphere conducive towards growth of industry but also illustrated the compatibility between the British government and the interests of a growing middle class.

SHORT READING LIST

Carlo Cipolla, editor, *The Industrial Revolution*, vol. 3 of *Fontana Economic History of Europe*.

Michael W. Flinn, *Origins of the Industrial Revolution* (1966)

A. Gerschenkron, *Economic Backwardness in Historical Perspective* (1966). Gerschenkron presents a model of industrialization. Whether the nation industrialized early or late had serious political and social consequences.

E. J. Hobsbawm, *Industry and Empire* (1970)

Tom Kemp, *Industrialization in Nineteenth Century Europe*. Industrialization in each major European nation is discussed. Useful questions appear at the end of each chapter.

David Landes, *The Unbound Prometheus* (1969). Landes sees industrialization as generally beneficial.

Peter Laslett, *The World We Have Lost: England Before The Industrial Age* (3rd edition, 1984), examines the European family structure and society on the eve of industrialization.

Neil Smelser, *Social Change and the Industrial Revolution*.

E. P. Thompson, *The Making of the English Working Class* (1966). A seminal work in social history. It cannot be omitted.

Louise Tilly and Joan Scott, *Women, Work, and Family* (1978). How did industrialization change women's place in the family?

C. Trebilcock, *The Industrialization of the Continental Powers 1780–1914* (1981). A comparative survey.

Unit Review K
Reaction, Romanticism, and Revolution
(1815–1867)

CHRONOLOGY

1815 Holy Alliance of Austria, Prussia and Russia is formed; its goal is to repress liberal ideas.

1818 Congress of Aix-la-Chapelle: Czar Alexander I suggests an international army to prevent revolutions in European nations.

1819 Carlsbad Decrees imposed by Metternich throughout the German Confederation.

1820 Revolutions in Spain and Sicily; Congress of Troppau agrees to allow Austria to send trops to Naples.

1822 Congress of Verona: Problems in Spain and the Middle East are discussed; France intervenes in Spain.

1824 Charles X becomes the extreme reactionary king of France; Repeal of the Combination Acts in Britain.

1830 Charles X abrogates the Constitutional Charter; revolution brings Louis Philippe, the "bourgeois king," to the throne.

1832 Reform Bill of 1832 enlarges the electorate of England by redistributing seats in the interest of larger urban communities. Property requirements for holding office and voting are lowered, benefitting the middle class.

1833 Factory Act to regulate child labor in Great Britain.

1838 Chartist Petition.

1842 Coal Mines Regulation Act prohibits boys, girls and women from working in coal mines.

1845 Potato Famine in Ireland.

1848 First publication of *The Communist Manifesto*.

January: Outbreak of revolution in Kingdom of Two Sicilies.

February: Revolt in Paris; abdication of Louis Philippe.

February–June: Establishment of the national workshops.

March 3: Hungarians led by Louis Kossuth demand autonomy.

March 13: Uprising in Vienna; Metternich escapes to London.

March 20: Ferdinand I of Austria agrees to liberal reforms.

April 22: French voters choose a moderate republic.

May 15: French radicals attack the Assembly but fail.

May 18: Frankfurt Assembly convenes to write a German Constitution.

June 22–26: The June Days; the government abolishes the national workshops and the Parisian workers revolt. General Cavaignac and the National Guard put down the revolt.

October: Austrian army recaptures Vienna from the rebels.

December: Ferdinand I abdicates in favor of Franz Joseph; Frederick William IV of Prussia disbands the Prussian Assembly. Louis Napoleon is elected President of the Second Republic.

1849 March: Frankfurt Assembly selects Frederick William IV as emperor of the new German Empire; he refuses "the crown from the gutter."

June–August: Austrian and Russian troops defeat the Hungarian independence movement.

1851 Louis Napoleon dissolves Parliament and declares himself Emperor.

1852 French electorate overwhelmingly approves Louis Napoleon as emperor Napoleon III (plebiscite).

1867 Reform Bill in Britain adds urban workers to the electorate.

MAJOR TERMS AND CONCEPTS

Alexander I (1777–1825)
Hector Berlioz (1803–1869)
Lord Byron (1788–1824)
George Canning (1770–1827)
Carbonari
Viscount Castlereagh (1769–1822)
Concert of Europe
Congress of Aix-la-Chapelle (1818)
Congress of Troppau (1820)
Congress of Verona (1822)
Congress of Vienna
John Constable (1776–1837)
Gustave Courbet (1819–1877)
Eugène Delacroix (1798–1863)
the "Eastern Question"
J. L. Gericault (1791–1824)
Great Powers
Greece (1821–1829)
Grimm's *Fairy Tales*
François Guizot (1787–1874)
Victor Hugo (1802–1885)
J. D. Ingres (1780–1867)
the July Revolution (1830)

Louis Kossuth (1802–1894)
Lamennais's *Paroles d'un Croyant* (1834)
Giacomo Leopardi (1798–1837)
medievalism
Prince Metternich (1773–1859)
National revolutionary movements:
  Naples (1820)
  Spain (1820)
  Belgium (1830)
  Poland (1830–1831)
Nicholas I (1796–1855)
Oxford Movement
Lord Palmerston (1784–1865)
Louis Philippe (1773–1850)
Joseph Radetzky (1766–1858)
Reform Act of 1832
François Rude (1784–1855)
Sir Walter Scott (1771–1832)
Percy Bysshe Shelley (1792–1822)
Talleyrand (1754–1838)
J. M. W. Turner (1775–1851)
William Wordsworth (1771–1855)

MAJOR THEMES AND QUESTIONS

1. "The European State System established by the Congress of Vienna gave the world a hundred-year peace." Discuss the validity of this statement.

2. "The reactionary agreements signed at the Congress of Vienna made the revolutions of 1848 predictable." Discuss this statement and the philosophy of history it represents.

3. How did Great Britain avoid the convulsions that shook continental Europe in 1848?

4. Was industrialization a factor that promoted or impeded revolution? Discuss this question from the point of view of a Liberal and a Marxist of the period.

5. Discuss the influence, if any, of the Romantic movement in art and music on revolution in the period 1815–1848.

6. Discuss the ideas of any of the utopian socialists.

7. "If the eighteenth century was dominated by French thought, the nineteenth century can be considered the German century." Discuss this statement paying particular attention to the period 1815–1848.

8. Contrast the revolutions of 1848 in France and Germany.

9. Although divided by class and nationality, the revolutionary movements of the years 1830–1848 shared many common characteristics. Describe the features held in common by revolutionary movements of the period in eastern and western Europe.

10. "The Romantic artist was inspired by his love of the French Revolution and his abhorrence of the Industrial Revolution." Discuss this statement from the point of view of two different forms of art.

11. "The Romantic movement was a reaction of youth against age." Citing specific references, discuss the validity of this statement.

SAMPLE OUTLINE

Topic: *How was nineteenth-century nationalism a force for revolution?*

I. Definition of nationalism

A. Cultural unity.
  1. Language and other symbolic communication.
  2. History, heroes, and holidays.
  3. Customs and beliefs.

B. A territory held or desired.

C. It could be manifested in mild or extreme forms.

II. In the early nineteenth century, nationalism was ideologically connected to liberal democracy

A. Nationalism included an inherent faith in the goodness of "the people," i.e., "our" nation.

B. Governments were conceived of as "by and for" the people.

C. The nation transcended class loyalties.

III. Early nationalists generally held one of the following two beliefs:

A. A peaceful world of independent nations was a real possibility (e.g., Young Europe).

B. The world was divided into the "we" and the "they" [Johann Herder, religious leader, writer and philosopher (1704–1803)].

IV. Nationalism was a component of various European revolutions in 1848

A. Throughout Europe, the "Young" movements arose (Young Italy, Young Poland, etc.).

B. Kossuth, in Hungary, demanded independence from the Austrian Empire; subsequent similar demands by other national groups (e.g., Rumanians, Serbs) within the anti-Austrian coalition helped to weaken it and secure a victory for the Hapsburgs.

C. Daniel O'Connell led the Irish Repeal Movement.

D. The Greek Movement for independence from the Ottoman Empire (*Philike Hetairia*) inspired Romantic poets and painters (Byron and Delacroix), liberals and intellectuals all over Europe.

E. Mazzini's Young Italy wanted to create a new Italy that would be a liberal, democratic republic.

V. **Some historians argue that nationalism was, in the period 1815–1848, a middle-class, educated-class phenomenon**

A. The Belgian merchants against the Dutch.

B. The Frankfurt Assembly and the conflict with Denmark over Schleswig–Holstein.

C. Textbooks, newspapers, and other printed materials appeared in the national languages.

D. As radicals and socialists became more and more involved in the revolutions, the liberal nationalists withdrew.

VI. **The liberal, nationalist revolutions of 1848 were, for the most part, failures**

SHORT READING LIST

Maurice Agulhon, *The Republican Experiment 1848–1852* (1973)

G. Best, *War and Society in Revolutionary Europe 1780–1870.*

R. J. Bezucha, *The Lyons Uprising of 1834.* Lyons was the second city of France. Were its silk weavers workers or capitalists? A study of the social history of the period.

Jerome Blum, *Lord and Peasant in Russia.*

L. Chevalier, *Working Classes and Dangerous Classes in Paris.* This has become a classic. Chevalier uses many different sources in his study of Paris in the early nineteenth century.

T. J. Clark, *The Absolute Bourgeois: Artists and Politics in France, 1848–1851.* Clark presents a picture of the time through the works of several different artists, Daumier being chief among them.

Gustave Flaubert, *Sentimental Education.* The time frame is the Revolution of 1848: Paris versus the countryside, revolution versus reaction; fiction is the medium.

Theodore Hamerow, *Restoration, Revolution and Reaction.* Hamerow is concerned with these movements in Germany.

Christopher Hill, *The Age of Revolution* and E. J. Hobsbawm, *The Age of Revolution 1789–1848* (1962). These two works cover much of the same ground but are both important surveys.

Henry Kissinger, *A World Restored: The Congress of Vienna.* The question of power is uppermost in this study.

E. H. Labrousse, "1848, 1830, 1789: How Revolutions Are Born," Challoner and Stern, eds. *Essays in European Economic History.* The debate between those who hold to political origins and those who emphasize social and economic factors is illustrated in this comparative study by a leading French historian.

Frank Manuel, *The Prophets of Paris.* An older work that remains a delightful survey of French utopian thought. Fourier, Saint-Simon, etc.

J. M. Merriman, *The Agony of the Republic: The Repression of the Left in Revolutionary France, 1848–1851.* What was the role of the bourgeoisie during the period of the Second Republic? Did it mainly repress the Left?

Robert Moeller, editor, *Peasants and Lords in Modern Germany.* A modern historian of Germany investigates the origins of German authoritarianism in the mid-nineteenth century.

Harold Nicolson, *The Congress of Vienna* (1946)

David Pinkney, *The French Revolution of 1830.*
——, *Napoleon III and the Rebuilding of Paris.* Older but still valuable, these works take us into the streets of Paris.

R. Price, *The French Second Republic, A Social History* (1972). A short period of French history, but significant.

P. Robertson, *Revolution of 1848.* A standard survey of the revolutionary year.

G. Rude, *The Crowd in History 1730–1848.* A classic! Cannot be omitted.

Joan Scott, "The Glassworkers of Carmaux," in Thernstrom and Sennett, *Nineteenth Century Cities.* A standard study in the history of labor.

Charles Tilly, ed., *The Rebellious Century 1830–1930.*

Unit Review L
Nationalism

CHRONOLOGY

1815 The Congress of Vienna is called to halt the spread of liberalism and, to some degree, nationalism.

1818 The Zollverein, an economic union initiated by Prussia, is created in the German states.

1848 Louis Kossuth, radical leader within the Hungarian Diet, makes speech on behalf of liberty.

Metternich resigns and flees to England after strikes in Vienna lead to armed battles with soldiers and invasion of the imperial palace.

Riots in Berlin, similar in nature to those in Vienna. The king of Prussia promises a constitution.

Rioters in Milan drive out Austrian garrison. Venice proclaims itself an independent republic. The king of Sardinia declares war upon Austria, and invades Lombardy-Venetia.

The first Panslav assembly meets in Prague.

The Young Italy movement, a nationalist youth organization, is born. Young England and Young Ireland movements also arise.

1848–1849 The Frankfurt Assembly meets in order to create a unified, constitutional German state.

1849 Pope Pius IX flees Rome after one of his ministers is assassinated.

A Roman Republic is declared with Mazzini and Garibaldi as two of the leaders. The republic is shortlived and both Mazzini and Garibaldi are driven out before the year's end.

Russian troops invade Hungary to defeat Magyar nationalists on behalf of the Austrian Emperor, Franz Joseph.

1850 The king of Prussia issues his own constitution creating a two-house parliament. This constitution would stand until 1918.

1852 Count Camillo di Cavour becomes Prime Minister of the Kingdom of Sardinia under King Victor Emmanuel.

1858 Napoleon III, of France, and Cavour, of Sardinia, reach an agreement whereby France would protect Sardinia in the case of Austrian aggression.

1859 Cavour manages to trick Austria into declaring war upon Sardinia.

Napoleon signs a separate peace with Austria, frustrating Cavour's plans for a unified Italy.

1860 Giuseppe Garibaldi and his Red Shirts land in Sicily and proceed to the Italian mainland.

1861 Czar Alexander II, of Russia, issues the Emancipation Act that abolished serfdom.

The Kingdom of Italy, excluding Rome and Venetia, is proclaimed by a parliamentary gathering. Victor Emmanuel II is declared king.

1862 Otto von Bismarck becomes Chief Minister of Prussia.

1863 The Danish attempt to annex the provinces of Schleswig–Holstein leads to war against Prussia (allied with Austria). Bismarck and Prussia win in three months' time.

1864 Pope Pius IX issues the *Syllabus of Errors,* warning all Catholics against the dangers of liberalism.

1866 Bismarck uses dispute with Austria over the province of Holstein to declare war. Prussian troops easily win the Seven Weeks (the Austro-Prussian) War.

Venetia is added to the Kingdom of Italy in return for Italian support of Bismarck during the war between Austria and Prussia.

1867 The Ausgleich, or compromise, establishes a dual monarchy in Austria-Hungary.

Prussian Parliament passes the Indemnity Act which legalized Bismarck's taxes used to finance Prussian armament and mobilization. This was accomplished ex post facto because of the unqualified success against Austria.

1870 After a revolution in Spain forces out reigning Queen Isabella II in 1868, the revolutionary government offers the crown to Prince Leopold of Hohenzollern, cousin to the king of Prussia. The Prince accepts after three refusals.

Napoleon III of France sends his ambassadors to Ems to force Leopold to withdraw his acceptance of the Spanish crown. The Prince agrees but later refuses to further disqualify any future members of the Hohenzollerns from becoming candidates. Bismarck releases a condensed version of the Ems proceedings so as to make it seem that the French ambassador was thrown out by the Prince. The Ems Dispatch causes nationalist feelings to flare in France and Napoleon III declares war upon Prussia, as Bismarck had hoped he would. France is defeated in three months.

Italian troops march into Rome after French troops are pulled out as a consequence of the Franco-Prussian war. Rome is now joined with the Kingdom of Italy.

1871 After the conclusion of a peace treaty with France (the Treaty of Frankfurt), Bismarck proclaims the establishment of the German Empire.

MAJOR TERMS AND CONCEPTS

Alexander II (1818–1881)
Ausgleich, 1867
"Blood and Iron"
Bundesrat
Count Canillo Cavour (1810–1861)
Carbonari
Carlsbad Decrees
constitutional monarchy
Die Macht
Emancipation Edict
Ems Dispatch
Franco-Prussian War
Frankfurt Assembly
Giuseppe Garibaldi (1807–1882)
Hohenzollern
Indemnity Act
Louis Kossuth (1802–1894)
Junkers
Leopold I (1790–1865)
Liberalism (in a nineteenth-century context)
Magyars

Giuseppe Mazzini (1805–1872)
Nationalism
Napoleon III
Panslavism
Papal States
Pius IX (1792–1878)
Prussian–Danish War
Realpolitik
Red Shirts
Reichstag
Republicanism
Seven Weeks' War
Syllabus of Errors
Treaty of Frankfurt
Victor Emmanuel II (1820–1878)
Otto von Bismarck (1815–1898)
Young England
Young Ireland
Young Italy
Zollverein

MAJOR THEMES AND QUESTIONS

1. Discuss the relationship between nationalism and liberalism in the continental European revolutions of 1848.

2. Compare and contrast the effect of nationalism upon the eventual unified governments of Germany and Italy? To what actions and factors do you attribute the differences?

3. In 1849, Russian troops poured into Hungary in order to crush the nationalist rebellion there and aid the emperor of Austria. In 1914, a mere 60 years later, Russia would be one of the greatest supporters of Panslav nationalist operations. Explain and discuss the reasons for this shift in policy.

4. Analyze and discuss the relationship between, and effects of, nationalism in France, Italy, and Germany.

5. To what extent was the surge of nationalism during the mid-nineteenth century a consequence of industrialism and the growth of the middle class?

6. Nationalism in England tended to be a unifying influence and strengthened not only the position of the government but also the economic position of British industry, whereas in Austria, and to some degree in Italy and Germany, nationalism was a destabilizing factor. To what factors would you attribute this phenomena?

7. Discuss the effects of the nationalist movements of the revolutions of 1848 upon the future governments of Austria, Italy, and Germany.

8. Explain and discuss the reasons for the aversion of the Roman Catholic Church, under Pope Pius IX, to liberalism and nationalism.

9. What effect did the nationalism of the mid-nineteenth century have upon the socialist and Marxist movements in the various European nations, particularly England, France, Italy, Germany, and Austria?

10. In what way did the process and results of German unification in the nineteenth century effect the political future of Europe and Germany in the twentieth century?

SAMPLE OUTLINE

Topic: *Was the nationalism of the nineteenth century a progressive or a regressive force?*

I. Define terms and points of reference

A. Liberalism in the nineteenth-century context (if this could indeed be called progressive) tended towards limited constitutional monarchies, expansion of the rights and powers of the middle class, and general freedom of "the Rights of Man."

B. Conservative/regressive forces in nineteenth-century Europe were epitomized by the adherents of the Metternich System and the attempt to maintain, more or less, absolute monarchies.

C. The revolutions of 1848 provide a point of reference since they exhibited liberal, conservative, and nationalist components.

II. Nationalism in England and the United Kingdom

A. Unlike many of the other European nations, nationalism in England was not confined to the Liberal/Whig party. Indeed, it was Benjamin Disraeli who championed nationalist groups such as the Young England movement.

B. England did face nationalist rebellions such as the Young Ireland uprising of 1848, however, even in Ireland, most of the nationalist effort was concentrated in Parliamentary opposition such as that of Daniel O'Connell and the cause of Catholic Emancipation. England's ability to deal in a positive fashion with this movement was an important factor in satisfying the nationalist desires (of the majority at the time) while not jeopardizing the position of the British Empire.

C. Because of the ongoing reform legislation within England, and the beneficial effects of industrialization, nationalism tended to be aimed at advancing the interests of England and therefore had a unifying effect rather than a destabilizing effect. Both parties could and would use nationalism for their own benefit and the progressive and regressive actions of the government tended to result from reaction to external forces or internal social forces rather than to nationalism per se.

III. Nationalism in Austria and Germany

A. The revolutions in Austria had nationalist overtones as in the Magyar rebellion (Louis Kossuth). Though the liberalism of the Magyars is suspect, it did reinforce the anti-nationalist, anti-liberal tendencies of the Austrian emperor Franz Joseph.

B. Because of the ethnic makeup of the Austrian Empire, and the tendency for nationalism to be associated with liberalism, Franz Joseph could permit neither. The revolutions of 1848 illustrated the nationalism/liberal connection and would from then on associate both with anti-Austrian feeling.

C. Nationalism in Germany had been coopted, not by the liberal element, but rather by the conservative Junkers led by Bismarck. Consequently, the success of nationalism would lead to a conservative/regressive government for Germany. The failure of the liberal Frankfurt Assembly and the anti-German nature of the nationalist rebellions in Austria also reinforced the conservative tendencies of German nationalism.

IV. Italian and French nationalism

A. Nationalism in Italy had strong republican elements (such as Garibaldi and Mazzini).

B. Count Cavour, the more conservative of the Italian nationalists, favored a limited monarchy on the order of the English government.

C. Italian nationalism was heavily influenced by the conservative nature of the Austrian government and therefore tended towards liberalism.

D. The Catholic Church, being both conservative and anti-nationalist, tended to associate nationalism and liberalism with support for foreign occupiers.

E. French nationalism, since the French Revolution, had been led by the middle class and therefore led towards liberalization.

SHORT READING LIST

Hannah Arendt, *The Origins of Totalitarianism*, presents a controversial thesis: Was totalitarianism the "Old Regime" dressed in different clothing?

G. Craig, *Germany, 1866–1945* (1980). A thorough and complete survey.

Ernest Gellner, *Nations and Nationalism*

Antonio Gramsci, *The Risorgimento*. A socialist historian, imprisoned under facism, presents his view of Italian unification.

Raymond Grew, *A Sterner Plan for Italian Unity*
——, "How Success Spoiled the Risorgimento," *Journal of Modern History* 1962, #34. Grew examines the conflict between Liberal Nationalists and those who engaged in *Realpolitik*.

Theodore S. Hamerow, editor, *Otto von Bismarck: A Historical Assessment* (1962), part of the D.C. Heath *Problems In European Civilization* Series.
——, *The Social Foundations of German Unification*. Was Bismarch the greatest man of his age or a precursor of Hitler? This series presents conflicting viewpoint.

E. J. Hobsbawm, "Some Reflections on Nationalism," in T. J. Nossiter, editor, *Imagination and Precision in the Social Sciences*. From an important British Marxist historian.

Barrington Moore, *Social Origins of Dictatorship and Democracy* (1966). An original view. Still very important.

George Mosse, *The Nationalization of the Masses*
——, *Nationalism and Sexuality*. Recent, valuable works of social history.

O. Pflanze, *Bismarck and the Development of Germany: The Period Of Unification, 1815–1871* (1963). A traditional view.

Unit Review M
Nineteenth Century Social and Political Change (Democratic Reforms)

CHRONOLOGY

1800 The Combination Act in Britain effectively outlaws labor unions.

1813 Publication of Robert Owen's *New View of Society*.

1819 The Peterloo Massacre in Manchester; repressive Carlsbad decrees in the German states.

1824 Repeal of the Combination Act in Britain; workers were allowed to meet to discuss wages and hours.

1828 Repeal of laws barring Dissenters and Roman Catholics from political rights in Britain.

1830 Revolution in France; Charles X flees to England and Louis Philippe becomes "The Citizen King."

1831–32 The Sadler Committee of Parliament begins its investigation of child labor in Britain.

1832 Reform Act gives voting rights to those who pay rent of at least 10 pounds per year; many "rotten boroughs" eliminated.

1833 Factory Act regulates child labor in mills and factories.

1838 Beginning of the Chartist Movement, *The People's Charter*.

1842 Coal Mines Regulation Act prohibits females and boys under ten from working in coal mines.

1844 A second Factory Act restricts child labor in factories to six and one-half hours per day.

1845 Formation of the National Association for the Protection of Workers in Britain.

1847 Ten Hours Act limits the number of hours that women and "children under 18 years old" can be employed in textile factories.

1848 Publication of *The Communist Manifesto*; revolutions break out all over the Continent; establishment of the Second French Republic.

1852 Second Republic ended by Louis Napoleon; founding of the Second Empire.

1854 Publication of Charles Dickens' *Hard Times*.

1859 Publication of John Stuart Mills' essay *On Liberty*.

1861 Emancipation of the serfs in Russia by Czar Alexander II.

1867 Reform Act in Britain extends the franchise to city workers: this was Disraeli's famous "leap in the dark."

1870 Public Education Act in Britain.

1871 Trade Union Act in Britain.

1872 Secret Ballot in Britain.

1878 Anti-Socialist Law passed in Germany: government could suppress Socialist Party newspapers, meetings, etc.

1883–1888 Bismarck introduces legislation granting workers insurance against sickness and accidents; some paid holidays are put into law; the final step in his program to steal the platform out from under the socialists is the introduction of a social security pension law.

1884 Reform Act extends the vote to virtually all adult males in Britain; unions legalized in France.

1888 Founding of the International Council for Women; Emmeline Pankhurst will found the Women's Social and Political Union (WSPU) in 1903.

1891 Pope Leo XIII issues the encyclical *Rerum Novarum* which, although defending private property socialism, calls for social justice.

1900 Organization of the Labour Party in Britain.

MAJOR TERMS AND CONCEPTS

Anti-Corn Law League; Richard Cobden, John Bright
Honoré de Balzac, *The Human Comedy*
Louis Blanc (1811–1882)
Louis Cavaignac (1802–1857)
Center Party
Chartism
Classical Liberalism
William Cobbett (1763–1835)
Combinations Act (and repeal)
Auguste Comte (1798–1857)
demographic patterns/falling death rates, falling birth rates
Benjamin Disraeli (1804–1881)
Factory Act (1820)
Falk Laws
Falloux Law
Jules Ferry (1832–1893)
Gustave Flaubert's *Sentimental Education*
William Gladstone (1809–1898)
Great Exhibition of 1851
Great Famine
Baron Haussmann (1809–1891)

Home Rule
intelligentsia
Irish Land Question
Kulturkampf
Alphonse de Lamartine (1790–1869)
Manchester School
Narodniki
national workshops
nihilism
Paris Exhibitions (1867, 1889, and 1900)
Sir Robert Peel (1788–1850)
Peterloo Massacre
positivism
Reform Bills (1832, 1867, and 1884)
Rerum Novarum
"Six Acts" (1819)
Suez Canal
Ten Hours Act
Third Republic
Tories
transformismo
Whigs

MAJOR THEMES AND QUESTIONS

1. "Peaceful change, not armed revolution, was responsible for the growth of democracy in Britain during the nineteenth century." Assess the validity of this generalization. Cite specific references to the major legislative reforms between 1832 and 1884.
2. "The Whig interpretation of history is no longer, if it ever had been, valid." With specific reference to nineteenth-century Britain, discuss this statement.
3. During most of the nineteenth century, Europeans believed firmly in science and progress. By the end of the century, they were no longer so sure. Describe the most significant aspects of scientific and technological advances of the nineteenth century and the causes for the change over time.
4. Assess Napoleon III as a modern dictator, a reformer, or a buffoon. Pay particular attention to his domestic program.
5. Discuss the origins of the Third Republic in France. How did the conflict between Church and State during the period 1875–1905 affect the growth of democratic institutions in France? Compare the results of

this conflict in France with the Kultur-kampf in Germany. Discuss any other crisis for the Third Republic during its first thirty years.

6. Describe the activity of the Populists in Russia during the last third of the nineteenth century. Was their success or their failure a greater factor in the overthrow of Russia's Old Regime in the twentieth century?

7. Analyze Europe's demographic development during the period 1850–1914. How did the Great Migration affect this development? How were these demographic changes viewed in France and Germany.

8. Explain the strange demise of classical liberalism in Britain.

9. Choose any two areas of social reform during the nineteenth century from the following list: religion, education, public health, temperance, women's rights, welfare. Describe the tensions that led to change in one of the following countries: Britain, France, or Germany.

10. Discuss changes in art and literary styles during the period 1825–1885. How can changes in these fields be related to political and social changes in the larger society?

SAMPLE OUTLINE

Topic: *How was political reform achieved in nineteenth-century England?*

I. The Reform Bill of 1832

A. Bishop Horsley said in 1790, "The people have nothing to do with the laws but obey them." The Reform Bill of 1832 was to set in motion a process that changed such a concept.

B. The Whigs, in power under Lord Grey, were the voice of the middle class whom they idealized as the intelligent, productive, and solid part of the community.

C. The bill was introduced in the House of Commons on March 1, 1831 and included a provision to abolish entirely the "rotten boroughs" and to redistribute their representatives to the new industrial centers (like Manchester, the "home" of liberal thought in England). It passed, after some debate and a new election, by 136 votes, but would it pass in the House of Lords?

D. The bill lost in the House of Lords by 41 votes.

1. A perfectly predictable result in the House of Lords.
2. Reform mobs seemed to be on the edge of revolution.
3. The army and police were believed to be inadequate to put down an uprising. The outbreak of the cholera epidemic of 1832 added to the general unrest.

E. Passage of the bill was urged by business leaders as a measure to prevent revolution and stabilize society, and it was reintroduced in the Lords in 1832.

F. Lord Grey persuaded King William to threaten the Lords with the creation of enough peers to pass the bill if they did not vote for it; it passed.

G. Did the Reform Act have profound significance as some historians have written, or did it merely add to Parliament—because of the "ten-pound" property qualification—people with the same point or view as those already there? Although the number of voters increased by 50 percent, urban workers were not enfranchised. One answer might lie in the fact that men such as Cobbett supported the bill because they saw its implications—the ten-pound qualification could not be kept forever.

II. **Reform legislation such as the new Poor Law, a new Factory Act, abolition of slavery, and repeal of the Corn Laws followed soon after passage of the Reform Bill**

III. **The Reform Bill of 1867**

A. The influence of John Stuart Mill: Mill advocated the participation of all citizens in the electoral process (in Parliament and on the local level) to increase their interest in affairs that concerned them.
   1. *On Liberty* (1859).
   2. *Representative Government* (1861).
   3. *The Subjection of Women* (1869.

B. John Bright, who had been one of the leaders in the Anti-Corn Law League, was a leading spokesperson for the enfranchisement of the "town laborer."

C. William Gladstone introduced a bill (1864) to reduce property qualifications from ten pounds to seven pounds. The Conservative opposition spoke heatedly against even this moderate change (which would have had very little effect); their opposition, however, aroused popular resentment. Protests broke out in England in 1866.

D. Benjamin Disraeli, the Conservative leader, took the "leap in the dark" to support the enfranchisement of the working class, which he realized could not be safely excluded from political involvement. He also hoped that working people would join with the landed aristocracy in political opposition to the Liberals. It didn't happen. The result of Disraeli's "leap in the dark" and support of the enfranchisement of the working class was that Disraeli's Conservative party was turned out in the next general election and replaced by Gladstone and the Liberals whose ideas Disraeli had "appropriated."

IV. **The general election of 1868 gave a majority to the Liberal Party, with Gladstone as prime minister**

A. Abolition of compulsory taxes to support the Church of England was actually passed while Disraeli was technically still prime minister.

B. Disestablishment of the Church of Ireland.

C. The Great Education Bill (1870) added many new schools; primary education became compulsory in 1880 and free in 1891.

D. The Australian Ballot Act (1872).

E. Open examinations required for careers in the Home Civil Service (1870).

V. **Reform measures passed by Disraeli's Conservative Government**

A. Public Health Act (1875).

B. Artisan's Dwelling Act.

C. River Pollutions Act.

D. Factory and Workshop Act (1878).

VI. Further reform legislation

A. The Reform Act of 1884.

1. Passed by Gladstone.
2. Agricultural Laborers received the franchise.
3. Two million voters added.

B. The Parliament Act of 1911.

1. Passed by Prime Minister Asquith (Liberal).
2. Power of the House of Lords to veto legislation abolished.
3. King George V threatened to create new Peers unless it was passed.

C. The Representation of the People Act (1918).

1. All men over 21 allowed to vote, including those who owned no property and had been previously excluded.
2. Most women over 30 were enfranchised.

D. The Reform Act of 1928—All women over 21 enfranchised.

VII. Democracy in Great Britain was achieved through a combination of legislation and direct action

A. The Workers' Organizations (e.g., unions).

B. The Women's Suffrage Movement.

SHORT READING LIST

Isiah Berlin, *The Hedgehog and the Fox*

Asa Briggs, ed., *The Nineteenth Century*

——, *The Age of Improvement*

Louis Chevalier, *Working Classes and Dangerous Classes in Paris*. Chevalier's study, although his sources have been challenged recently, describes a view of Paris in the early nineteenth century.

T. J. Clark, *The Painting of Modern Life: Paris in the Art of Manet and His Followers* (1984). Clark describes the expansion of "modern" Paris to its borders.

Richard Cobb, *The Police and the People*

A. P. Donajgrodzki, ed., *Social Control in Nineteenth Century Britain* (1977). There were many methods besides the police force that the "ruling classes" used to control those they considered below them, including hospitals, schools, charity. These essays explore some of them.

J. Dyos and M. Wolff, editors, *The Victorian City: Images and Reality* (1973). Two leading social historians gather important essays about the ordinary people in nineteenth-century Britain.

George Eliot, *Felix Holt, The Radical* [fiction]. A novel set in the times just after the Reform Act of 1832.

Terence Emmons, *The Russian Landed Gentry and the Peasant Emancipation of 1861* (1968)

Friedrich Engels, *The Condition of the Working Classes in England*

J. Foster, *Class Struggle and the Industrial Revolution*

E. J. Hobsbawm, *Industry and Empire: The Making of Modern English Society*. Hobsbawm, a leading Marxist British historian, analyzes the place of industrialization in Britain and the place of Britain in the world.

B. Harrison, *Drink and the Victorians* (1971)

M. Ignatieff, *A Just Measure of Pain: The Penitentiary in the Industrial Revolution*

Gareth Steman Jones, *Outcast London*. This is a classic study by a leading British social historian. It reveals the attitude of the upper classes towards those "below" them.

William L. Langer, *Political and Social Upheaval, 1832–1852* (1969). Langer provides a useful survey of a crucial two decades. What forces led to the revolutionary year (1848) and why did those revolutions fail?

W. H. Lewis, *The Splendid Century*. A popular history of the 19th century in Britain

Frank Manuel, *The Prophets of Paris*. Manuel's work deals with Utopians (Saint-Simon, Fourier, others) at the end of the 18th and beginning of the 19th centuries in France. It is a lively summary of their ideas and their movements.

Linda Nochlin, *Realism* (1971)
——, *The Politics of Vision Essays on Nineteenth Century Art and Society* (1989). Professor Nochlin, an art historian, is a leading expert on the French realist, Courbet. The 1989 work covers some of the same territory as T. J. Clark's, but from a very different viewpoint.

Harold Perkin, *The Origins of Modern English Society, 1780–1850*

R. Shannon, *Gladstone*

Barbara Taylor, *Eve and the New Jerusalem: Socialism and Feminism in the Nineteenth Century* (1983). A modern study of two intertwined movements. It should be read in connection with Frank Manuel's *Prophets of Paris*.

David Thomson, *Democracy In France*. This is a classic survey of nineteenth- and twentieth-century France. Thomson emphasizes political, rather than economic or social developments.

H. Pelling, *Popular Politics and Society in Late Victorian England*

J. Weeks, *Sex, Politics and Society*

D. Thompson, *The Chartist*

Martha Vicinus, ed., *Suffer and Be Still* (1972)
——, *A Widening Sphere* (1981)
These are two important works, landmarks in the field of women's history.

Unit Review N
The Age of Imperialism

CHRONOLOGY

1751 Robert Clive captures military posts in Madras as England begins to oust France from India.

1757 Clive and the British capture all of Bengal at the Battle of Plassey.

1761 British conquest of Pondicherry brings all of India under British domination.

1830 French forces occupy Algeria and arrest the Dey, supposedly to end attacks from the Barbary pirates.

1839 The Opium Wars begin in China.

1842 The Opium Wars in China end in the signing of the Treaty of Nanking.

1850 The Taiping Rebellions begin in China.

1854 Commodore Perry threatens to attack Tokyo, Japan unless United States trade is allowed.

1856 The British consul at Canton calls upon the British navy to bombard the city in retribution for violence against Europeans.

1857 The Sepoy Rebellion against British rule in India.

1858 India comes under direct rule by England in the wake of the Sepoy Rebellion.

1858 Japan and the United States agree to exchange diplomatic representatives.

1861 England annexes the port city of Lagos. Shortly thereafter, all of Nigeria becomes a protectorate.

1864 An allied force of British and Americans attack Choshu, leading to a revolution in Japan.

The Taiping Rebellions end.

1869 The French government creates a commission to control Tunisia's finances.

1870 Cecil Rhodes arrives in Cape Town, South Africa.

1877 Queen Victoria is named Empress of India.

1878 The Congress of Berlin meets to establish boundaries of European imperialism. France receives Tunisia, Britain retains Cyprus.

1881 France uses frequent raids into Algeria by Tunisian rebels as an excuse to annex Tunisia as a "protectorate".

1882 British troops land at Suez to protect British interests in the canal.

1885 Germany establishes German East Africa as a protectorate.

1886 All of Burma comes under British control.

Rhodes establishes British control over the Transvaal region of South Africa.

1895 The Sino–Japanese War.

1898 The Boxer Rebellion in China.

1899–1902 The Boer War.

1900 France lays claim to French West Africa (the Sahara, Sudan, the northern Congo basin).

1901 Britain annexes the entire Gold Coast of West Africa.

1904 The Russo–Japanese War. Japan takes Korea and Port Arthur from Russia.

1906 The Algeciras Conference. Morocco is to be controlled by France through the auspices of an international bank.

1910 The Union of South Africa is formed.

1911 Italy annexes Tripoli.

MAJOR TERMS AND CONCEPTS

Algeciras Conference
Belgian Congo
Boer War
Boxer Rebellion
Robert Clive (1725–1774)
Congress of Berlin
Lord Cornwallis (1738–1805)
East India Company
Fashoda Incident
German East Africa
Gunboat Diplomacy
Jingoism
Kaffir
Rudyard Kipling (1865–1936)
Dr. David Livingstone (1813–1873)
Meji Restoration

Mogul Empire
Open Door Policy
Opium Wars
Commodore William Perry (1794–1858)
Protectorate
Cecil Rhodes (1853–1902)
Russo–Japanese War
Sepoy Rebellion
Sino–Japanese War
Spanish–American War
Sphere of Influence
Taiping Rebellions
Townshend Harris (1804–1878)
Trans–Siberian Railroad
Treaty of Nanking
The White Man's Burden

MAJOR THEMES AND QUESTIONS

1. In what ways did the imperialism of the nineteenth and twentieth centuries differ from earlier adventures in imperialist conquest?

2. Analyze and discuss the motives behind nineteenth-century imperialism.

3. In what ways did the major powers justify their imperialist conquests? Discuss the extent to which the same justifications are used today.

4. Compare and contrast the methods of imperialism of the British and French governments of the nineteenth century. To what do you attribute these differences?

5. Discuss the validity of the following statement by English journalist W. T. Stead: "If you have not to be cannibals, you have got to be Imperialists."

6. What role, if any, did western racism play in the expansion of imperialism? Was it cause, consequence, or both?

7. What effect, if any, did the growth of imperialism have upon the balance of power in Europe during the latter nineteenth and early twentieth century?

8. To what extent did the victims of western imperialism benefit? To what extent did they suffer?

9. To what extent are the consequences of nineteenth-century imperialism still being felt today? Explain with examples.

10. Discuss the validity of the Marxist claim that imperialism is the ultimate stage in the development of capitalism.

SAMPLE OUTLINE

Topic: *How has imperialism been attacked/defended?*

I. Definition of terms

A. Justification of political actions can be made in terms of national interest. This could also be called a Darwinian or rationalization approach based upon the concept of "survival of the fittest" or "realpolitik."

B. Justification for political actions can also be made in more moral terms of right and wrong or in whether a specific action, if made by a government, benefits the greatest possible number of people without unnecessarily infringing upon the rights of others.

II. Darwinist/rationalist approach

A. Many nineteenth-century philosophers as an extension of the Darwinian concept of survival of the fittest. Writers such as Thomas Carlyle espoused the idea that the lands of the earth belong to those who could best utilize them.

B. The race for colonies encompassed much more than merely trade and industrial interests. Colonies were also of strategic importance lest a nation become outflanked.

C. Studies by the United States Bureau of Statistics at the turn of the century point out that Britain took most of the exports from her colonies, a fact used to argue on behalf of the profitability of colonialism.

D. Writers such as Parker T. Moon argued against imperialism on the grounds that trade does not necessarily follow the flag and that in any case the greatest burden is paid by the average citizen while the profit goes only to the corporations involved.

E. Historians such as John Hobson attacked the concept of imperialism and its attempted justification as merely convenient masks for the profit motive or sheer quest for power.

III. Moral arguments

A. There definitely were missionary motives such as those exhibited by Dr. Livingstone and many of the Christian missionaries who probably believed in the "justness" of their cause.

B. Racism also was both cause and consequence of imperialism as the people of Western Europe saw themselves as the epitome of civilization. The whole concept that western technology was both required and sought by other societies illustrates this as does the modern day philosophy that the United States is exporting the virtues of American Know-How.

C. The question must also be raised as to whether it is necessary or desirable to destroy and exploit a people in order to bring other benefits.

D. Writers such as Sir Alan Burns were apologists for imperialism, arguing that it brought certain improvements to the areas affected. Exploitation in this era, it was argued, was no worse than that of any other period.

E. If one argues on moral grounds, the question must then be whether the survival of one people can justify the harming of another.

SHORT READING LIST

W. Baumgart, *Imperialism: The Ideas and Reality of British and French Colonial Expansion* (1982). Baumgart tries to avoid being either anti- or pro-imperialism.

Henri Brunschwig, *Myths and Realities of French Colonialism* (1966). A fairly objective account.

Joseph Conrad, *Heart of Darkness* (novella, 1902). Conrad reflected the interest in the "exotic" that was part of the imperialist age.

H. Gollwitzer, *Europe in the Age of Imperialism*. An important survey of modern theories of imperialism.

D. R. Headrick, *The Tools of Empire*

Michael Hechter, *Internal Colonialism*. Social imperialism has become an increasingly important concept.

J. A. Hobson, *On Imperialism* (1902, reprinted 1967). Hobson makes the case that imperialism does not pay.

D. Judd, *The Victorian Empire* (1970)

William L. Langer, *Europe: The Diplomacy of Imperialism* (1951). Imperialism in the context of great power rivalries.

V. I. Lenin, *Imperialism: The Highest Stage of Capitalism*. A classic critique.

Wolfgang Mommsen, *Theories of Imperialism*. Emphasizes economic causes.

B. Porter, *The Lion's Share* (1976). British imperialism.

R. E. Robinson and J. A. Gallagher, *Africa and the Victorians: The Climax of Imperialism* (1961)

Bernard Semmel, *Imperialism and Social Reform*

T. Smith, *The Patterns of Imperialism*, (1981), a comprehensive survey.

Robin Winks, ed., *The Age of Imperialism* (1969). This book includes many primary sources.

Unit Review O
The Fin-de-Siècle:
Modernization or Decadence?

CHRONOLOGY

1876 Alexander Graham Bell obtains a patent for the invention of telephone.

1879 Thomas A. Edison introduces the electric light.

1884 The Fabian Society is founded.

1885 Gottlieb Daimler's first motorcycle; Louis Pasteur first uses the rabies vaccine.

1889 Invention of the electric elevator; Vincent Van Gogh's *Starry Night*.

1890 Invention of the Rover "safety bicycle" with equal-size wheels; introduction of the electric street car in major European cities.

1894 Trial of Alfred Dreyfus.

1895 Guglielmo Marconi's wireless telegraph (1901 first transatlantic transmission); discovery of x-rays (Roentgen).

1896 The first modern Olympic Games.

1897 Publication of A. M. Barres' *Deracinés (The Uprooted)*.

1899 Invention of the aspirin.

1901 Awarding of first Nobel Prizes in the arts and sciences.

MAJOR TERMS AND CONCEPTS

Action Française
advertising
airplane
alcoholism
anarchists
anti-semitism
Art Nouveau
Maurice Barres (1862–1923)
Belle Epoque
Karl Benz (1844–1929)
Henri Bergson (1859–1941)
Hector Berlioz (1803–1869)
bicycle
Bon Marché Department Store
Café-concerts
Nicolas Sadi Carnot (1796–1832)
Paul Cézanne (1839–1906)
Jean-Martin Charcot (1825–1893)
cholera
consumerism
contraception
Thomas Couture (1815–1879)

crime
Benedetto Croce (1866–1952)
Gottlieb Daimler (1834–1900)
Social Darwinism
Claude Debussy (1862–1918)
decadence
Edgar Degas (1834–1917)
André Derain (1880–1954)
divorce
Dreyfus Affair
Edouard Drumont (1844–1917)
Emile Durkheim (1858–1917)
education
electricity
Havelock Ellis (1859–1939)
Entente Cordiale
Fabian Society
Fauvism
feminism
Sigmund Freud (1865–1939)
Paul Gaugin (1848–1903)
General Confederation of Labor

Baron Victor Horta (1861–1947)
Henrik Ibsen (1828–1906)
immigration
Jean Jaurès (1859–1914)
Jugendstil
Khaki Election of 1900
Gustav Klimt (1862–1918)
Karl Lueger (1844–1910)
Gustav Mahler (1860–1911)
Guglielmo Marconi (1874–1937)
Henri Matisse (1869–1954)
medicine
nationalism
Friedrich Nietzsche (1844–1900)
Olympic Games
Emmeline Pankhurst (1858–1928)
Paris Exhibitions of 1889 and 1900
Charles Pathé (1873–1957)
Max Planck (1858–1947)
Postimpressionsism
Marcel Proust (1871–1922)
radicals
Auguste Renoir (1841–1919)
Arnold Schoenberg (1874–1971)

Georges Seurat (1859–1891)
George Bernard Shaw (1856–1950)
socialism
Georges Sorel (1847–1922)
Herbert Spencer (1820–1903)
suburbs
Bertha von Suttner (1843–1914)
Symbolist Manifesto
telephone
Third Republic
Henri de Toulouse-Lautrec (1864–1901)
transformism
Triple Alliance
Maurice de Vlaminck (1876–1958)
Richard Wagner (1813–1883)
Sidney (1859–1947) and Beatrice (1858–1943) Webb
Whileley's Universal Emporium
Oscar Wilde (1854–1900)
women and family life
women's suffrage movement
Women's Social and Political Union
Emile Zola (1840–1902)

MAJOR THEMES AND QUESTIONS

1. What is the significance of the term *fin de siècle*? How is it different from *belle époque*? In what sense was the late nineteenth century a fin de siècle in Europe?

2. Describe the private life of the middle class in late nineteenth-century France, Britain, Germany, or Austria.

3. Discuss the effects of the increase in mass transportation and the department store on the development of Paris, London, or any other major European city.

4. How did leisure time become a matter of concern during the late nineteenth century? What methods of social control were instituted to deal with the "problem" of leisure time?

5. Discuss the origins of mass political parties in France and England during the late nineteenth century, "from mystique to politique."

6. What economic, political, and social reforms were sought by women's groups during the period of the turn of the century? Refer to specific countries and events.

7. How did the new art styles of the turn of the century reflect changing attitudes and perceptions? Refer specifically to Art Nouveau, Fauvism, and Futurism.

8. How did the working class organize itself during the last decade of the nineteenth and the first decade of the twentieth centuries?

9. How did the Irish Question in Britain remain unresolved at the turn of the century?

10. "The end of the nineteenth century was, on the surface, a time of peaceful progress. Not far below that surface, questions that would ultimately result in a world war were present." Discuss the validity of this statement.

SAMPLE OUTLINE

Topic: *How did the widespread popularity of the bicycle in France during the 1890s reflect changing social conditions?*

I. Development of the modern bicycle and accessories

A. Rover safety bicycle with equal-sized wheels and chain drive was introduced.

B. Dunlop's pneumatic tires replaced solid rubber tires.

C. Weight cut in half from about 80 pounds to about 40 pounds.

D. Michelin's inner tubes were made detachable; replaceable tires were now possible.

E. Prices declined from about 500 francs (about three month's pay for a school-teacher) to about 125 francs.

II. Competitions among sporting associations popularized cycling

A. At first, only wealthy amateurs participated.

B. Poorer athletes soon began to compete, too.

C. The Velodrome d'Hiver ("Vel d'hive"), an indoor stadium, was built in 1893.

D. Popular magazines included cycling columns.

III. Cycling affected manners and morals

A. Women cyclists abandoned traditional attire—including corsets—in order to be able to pedal more easily.

B. Exercise was accompanied by better diet and hygiene, all contributing to the liberation of middle-class women.

C. Tourism and excursionism changed some customs and introduced new ones, e.g., tourist guides that rated hotels and inns.

D. People began to pursue sports for pleasure alone.

IV. As bicycling became more "popular," the upper classes increasingly lost interest in it

A. Other sports became favored, including golf and tennis.

B. Peugeot and Panhard built French automobiles and automobile clubs were founded (1895).

SHORT READING LIST

Bernard Champigneulle, *Art Nouveau, Art 1900, Modern Style, Jugendstil* (1976)

George Dangerfield, *The Strange Death of Liberal England.* This short work remains a classic.

R. J. Evans, ed., *Society and Politics in Wilhelmime Germany.* This work presents a more recent interpretation of the period.

Emile Guillaumin, *The Life of a Simple Man* (English edition, 1982). A moving story that presents many of the idea in E. Weber's work, but in fictional form.

Eric Hobsbawm, *The Age of Empire* (1987). This is a broad synthesis of the age by a leading historian.

H. Stuart Hughes, *Consciousness and Society.* This has become a classic interpretation of the age.

Douglas Johnson, *France and the Dreyfus Affair.* A standard work.

James Joll, *The Second International, 1889–1914.* A challenging summary.

Arno Mayer, *The Persistence of the Old Regime* (1982). This is an important reinterpretation of the period.

M. Miller, *The Bon Marche: Bourgeois Culture and the Department Store, 1869–1920* (1981). The department store has been considered representative of many values of the French bourgeoisie.

Philip Nord, *Paris Shopkeepers and the Politics of Resentment.* The lower-middle class found itself increasingly out of place in the new France; Nord examines just who they were.

Michelle Perrot, *Workers On Strike* [English ed.] (1987). This is an English translation and abridgement of Perrot's doctoral dissertation; she analyzes the methodology of worker protest in France.

Peter Pulzer, *The Rise of Political Anti-Semitism in Germany and Austria* (1964). Did political anti-semitism represent a "failure of liberalism"? Why did these German-speaking areas develop differently from England and France? How did the tensions between industrial and agrarian interests affect the rise of anti-semitism?

Carl Schorske, *Fin-de-Siècle Vienna: Politics and Culture* (1980). In a series of brilliant essays, Schorske uses art, music, and even the physical development of nineteenth century Vienna to illuminate social and political changes.

Jerrold Seigel, *Bohemian Paris: Culture, Politics, and the Boundaries of Bourgeois Life* (1986). This work presents more than 100 years of French life on the margins of society. How did "bohemia" challenge and change "mainstream" society?

Roger Shattuck, *The Banquet Years: The Origins of the Avant-Garde in France 1885 to World War One* (1967). An older work, but still useful.

Deborah L. Silverman, *Art Nouveau in Fin-De-Siecle France* (1989). This is a very recent work whose topic is at the cutting edge of historical scholarship. How did "art nouveau" reflect an "internalization" of society?

Judith Stone, *The Search for Social Peace: Reform Legislation in France, 1890–1914* (1985). Were social reforms laws passed to manipulate workers? This is a recent reexamination of French history during the Third Republic.

Norman Stone, *Europe Transformed 1878–1918* (1983). This is a recent survey based on traditional scholarship.

Barbara Tuchman, *The Proud Tower* (1966). Popular history at its most readable.

Edward R. Tannenbaum, *1900, The Generation Before the Great War* (1976). How can the conflicts which led to World War I be seen as arising from tensions between the young and the old? Which values were shared and which were being replaced?

Eugen Weber, *France Fin de Siècle* (1986)
——, *Peasants Into Frenchmen* (1976). Both Weber's works tell us a great deal about life in France during the later nineteenth century. His hypotheses, however, have been questioned.

Martin J. Wiener, *English Culture and the Decline of the Industrial Spirit, 1850–1980* (1981). Why did England lose its position as the world's workshop? How did the attitude towards business that became widespread among British businessmen (according to Wiener) contribute to that decline?

Emile Zola, *Au Bonheur des Dames*. A novel of the "new" department store.

Unit Review P
World War I

CHRONOLOGY

1878 The Congress of Berlin meets to try and resolve territorial disputes in the Asian region.

1879 Bismarck forms an alliance between Germany and Austria-Hungary.

1882 Italy is included in the German, Austro-Hungarian alliance thus forming the Triple Alliance.

1885 A second Congress of Berlin is called to settle disputes between the major powers in Africa.

1894 France enters into an alliance with Russia.

1896 Kaiser William II issues the Kruger Telegram, provoking British indignation and worsening Anglo-German relations.

1898 Germany begins to build a modern navy.

1902 England enters into a military alliance with Japan.

1904 England and France enter into an Entente Cordiale in response to the Triple Alliance.

1907 England and Russia enter into a military alliance. The Triple Entente with France was completed.

1908 Russia enters into a secret agreement with Austria whereby Austria would receive Bosnia in return for supporting the opening of the Dardanelles Straits to Russian warships.

1911 German gunboat, the *Panther*, arrives at Agadir to guard German colonial interests. The crisis is resolved when the Germans relinquish Morocco to the French for what had been the French Congo.

Italy declares war upon Turkey. Bulgaria, Greece, and Serbia join against Turkey.

1912 A second Balkan War begins as Serbia, Greece, Rumania, and Turkey turn upon Bulgaria.

1914 June 28: Serbian revolutionary, Gavrilo Princip, assassinates Austrian heir Archduke Franz Ferdinand at Sarajevo Yugoslavia.

July 28: Austria declares war upon Serbia.

August 1: In response to Russian mobilization, Germany declares war upon Russia.

August 3: Germany declares war upon France.

August 4: England declares war upon Germany after Belgian neutrality is violated.

August 8: Japan enters the war against Germany.

September 5: The Battle of the Marne.

The Ottoman Empire joins forces with Germany as does Bulgaria.

1915 British and French forces attack Turkey at Gallipoli.

The *Lusitania* is sunk by German submarines, precipitating the eventual entry of the United States into the war.

Italy joins the Triple Entente in a secret Treaty of London.

1916 The Battle of Verdun.

1917 The Zimmerman Telegram brings the United States closer to war with Germany.

April 6: The United States officially enters the war against Germany.

The Russian Revolution overthrows the Czar and in December, Russia withdraws from the war after the Treaty of Brest-Litovsk.

The Battle of Passchendaele costs 400,000 Allied lives.

1918 The Allied offensive at Argonne, in September, breaks German resistance.

November 11: An armistice ends the fighting along the Western Front and World War I is brought to an end.

November 12: Austrian emperor, Charles I, abdicates.

1919 The Paris Peace Conferences convene, concluding with the signing of the Treaty of Versailles.

MAJOR TERMS AND CONCEPTS

Argonne
Balkan Wars
Berlin Conference, 1878
Berlin Conference, 1885
Black Hand
Charles I (1887–1922)
conscription
Entente Cordiale
Archduke Franz Ferdinand (1863–1914)
Freedom of the Seas
David Lloyd George (1863–1945)
isolationism
Joseph Joffre (1852–1931)
Kaiser Wilhelm II
Kruger Telegram
T. E. Lawrence (1888–1935)
League of Nations
V. I. Lenin (1870–1924)
Lusitania

Battle of the Marne
Morocco Crisis, 1911
Nicholas II (1868–1918)
Gavrilo Princip (1895–1918)
Treaty of Brest-Litovsk
Treaty of Neuilly
Treaty of Sèvres
Treaty of St. Germain
Treaty of Trianon
Treaty of Versailles
Triple Alliance
Triple Entente
Battle of Verdun
Western Front
Wilson's Fourteen Points
Woodrow Wilson (1856–1924)
Young Turk Movement
Zimmerman Telegram

MAJOR THEMES AND QUESTIONS

1. In what way did nineteenth-century imperialism lead to World War I?
2. To what extent were the Marxists correct in their claim that World War I was a war of capitalist interests only.
3. What effect did World War I have upon the Ottoman Empire and the Hapsburgs of Austria?
4. To what extent did the results of World War I live up to its theme of: "So that small nations might be free"?
5. What role did military alliances, both overt and covert, play in the outbreak of World War I?
6. To what extent did the Treaty of Versailles address the causes of World War I?
7. What effect did World War I have upon the balance of world power?
8. In what way did the conclusion of World War I lead to the disillusionment of the 1920s and 1930s?
9. What reasons would explain the rejection, by the European powers, of President Wilson's Fourteen Points Program?

SAMPLE OUTLINE

Topic: *What were the social, political, and economic effects of World War I?*

I. Social and economic effects

A. Government involvement in business production increased during the war and remained after the war ended.

B. All the major governments created bureaucracies to address the increased economic involvement. In addition, many businesses that might otherwise have gone under were kept afloat.

C. Government control over stock exchanges was increased and became permanent.

D. Women became an increasing part of the work force in Europe, a fact that helped gain them the vote.

E. The use of propaganda and government control of ideology became very important. The efficiency of Britain in this field was admired, and later imitated, by Adolf Hitler. It took nearly fifty years for freedom of thought to once again be valued.

II. Political effects

A. The United States emerged as a military, and more importantly, an economic power as it was the only nation to reap a profit from the conflict.

B. Britain became a debtor nation and would never again regain the ground she lost to the United States in the commercial trade field.

C. The division of Austria-Hungary broke up the last of the Hapsburg Empire. According to some historians, this was also the final end of the Holy Roman Empire.

D. The decimation of Germany created a power vacuum in Central Europe and led to the eventual rise of Fascism.

E. The United States' disgust with the Treaty of Versailles culminated in her refusal to join the League of Nations and thus ended any possible hope for lasting peace.

F. The snub of both Russia and Japan by the "Big Four" led to their alienation, the consequence of which became apparent in the 1930s.

G. The cry of the European Communists regarding the unjustness of the war was justified by the results and consequently led to the popularity of various Communist parties.

H. The crippling of Germany and the relative exhaustion of the victors led to a world-wide depression.

SHORT READING LIST

Volker R. Berghahn, *Germany and the Approach of War in 1914*. Berghahn is a leading historian of modern Germany. This book summarizes recent research.

F. Chambers, *The War Behind the War: 1914–1918* (1939). A product of its times.

Fritz Fischer, *Germany's Aims in the First World War*. Why did Germany back Austria in 1914?

P. Fussell, *The Great War and Modern Memory* (1975)

M. R. Gordon, "Domestic Conflict and the Origins of the First World War: The British and the German Cases," *Journal of Modern History*, Vol. 46, No. 2 (June, 1974)

B. H. Liddell Hart, *The Real War 1914–1918*. Military history.

James Joll, *The Origins of the First World War*. A revisionist approach.

L. Lafore, *The Long Fuse* (1971). Highly recommended. The origins of war.

Paul Kennedy, *The Rise and Fall of the Great Powers* (1989)

See especially Chapter 5, "The Coming of a Bipolar World and the Crisis of the Middle Powers."

———, *The Rise of the Anglo-German Antagonism, 1860–1918*. Kennedy links economic developments and international politics.

Arno Mayer, "Domestic Causes of the First World War," in Leonard Krieger and Fritz Stern, *The Responsibility of Power*

Standish Meacham, " 'The Sense of an Impending Clash': English Working Class" in *American Historical Review*, Vol. 77, No. 5 (December, 1972)

S. E. Miller, ed., *Military Strategy and the Origins of the First World War*. Was World War I unstoppable? Presents important questions.

Wolfgang J. Mommsen, "Domestic Factors in German Foreign Policy Before 1914," *Central European History* (1973). Mommsen has joined the Fritz Fischer debate.

Erich Maria Remarque, *All Quiet on the Western Front* (1929). A classic novel with an anti-war theme.

J. Remak, *The Origins of World War I* (1967). A comprehensive survey of the causes of the war.

N. Stone, *Europe Transformed: 1878–1919*, in the *Fontana History of Europe*. Economics and technology as background to diplomatic history.

A. J. P. Taylor, *The Struggle for Mastery in Europe, 1848–1918* (1966). European diplomatic history.

Barbara Tuchman, *The Guns of August*. A narrative account.

Eugen Weber, *The Nationalist Revival in France*. Weber has done important studies of the right-wing in France.

Unit Review Q
The Russian Revolution

CHRONOLOGY
(Western Calendar)

1915 The Duma demands democratic reforms and the Progressive Bloc is formed; Nicholas "adjourns" the Duma "temporarily" and decides to go to the front lines to take personal command of the army.

1916 Rasputin is murdered.

1917 March 8: Food riots break out in Petrograd (Leningrad); Nicholas orders his troops to restore order.

March 12: Volinsk and other regiments refuse to charge the revolutionaries. Petrograd Soviet is established.

April 16: Lenin enters Moscow.

May 4: Provisional Committee of the State Duma repeats its pledge to remain in the war on the Allies' side.

May 8: Coalition of liberals and moderate Socialists in control of the government.

June 8: Kronstadt Soviet declares it is in charge of the city.

June 16–18: The "June Days", Bolshevik street demonstrations against the government.

August 6: Alexander Kerensky is put in charge of the Provisional Government.

September 7–12: The Kornilov rebellion is put down.

November 7: Bolsheviks gain control of the Petrograd Soviet; The October (November) Revolution is begun.

November 8: Bolsheviks declare a Soviet Republic.

December 3: Peace negotiations with the Germans.

MAJOR TERMS AND CONCEPTS

Alexander II (1818–1881)
Alexander III (1845–1894)
Czarina Alexandra (1872–1918)
Czarevich Alexis
"All Power to the Soviets"
"All Land to the Peasants"
anti-semitism as a state policy
Army Order #1
Mikhail Bakunin (1814–1876)
Bloody Sunday
Bolsheviks
Cheka
Civil War: Whites versus Reds
Decembrist Revolt
Dictatorship of the Proletariat
Fyodor Dostoevsky (1821–1881)
Duma

Finland Station
Fundamental Laws
Industrialization, 1860–1900
Alexander Kerensky (1881–1970)
General Lavr Kornilov (1870–1918)
Kronstadt Revolt
V. I. Lenin (1870–1924)
March Revolution
Menshiviks
Mir
narodniki
Nicholas I (1796–1855)
Nicholas II (1868–1918)
nihilism
October Manifesto
panslavism
"Peace, Bread, and Land"

Petrograd Soviet
Prince Georgi Lvov (1861–1925)
Provisional Government
1905 Revolution
Rasputin (1871–1916)
Red Army
Russo-Japanese War
Slavophiles
Social Democrats

Social Revolutionaries
Joseph Stalin (1879–1953)
Pyotr Stolypin (1862–1911)
Leo Tolstoy (1828–1910)
Treaty of Brest-Litovsk
Leon Trotsky (1879–1940)
"the wager on the strong"
Count Sergei Witte (1849–1915)
zemstvos

MAJOR THEMES AND QUESTIONS

1. "Although the proletariat was larger and better organized in Germany than Russia, Germany was able to avoid revolution of the proletariat whereas Russia was not." Discuss this statement.

2. Describe Lenin's seizure of power. Discuss the hypothesis that Lenin's success was due more to the mistakes of others than to his own abilities. Why was a small minority able to seize power?

3. Compare and contrast the Russian Revolution and the French Revolution of 1789. Discuss both these revolutions as examples of the generalization that every revolution follows a similar pattern.

4. Compare Lenin's use of the slogan, "Peace, Bread, and Land" to the French Revolution's call for "Liberty, Equality, Fraternity."

5. Marx and Engels had written that various revolutions (e.g., the Peasants' Revolt of 1524 and even the French Revolution) had failed ultimately because the working class was not yet mature enough. Discuss this ideological problem for Bolsheviks of 1910–1917.

6. Discuss the beginnings of industrialization and modernization in Russia under the last three Czars as a cause for the Russian Revolution.

SAMPLE OUTLINE

Topic: *To what extent can the Russian Revolution be viewed as an extension of the French Revolution?*

I. Ideology and politics

A. Both France, under Louis XVI, and Russia, under Czar Nicholas II, were examples of absolute monarchies with significant sources of opposition from within the upper classes.

B. In both societies, the tax burden for an increasingly bankrupt government fell upon the middle and lower classes.

C. Both the Romanovs and the Bourbons allowed the clergy to play an exaggerated role in the formation of government policy.

D. The Jacobins were the leaders of the French Revolution. Although they were predominantly a middle-class party, at that period it was the middle class which was the dynamic element in European affairs. At the time of the Russian Revolution, the working class was emerging as the center of political unrest.

E. The Jacobin slogan of "Liberty, Equality, and Brotherhood" can be equated to the Bolshevik promise of "Peace, Bread, and Land." Although the Jacobins were in no way Communist, to the average Russian peasant, Bolshevism meant the acquisition of farmland, not the abolition of private property.

II. Tactics and consequences

A. Lenin espoused the concept of using terror as a legitimate political weapon as did the Jacobins under Robespierre. Both can be seen not as simply evil motives by would-be dictators, but also as responses to an all-pervasive government opposition and hostile foreign powers at the outset.

B. Both revolutions had to deal with the problem of both mobilizing and rallying a largely uneducated and conservative peasant population. For the eighteenth-century peasant in France, the concept of republicanism was as foreign to his instincts as Marxism was to the twentieth-century Russian farmer.

C. Both revolutions saw the rise and evolution of comparatively democratic institutions which would culminate in dictatorships (the Jacobin Club and the Legislative Assembly in France, and the Petrograd Soviet and the Central Committee in Russia).

D. The ultimate courses of both revolutions could have been significantly different; both monarchs had opportunities to deal with more moderate bodies (Louis and the National Assembly; Nicholas II and any of the four elected Dumas). The perceived failure of the moderates would, in both cases lead to the rise of the more extreme organizations.

E. The course of both revolutions would ultimately come full circle and culminate with purges of opposition (Marat in France and Trotsky in Russia) and the rise of dictators similar in status to those deposed.

F. The governments in the later stages of the French Revolution would experiment with the concept of direct government involvement in the economy (the National Workshops). This was comparatively far more revolutionary than anything during the Russian Revolution.

SHORT READING LIST

Paul Avrich, *The Russian Anarchists*. A sympathetic portrayal of anarchism.

E. H. Carr, *The Russian Revolution: From Lenin to Stalin*. A political history.

John Curtiss, *Church and State in Russia 1900–1917*. Had the church lost its power by 1900 or was it a powerful institution on the eve of the Revolution?

R. Daniels, *Red October* (1969). The second revolution and counter-revolution.

Isaac Deutscher, *The Prophet Armed: Trotsky, 1879–1921* (1954). This big biography is sympathetic to Trotsky.

Louis Fischer, *Life of Lenin* (1964)

L. Haimson, *The Russian Marxists and the Origins of Bolshevism*

V. I. Lenin, *The State and Revolution*. An original source book.

A. Mazour, *The First Russian Revolution*

Alan Moorehead, *The Russian Revolution* (1959). A good starting point.

B. Pares, *The Fall of the Russian Monarchy*

Boris Pasternak, *Dr. Zhivago* (1957). A novel set in revolutionary Russia.

John Reed, *Ten Days That Shook The World* (1919). An eye witness account by a sympathetic observer.

Solomon Schwartz, *The Russian Revolution of 1905*

Leon Trotsky, *History of the Russian Revolution* (1932). A biased view—the revolution betrayed.

A. Ulam, *The Bolsheviks* (1968)

Theodore Von Lave, *Why Lenin? Why Stalin?* (1971). This book puts the Russian revolution into the context of European history in general.

E. Wilson, *To The Finland Station*. A classic study. Fascinating reading.

Bertram D. Wolfe, *Three Who Made A Revolution* (1948). Old but still exciting reading.

Unit Review R
Totalitarian Societies

CHRONOLOGY

1881 Alexander II is assassinated after attempting reforms similar to the Emancipation Edict of 1861.

1898 The Social Democratic Labor Party is founded by Russian Marxists.

1901 The Social Revolutionary Party is formed.

1903 The Second Party Congress of Russian Marxists in Brussels and London results in the split of the party into the Bolsheviks and Mensheviks.

1905 "Bloody Sunday" at The Winter Palace in Petrograd.

The Constitutional Democratic Party (Cadets) is established.

Czar Nicholas II bows to pressure and calls together a Duma or parliament.

1906 The first Duma is elected despite the abstention of both the Bolsheviks and the Mensheviks.

1907 A second Duma is elected. The Mensheviks now take part in the elections.

A third Duma is elected after voting qualification changes increases the vote of the propertied class.

1911 Peter Stolypin, chief minister to the czar, is assassinated thus destroying his reform programs.

1912 The Bolsheviks split officially from the Social Democrats and form their own party.

A fourth Duma is elected.

Pravda is published in St. Petersburg as an organ of the Bolshevik party.

1913 The Bolshevik Party Congress is held.

The Christian Socialist Party makes a strong show in the Italian General Elections.

A young Adolf Hitler moves to Bavaria.

1914 World War I breaks out.

1915 The Duma is suspended due to World War I.

1917 Food riots in March. Soviet of Workers and Soldiers' Deputies, modeled along the lines of groups from the 1905 uprising, are organized in Petrograd.

Following the desertion of the army in the face of strikes by the Petrograd Soviet, Nicholas II abdicates.

Lenin returns from exile to lead Bolsheviks in Petrograd. Lenin and Bolsheviks oust Kerensky during the "Novembrist Revolutions."

The Treaty of Brest–Litvosk officially signals Russia's withdrawal from World War I.

1918 The Red Army is founded with Leon Trotsky as its head.

U.S. and Japanese forces land at Vladisvostok in an attempt to crush the revolution in Russia.

1919 Adolf Hitler joins the German Workers Party.

Benito Mussolini organizes his Black Shirts which he calls "Fascio di Combattimento."

1920 Civil war in Russia between the "Whites" and the "Reds."

Labor strikes in Italy result in widespread violence which is blamed upon "communist unions."

The German Workers Party renames itself the National Socialist German Workers Party.

The Kapp Putsch in Munich fails. The first of many coup attempts by the extreme right.

1921 Mussolini's Fascist Party wins 35 seats in the General Elections.

1922 Red Army is victorious against the "Whites."

Mussolini and his Black Shirts seize control of the Italian government and proclaim "Fascismo" after their March on Rome. Mussolini named Premier.

1923 Nazi Brownshirts attempt the Beer Hall Putsch in Munich. It fails and Hitler is jailed. During his prison term he writes *Mein Kampf*.

1924 V. I. Lenin dies and a power struggle ensues.

Fascists receive more than 60% of the popular vote in the Italian General Elections. Although opposition parties appear, the elections are considered rigged. Labor unions lose their right to strike.

1927 Joseph Stalin defeats Trotsky in an election of the Central Committee. Trotsky is exiled to Siberia, charged with "Leftist Deviation."

1928 Stalin begins first Five-Year Plan.

1929 Mussolini signs the Lateran Accord with the Catholic Church which now becomes associated with Fascism.

1930 Nazis win 107 seats in the Reichstag, up from only 12 seats in the General Elections of 1928.

1932 Hitler and the Nazi Party win 230 seats in the Reichstag.

In the November General Elections, the Nazis lose 34 seats in the Reichstag while the Communists rise to 100 seats.

1933 Following the resignation of German General Schleicher, Hitler is named Chancellor of Germany. The Third Reich is born.

One week before scheduled General Elections, the Reichstag building catches fire. The Communists are blamed by Hitler and Brownshirts try to "bully" the elections, using physical force to intimidate both potential voters and candidates during the campaign and elections.

1934 Hitler purges the Nazi Party of all opposition. The Gestapo formed as Hitler's secret police.

1935 German Jews are deprived of their citizenship.

1936 Stalin begins his purges to consolidate his hold on power.

Spanish Civil War begins. Hitler and Mussolini support Francisco Franco and his Falange (Fascist) party.

1938 Papal encyclical outlines support for the concept of the "Vertical Society" and gives Catholic endorsement of Fascism.

MAJOR TERMS AND CONCEPTS

Black Shirts
Bloody Sunday, 1905
Bolsheviks
Brownshirts
Cadets
Central Committee
Christian Socialist Party
collectivization
communism
Cordon Sanitaire
Corporate State
Duma
Falange
Fascism

Five-Year Plan
German Workers Party
Gestapo
Adolf Hitler (1889–1945)
Alexander Kerensky (1881–1970)
The Lateran Accord
V. I. Lenin (1870–1924)
March Revolutions
March on Rome
Mein Kampf
Mensheviks
Mirs
Benito Mussolini (1883–1945)
National German Workers Party

New Economic Policy
Nicholas II (1868–1918)
Novembrist Revolution
Nuremberg Laws
Pravda
purge
Putsch
Red Army
Social Democratic Labor Party
Social Revolutionary Party

Soviet Workers Council
Joseph Stalin (1879–1953)
Pyotr Stolypin (1862–1911)
Third Reich
totalitarianism
Leon Trotsky (1879–1940)
Vertical Society
Weimar Republic
"White Army"
World Revolution

MAJOR THEMES AND QUESTIONS

1. In what ways did the conclusion of World War I lead to the growth of both the Communist and Fascist movements in twentieth-century Europe?
2. In what ways did Lenin, Trotsky, and Stalin differ in their political ideologies?
3. What existing social conditions caused the popular acceptance of Lenin and the Bolsheviks?
4. To what extent was Trotsky justified in his charge that Stalin "betrayed the revolution"?
5. Explain and discuss the relationship between the popular, and simultaneous, acceptance of both Fascism and Communism.
6. To what degree did Germany and Italy benefit from the rule of Fascist governments?
7. Evaluate and discuss the relative success and failure of Stalin's Five-Year Plan.
8. Compare and contrast the tactics used by both the Fascists and the Bolsheviks in their quest for power. To what extent were their tactics dictated by external actions?
9. To what extent did the actions and policies of other nations contribute to the rise of Nazi Germany and Communist Russia?
10. To what extent did the Russian Revolution address the abuses of the Czarist regime? Explain and discuss.

SAMPLE OUTLINE

Topic: *Compare the status and treatment of women in Nazi Germany, Fascist Italy, and the Soviet Union.*

I. Soviet Union

A. Marx and Engels had written that women are exploited in non-communist society because they have become man's property (*The Origin of the Family, Private Property, and the State*, 1884).

B. Therefore, according to theory, exploitation of women will not exist in a communist society.

C. Under Stalin, women were employed in factories as well as on farms.

D. Barriers to women for higher education in all fields were eliminated; three out of four doctors in the Soviet Union are women.

II. Fascist Italy

A. The status of women reflected Mussolini's own attitude, "Women should be passive . . . She must obey. . . . My view of the role of women in the state is opposed to feminism. . . . Women are the tender, gentle influence that represents a pleasant parenthesis in a man's life. . . . Women are a charming pastime, when a man has time to pass . . . but they should never be taken seriously, for they themselves are rarely serious. . . . Women's place in the present as in the past, is in the home."

B. Mussolini tried to "fascisize" women to see their main, if not sole, role as mothers. In the girls' high school, the curriculum included singing, embroidery, dance, and "women's work."

C. By 1928, all school principals had to be men; women were not permitted to teach philosophy or literature; they were considered incapable of handling philosophy and too emotional to treat literature properly.

D. Fees for women's education were twice as high as the fees for men.

E. A quota of only 10 percent of the better-paying jobs for women was established by the end of the 1930s and 90 percent was reserved for men.

F. Divorce was abolished and single people paid higher taxes.

G. In the mass media, as well as in schoolbooks, families were always shown to include many children. Pictures of thin women were barred.

H. To a large degree, these attitudes reflected traditional Italian views that were unchanged by the Fascists.

   1. On May 9, 1936 a women's "demonstration" took place in Rome with many women marching and carrying signs that read, "Duce, our sons belong to you."
   2. A survey of the antifascist organizations shows practically no women in positions of leadership.

III. Nazi Germany

A. Although officially antifeminist, Nazi Germany found that by the late 1930s women were needed to overcome a severe labor shortage.

B. Women got jobs previously denied to them.

C. Women's income raised their family's standard of living.

D. Throughout the Nazi period, however, Nazi women argued that much of the decadence in the world was caused by feminism.

   1. They pointed to French, English, and American "flappers" as the worst possible examples of womanhood.
   2. They claimed that the university was the home of only the "Jewish intellectual" women and therefore a place good German women should avoid.
   3. German women, like German men, saw Nazism as a national and social revolution that was restoring pride to their fatherland and eliminating upper-class privileges.
   4. Claudia Koonz, in *Mothers In the Fatherland*, written with Renate Bridenthal, states that in Nazi Germany, although "unaware of the consequences, women welcomed the apparent return to tradition."
      a. No woman ever held any Nazi Party office.

b. Hitler promised to provide a husband for every woman.

c. Over one and one-half million women per year were enrolled in "motherhood" courses.

d. Nazi laws were passed that encouraged marriage and outlawed birth control. A newly married couple was given a loan to purchase furniture; the loan was increased by 25 percent for each child the couple had.

5. Five concentration camps were established for women engaged in "resistance activities."

SHORT READING LIST

William Allen, *The Nazi Seizure of Power*. A vivid account of how the Nazis refused to remain the tools of those who would use them.

Hannah Arendt, *The Origins of Totalitarianism*

N. Berdyaev, *The Origins of Russian Communism* (1937). An older work but an important intellectual history.

K. Bracher, *The German Dictatorship: The Origins, Structure and Effects of National Socialism* (1970). If only one book can be read on Nazi Germany, this should be the one.

R. Bridenthal and C. Koonz, *Becoming Visible*. See the chapters on women in Nazi Germany. A different outlook.

Allen Bullock, *Hitler: A Study in Tyranny* (1953). The classic study, still extremely valuable.

E. H. Carr, *The Russian Revolution: From Lenin to Stalin*

Lucy Davidowicz, *The War Against the Jews*. Did the Nazis plan the Holocaust from the beginning or was it developed later on?

Frederick W. Deakin, *The Brutal Friendship: Mussolini, Hitler and the Fall of Italian Fascism* (1962)

Victoria DeGrazia, *The Culture of Consent: Mass Organization of Leisure in Fascist Italy* (1981). A brilliant analysis of Fascist institutions created to "fascisize" the Italian people.

Charles F. Delzell, *Mediterranean Fascism 1919–1945* (1970)

—*Mussolini's Enemies: The Anti-Fascist Resistance* (1961). How strong was it? Could anti-Fascists be effective from outside the country?

Isaac Deutscher, *Stalin*

M. Djilas, *Conversations With Stalin*. A Yugoslav leader and writer examines Communism.

Joachim Fest, *Hitler* (1974). Was Hitler an "abberation" or a product of German history?

K. Geiger, *The Family in Soviet Russia* (1968). Modern social history.

Ian Kershaw, *The Nazi Dictatorship*, summarizes the major debates over Nazi Germany.

Tracy H. Koon, *Believe, Obey, Fight: Political Socialization of Youth in Fascist Italy* (1985)

C. Koonz, *Mothers in the Fatherland*

Walter Laquer, ed., *Fascism* (1976). A general survey, well written.

Michael Ledeen, *The First Duce: D'Annunzio at Fiume*. The origins of Fascism. Mussolini copied many of D'Annunzio's ideas.

Adrian Lyttleton, *The Seizure of Power, Fascism in Italy 1919–1929* (1973). Fascism in power. The most useful survey.

Unit Review S
World War II

CHRONOLOGY

1931 Japan invades Manchuria.

1933 Hitler pulls Germany out of the League of Nations.

Austrian Nazi Party attempts a Putsch and assassinates the Austrian chancellor.

Austro-German unification is demanded by the Nazis of Austria.

Mussolini mobilizes Italian forces along Italy's borders with Austria in response to German unification demands.

1934 The Soviet Union joins the League of Nations.

1935 The Soviet Union signs a mutual assistance pact with France and Czechoslovakia.

Plebescite in the Saar, as mandated by the Treaty of Versailles, votes for reunion with Germany.

Hitler openly repudiates the German disarmament clauses in the Versailles Treaty. The arms build-up begins in full.

Italy declares war upon Ethiopia.

1936 Hitler repudiates the Locarno agreements and reoccupies the Rhineland. The Franco-Soviet pact is used to justify the action.

The outbreak of the Spanish Civil War between Republican and Falange forces. Hitler and Mussolini openly aid the Fascists.

Hitler and Mussolini form the Rome-Berlin Axis.

Germany and Japan sign the Anti-Comintern Pact, ostensibly to oppose the spread of Communism.

1937 Japan launches full-scale invasion of China.

1938 The Anschluss—German forces move into Austria. Mussolini now accepts the unification with Germany he had opposed in 1934.

Liebenstraum German forces move into the Sudetenland in Czechoslovakia.

Britain and France yield the Sudetenland to Hitler at the Munich Conference.

1939 German troops attack Bohemia-Morovia.

Mussolini invades Albania.

Stalin signs a nonaggression pact with Germany.

September 1: Germany invades Poland.

September 3: England and France declare war upon Germany.

Soviet forces invade Finland, Estonia, Latvia, Lithuania.

The United States breaks its policy of neutrality by sending arms to England.

1940 Nazi forces take Paris. France falls between June 13 and 22. Evacuation of British forces at Dunkirk.

Germans bombard Britain from June to September.

Hitler breaks off attack on Britain to launch invasion of Russia in October.

1941 The United States adapts Lend-Lease policy to provide arms to the Allied powers.

The Soviet Union signs a nonaggression pact with Japan.

A German submarine sinks United States destroyer.

Japan bombs Pearl Harbor and the United States enters World War II.

Roosevelt and Churchill establish the Atlantic Charter.

1942 German offensives against Russia push to within 200 miles of Moscow. Stalingrad falls. Rommel advances through North Africa.

Battle of Coral Sea and Midway. United States forces land at Guadalcanal.

Montgomery defeats German forces at El-Alamein.

1943 Allied forces take Sicily.

Meeting at Teheran between the Allied leaders (Churchill, Roosevelt, and Stalin).

1944 June 6: D-Day. The Allied invasion of Normandy takes place. Paris is liberated in August.

Churchill and Stalin meet to discuss the postwar division of European spheres of influence.

1945 The Allied leaders meet at Yalta to discuss postwar programs.

May 8: V-E Day. Germany surrenders.

The Potsdam Conference is held among Churchill, Stalin, and Truman to discuss the future of the war against Japan. It is agreed to divide Germany and to occupy Berlin by the major western Allied powers.

August 6: The first atomic bomb is dropped upon Hiroshima.

September 2: V-J Day. Japan surrenders.

1947 Peace treaties are signed with Italy, Rumania, Hungary, Bulgaria, and Finland.

1951 The United States signs a peace treaty with Japan.

1956 Japan and the Soviet Union sign a peace treaty.

MAJOR TERMS AND CONCEPTS

Anschluss
Anti-Comintern Pact
Atlantic Charter
Battle of Britain
Casablanca Conference
Neville Chamberlain (1869–1940)
Winston Churchill (1874–1965)
Battle of Coral Sea
Council of Foreign Ministers
Curzon Line
D-Day
Edouard Daladier (1884–1970)
El-Alamein
General Dwight D. Eisenhower (1890–1969)
Enola Gay
Francisco Franco (1892–1975)
Lend-Lease Program
Liebenstraum
Maginot Line
Mare Nostrum
George C. Marshall (1880–1959)

Battle of Midway
General Bernard Montgomery (1887–1976)
Morgenthau Line
Munich Conference
pacifism
General George S. Patton (1885–1945)
Pearl Harbor
Potsdam Conference
Rome–Berlin Axis
Erwin Rommel (1891–1944)
Franklin D. Roosevelt (1882–1945)
Russo–German Nonaggression Pact
Joseph Stalin (1879–1953)
Sudetenland
Teheran Conference
Tojo Hideki (1884–1948)
Harry Truman (1884–1972)
V-E Day
V-J Day
Yalta Conference

MAJOR THEMES AND QUESTIONS

1. To what extent were the terms of the Treaty of Versailles a major cause of World War II?

2. To what extent did the neutrality and isolationism of the United States contribute to the success of Fascist militarism in Europe?

3. Discuss the reasoning behind the signing of the Anti-Comintern Pact of 1936 between Germany and Japan.

4. Discuss and explain the significance of the Spanish Civil War (and Western Allied responses) to World War II.

5. What internal and external factors could explain the signing of the Nonaggression Pact between Russia and Germany?

6. What social and political factors could explain the policy of appeasement pursued by Britain and France towards Hitler before 1939?

7. Discuss the significance of the meetings between the Allied leaders (Teheran, Casablanca, Yalta, and Potsdam) to the future of European politics.

8. To what degree were some political leaders correct when they branded the conference at Yalta a "sellout"? Discuss and explain.

9. In 1945, the United States dropped the first atomic bomb upon Japan, ostensibly to end the war quickly. It was also claimed that the United States wished to end the war before Russia entered and to prevent future territorial concessions to Russia. Concessions had already been made at Yalta, however, along with an agreement for Russian entry into the war. Discuss and explain the apparent discrepancy.

10. Discuss and explain the long-range effects of how World War II ended with respect to present-day political affairs and events.

SAMPLE OUTLINE

Topic: *What effects did the various World War II conferences have upon the future of European and world politics?*

I. The Atlantic Charter and the Casablanca Conference

A. Aimed at preventing much of the ambiguity, and consequent bad feelings, that permeated the peace treaties of 1918.

B. Both were still highly optimistic regarding the possible future political implications of an Allied victory over Germany (the absence of territorial discussions is conspicuous).

II. Teheran, Yalta, and the Churchill–Stalin conference (October 1944)

A. The demilitarization of Germany laid the groundwork for future division and occupation.

B. Teheran set the foundation for the future organization of the United Nations.

C. The Churchill–Stalin Conference of October 1944 seemed to recognize not only the imminent defeat of Nazi Germany but also the future conflict for power between the Soviet Union and the Western European powers.

D. At the Churchill–Stalin Conference, much of the optimistic euphemism gave way to power politics as Europe was divided into spheres of influence. Clearly, for the British, the "old enemy" of Nazi Germany was already being replaced by a "new enemy," that is, the Soviet Union.

E. The Soviet Union's desire for protection along its western flanks was recognized by Britain and the United States.

F. The sovereignty of Eastern Europe was disregarded and the future Iron Curtain was designed at Yalta.

G. German division and Berlin occupation were proposed at Yalta.

III. Potsdam conference

A. The future of German occupation and division was made official.

B. It was agreed that Europe and Asia were to be divided into East–West spheres of influence. Each side made a de facto agreement to turn a blind eye towards elections (re: lack of elections) in the others' sphere. The modern boundaries of Poland were also determined.

SHORT READING LIST

Raymond Aron, *A Century of Total War.* A classic.

P. Birdsall, *Versailles Twenty Years After.* A revisionist approach.

Peter Calvocoressi and Guy Wint, *Total War: Causes and Courses of the Second World War* (1979). This book is a useful source of information for those who are interested in military history, battles and strategy.

E. H. Carr, *The Twenty Years' Crisis*

Winston Churchill, *The Second World War* (several volumes). A sweeping account of the dramatic events of the period.

B. H. Liddell Hart, *The History of the Second World War* (1971). A military history.

MacGreor Knox, *Mussolini Unleashed, 1939–1941: Politics and Strategy in Fascist Italy's Last War* (1982)

R. J. Lifton, *Death in Life: Survivors of Hiroshima* (1967). A psychological perspective.

Robert Paxton, *Vichy France, Old Guard and New Order 1940–1945* (1972). A major study.

J. Remak, *The Origins of the Second World War,* (1975). A reappraisal of old themes.

M. J. Sherwin, *A World Destroyed: The Atomic Bomb and the Grand Alliance* (1975). Was the allegiance system obsolete in the nuclear age?

A. J. P. Taylor, *The Origins of the Second World War* (rev. ed., 1983). A controversial work. "Blame" for the war is placed not on Hitler's shoulders alone.

Gordon Wright, *The Ordeal of Total War, 1939–1945* (1968). A wide-ranging survey. Very complete.

Unit Review T
The Cold War (World War II–1968)

CHRONOLOGY

1943 November: At the Teheran Conference, Roosevelt, Stalin, and Churchill decide to attack Germany through France, thereby leaving eastern Europe to the Red Army.

1945 February: At the Yalta Conference, Germany is divided into occupation zones and ordered to pay reparations to the Soviet Union; Soviet Union to declare war on Japan within three months after German surrender; east European countries to hold free elections.

April: Roosevelt dies; Truman becomes president.

May: The United States cancels all aid to the Soviet Union.

July: At the Potsdam Conference, Truman and Attlee replace Roosevelt and Churchill. Stalin and Truman disagree over the Yalta accords on eastern Europe.

1946 March: Churchill gives his Iron Curtain speech.

1947 March: The Truman Doctrine is announced; military aid is granted to Greece and Turkey. The Rio Treaty Creates the OAS.

June: The Marshall Plan is announced.

1948 June: The Berlin Blockade begins; the Berlin airlift lasts 324 days.

1949 Berlin Blockade ends.

The NATO alliance is formed: Belgium, Canada, Denmark, France, Great Britain, Iceland, Italy, Luxembourg, the Netherlands, Norway, Portugal, and the United States.

The Chinese Communists defeat the Nationalists.

The German Federal Republic and the German Democratic Republic are created.

Tito of Yugoslavia breaks with the USSR.

1950 June: Korean War begins.

1951 ANZUS Pact.

1952 Greece and Turkey join NATO.

1953 March: Death of Stalin.

July: Cease-fire in Korea.

1954 SEATO is formed by the United States, Australia, France, Great Britain, New Zealand, Pakistan, the Philippines, and Thailand.

1955 West Germany joins NATO.

The Warsaw Pact is formed: Bulgaria, Czechoslovakia, German Democratic Republic, Hungary, Poland, Rumania, and the Soviet Union.

1956 Spring: Uprising in Poland; Wladyslaw Gomulka becomes leader.

Suez Crisis.

October: Hungarian Revolution.

November: Soviet troops invade Hungary; Imre Nagy executed (1958).

1957 Treaty of Rome creates the EEC.

1960 U-2 Spy Plane captured; summit conference canceled.

1961 April: Bay of Pigs invasion in Cuba.

Creation of the Peace Corps.

August: Berlin Wall is built.

Soviet Union announces resumption of nuclear testing in the atmosphere.

1962 October: Cuban Missile Crisis.

1963 Franco-German Treaty of Cooperation.

Nuclear Test Ban Treaty is signed.

Assassination of John F. Kennedy.

1964 Nikita Khrushchev is overthrown.

Gulf of Tonkin Resolution.

1967 Glassboro Summit is held in Glassboro, New Jersey between the United States and the Soviet Union. It produces nothing of substance.

1968 January: Tet Offensive in Vietnam.
The Prague Spring in Czechoslovakia.

August: Invasion of Czechoslovakia by Soviet troops; Gustav Husak is installed as leader.

November: Election of President Richard M. Nixon.

MAJOR TERMS AND CONCEPTS

Konrad Adenauer (1876–1967)
Clement Attlee (1883–1967)
Willy Brandt (1913–   )
Brezhnev Doctrine
brinkmanship
Chinese Nationalists
COMECON
Cominform
containment
Council of Europe
Cultural Revolution
Alcide De Gasperi (1881–1954)
Charles De Gaulle (1890–1970)
de-Stalinization
"economic miracle"
Anthony Eden (1897–1977)
Eisenhower Doctrine
Ludwig Erhard (1897–1977)
Euratom
European Coal and Steel Community
European Economic Community
German Democratic Republic
German Federal Republic
Wladislaw Gomulka (1905–1982)
Hungarian Revolution
"Inner Six"
Iron Curtain speech
János Kádár (1912–1989)
Nikita Khrushchev (1894–1971)

Khrushchev's "secret speech"
Marshall Plan
Jan Masaryk (1886–1948)
massive retaliation
Jean Monnet (1888–1979)
Imre Nagy (1896–1958)
national communism
national sovereignty
NATO
Ostpolitik
Peace Corps
"peaceful coexistence"
Point Four Program
Potsdam Conference (1945)
Radio Free Europe
Schuman Plan
second strike capability
Stimson Doctrine
Teheran Conference (1943)
Marshal Tito (1892–1980)
Treaty of Rome
Truman Doctrine
XXth Party Congress
Walter Ulbricht (1893–1973)
Voice of America
Warsaw Pact
Yalta Conference (1945)
Mao Zedong (1893–1976)

MAJOR THEMES AND QUESTIONS

1. Evaluate how the United States and the Soviet Union were each responsible for the Cold War.
2. Discuss the development of eastern Europe as a Soviet sphere of influence. Analyze the failure of various east European nations to

achieve independence from Moscow. Evaluate United States policy towards eastern Europe.
3. Discuss Soviet economic developments from 1945 to 1965. What major problems faced

the Soviet economy? How successful were the Soviets in meeting these problems?

4. Analyze the origins and effects of the Sino-Soviet split.

5. Discuss the issues and tensions that have developed in NATO.

6. Compare and contrast political conditions in Europe in the decade just before World War I and just after World War II.

7. Discuss the Cold War in terms of the weapons each side has used.

SAMPLE OUTLINE

Topic: *How has the history of Germany reflected the history of the Cold War?*

I. Agreements over Germany made during the last years of World War II divided Germany into eastern and western spheres

   A. Teheran.

   B. Yalta.

   C. Potsdam.

   D. France felt slighted at not being one of the "Big" nations at the conferences and not receiving its own zone of occupation.

II. Early tensions arose over Berlin (1948–1949)

   A. The blockade.

   B. The airlift.

   C. The United States showed its determination to remain involved in world affairs rather than return to isolationist policies.

   D. Weapons other than military force were used to achieve desired goals.

     1. West Germany accepted Marshall Plan Aid.

     2. East Germany, under Soviet orders, turned down United States aid.

III. East and West Germany became leading nations in their respective blocs

   A. Federal Republic.

     1. NATO membership (1955).

     2. Common Market membership (1957).

   B. Democratic Republic.

     1. Warsaw Pact membership. East Germany has 100,000+ troops.

     2. East Germany was a leading member of COMECON.

IV. Tensions heightened again after 1958

   A. More than two million East Germans escaped to the West between 1949 and 1961.

   B. West Berlin became a symbol of western progress and communist lack of progress.

C. Khrushchev demanded the withdrawal of western forces and a "confederation" between East and West Germany.

D. August 1961, the Berlin Wall was built.

E. The Berlin Wall.

F. The United States sends army reserves to Berlin.

G. President Kennedy makes the "Ich Bin Ein Berliner" speech.

V. Since 1970, relations between East and West Germany have consistently improved.

A. Destruction of the Berlin Wall (1989).

B. Official reunification of the two countries on October 3, 1990.

SHORT READING LIST

Dean Acheson, *Present At the Creation* (1969). A highly personal account by an active participant in the events shaping post-war Europe.

A. De Porte, *Europe Between the Superpowers* (1979). A work of the highest scholarship.

H. Feis, *From Trust To Terror: The Onset of the Cold War, 1945–1950* (1970)

J. Gaddis, *The United States and the Origins of the Cold War* (1972). An American perspective on the Cold War.

N. Graebner, *Cold War Diplomacy: 1945–1960* (1962). A bit outdated.

W. La Feber, *America, Russia, and the Cold War* (1967). The Cold War could have been prevented if the U.S. had acted differently.

C. Linden, *Khrushchev and the Soviet Leadership, 1957–1964* (1966)

V. Mastny, *Russia's Road to the Cold War,* (1979)

R. and Z. Medvedev, *Khrushchev: The Years In Power* (1978). An examination of the regime by Soviet dissidents, but aims for fairness.

H. Seton-Watson, *The East European Revolution* (1965)

H. Smith, *The Russians* (1978). A descriptive account by the former Moscow correspondent of the *New York Times.*

M. Tatu, *Power In The Kremlin: From Khrushchev To Kosygin* (1968)

W. A. Williams, *The Tragedy of American Diplomacy* (1962)

F. R. Willis, *France, Germany, and the New Europe, 1945–1967* (1968)

D. Yergin, *Shattered Peace: The Origins of the Cold War and the National Security Council* (1977). Who was to blame for the Cold War, the United States or the Soviet Union?

Unit Review U
The End of Imperialism: Africa and Asia

CHRONOLOGY

1919 Syria, Lebanon, and Jordan are created as European-mandated areas as the Turkish Empire falls apart.

1937 Iraq becomes independent.

1942 The Dutch lose their colonial territories in the Indonesian archipelago to the Japanese.

1945 The Arab League is formed by the now independent nations of Egypt, Iraq, Syria, Jordan, Lebanon, Saudia Arabia, and Yemen.

1947 India becomes independent of British rule.

The British Commonwealth of Nations is formed from former direct colonies such as Australia, New Zealand, and parts of Canada.

1948 Pakistan becomes separate from India.

Ceylon, later to be renamed Sri Lanka, becomes independent from England. Burma follows.

Britain announces the end of her partition of Palestine. The nation of Israel is created.

1949 Ireland announces its break from the Commonwealth and its status as an independent Republic.

Indonesia's independence, and its new President Sukarno, is recognized by their former rulers, the Dutch.

1951 Libya becomes an independent state.

1954 Ho Chi Minh and his Viet Minh nationalists defeat French forces at Dien Bien Phu.

Britain relinquishes her treaty privileges in Egypt.

1956 Sudan breaks away from Egypt to form an independent state.

France grants independence to Morocco and Tunisia.

The first of many Arab-Israeli wars is fought. Britain occupies the Suez Canal zone.

1957 Federation of Malaya becomes independent.

Ghana, then called the Gold Coast, announces its independence from Britain.

1958 Charles De Gaulle offers French African colonies the choice of self-determination and voluntary association with France.

1959 The people in the Belgian Congo rise against Belgian rule.

1960 Ghana becomes a Republic.

Nigeria announces its independence.

1962 Uganda becomes an independent state.

1963 Nigeria becomes a member of the Commonwealth of Nations.

Kenya receives her independence.

Malaysia, formerly Federation of Malaya, is formed from former British Asian colonies.

1964 Jawaharlal Nehru, leader of the Indian National Congress Party, dies.

The nation of Tanzania is formed after the merger of the independent nations of Tanganyika (German East Africa) and Zanzibar.

British Nyasaland completes her 50-year rebellion against British rule and becomes Malawi.

1966 Indira Gandhi, daughter of Nehru, becomes prime minister of India.

The United Nations declares Namibia a free and independent nation from South Africa.

1967 The Six-Day War between Arab forces and Israel.

1970 Egyptian leader, Gamal Abdel Nasser, dies.

1971 The state of Bangladesh is created.
The nation of Zaire is proclaimed from
what was once the Republic of the
Congo.

1973 The Yom Kippur War between Arab
forces and Israel.

MAJOR TERMS AND CONCEPTS

General Idi Amin (1925–   )
Arab League
Balfour Declaration
Cold War
commonwealth
Commonwealth of Nations
Charles De Gaulle (1890–1970)
dominion
free-state
Indira Gandhi (1917–1984)
Mohandas K. Gandhi (1869–1948)
Ho Chi Minh (1890–1969)
Indian National Congress

Jomo Kenyatta (1890–1978)
Mau Mau society
Lord Louis Mountbatten (1900–1979)
Muslim League
Gamal Abdel Nasser (1918–1970)
Jawaharlal Nehru (1889–1964)
Palestine
Siege of Dien Bien Phu
Six-Day War
Sukarno (1901–1970)
Yom Kippur War
Zionism

MAJOR THEMES AND QUESTIONS

1. In what way did the onset and conclusion of World War II play a part in the independence movements of former colonies?

2. Explain and discuss the relationship between the Cold War of the 1950s and 1960s and the independence movements of the same periods.

3. What effect did the independence of the former African colonies have upon the balance of world power during the 1960s and 1970s?

4. To what extent did the tribal and religious ties of the newly emerging nations affect their future independent status? Explain and discuss.

5. To what extent did the process of independence of the various colonial territories affect their future forms of government and their foreign relations after independence?

6. What external and internal factors could explain the sudden surge in nationalist independence movements in the 1950s and 1960s?

7. What seem to have been the long-term effects upon United States policy of the decline of imperialism in Africa and Asia?

8. Many historians claim that much of the present-day trouble in the Middle East region is the result of both western imperialism and western ignorance as those powers gave up their colonial possessions. Discuss the validity of this analysis.

9. Compare and contrast the policies pursued by France and Britain vis à vis the retention and release of their colonial territorial possessions. What factors could account for the differences?

SAMPLE OUTLINE

Topic: *What effect did the onset of the Cold War have upon the independence movements in the Third World (1950s–1970s)?*

I. African nationalism

A. The alignment of the current Arab world as a consequence of their association of capitalism with the United States, exploitation (perceived and real), and even Israeli Zionism.

B. Soviet support of Arab interests against those of Israel as part of her attempt to gain control of Mideast ports and oil reserves.

C. African tendencies towards either British-style Parliamentary democracies or Soviet-style Communism are also as a consequence of former experiences with both Britain and United States support (or lack of support) for their independence movements.

D. Islamic Fundamentalism has largely been a response to what is perceived as interference, domination, and corruption of the Arab world by western and other foreign nations. This form of Islam has nationalistic as well as religious appeal to many in the Arab world. The Shiite Fundamentalism can be traced back to Safavid Persia (fl. 1511) where the movement was a reaction to Turkish influence in the Arabic community. Islamic Fundamentalism tends to be highly xenophobic, also typical of most nationalist movements.

II. Asia since 1945

A. The attraction of Marxism in a society where western values were seen as having corrupted Chinese society. The Soviet Union's eventual support for Mao exemplified the Soviet desire for an ally in the post-World War II era more than it showed any connection between Maoist Marxism and Leninist Marxism.

B. United States support for, and eventual involvement in, French interests in Vietnam came largely as a reaction to the virulent anticommunist atmosphere in the United States combined with the perceived communist expansionism (the "loss of China," and Soviet incursions into western Europe).

C. The current division of North and South Korea, China, and Taiwan, and the past division of Vietnam were largely orchestrated by the western powers and the Soviet Union in their efforts to mold the world in the shape of their Yalta and Potsdam Agreements.

III. Latin America

A. United States intervention in Bolivia (1967), Guatemala (1956), and Chile (1973), were not only an effort to protect corporate interests but also in response to Soviet support for insurgent movements in these regions.

B. The Cuban Missile Crisis and its United States–Soviet conflict causes and consequences.

C. Nicaragua, El Salvador, and Grenada are examples of the continuing conflict between the two Super Powers in the nuclear age when proxy-wars are far more economical and politically viable than direct conflict.

SHORT READING LIST

R. von Albertini, *Decolonization* (1971). A very general survey of the 1960s.

Gwendolen M. Carter, ed., *Politics in Africa: Seven Cases* (1966). Local tribalism versus anti-westernism: Forces for unity or disruption in Africa.

Basil Davidson, *Which Way Africa?* (1973)

Vera Micheles Dean, *The Nature of the Non-Western World* (1966)

Rupert Emerson and Martin Kilson, eds., *The Political Awakening of Africa* (1965)

F. Fanon, *The Wretched of the Earth* (1965). A psychiatrist examines the meaning of revolt for colonial peoples.

E. Kedourie, *Nationalism in Asia and Africa* (1971)

Ronald Segal, *African Profiles* (1963). Older views but still useful. Over 400 leaders profiled.

B. Ward, *Rich Nations and Poor Nations* (1962). Presents the case that it is in the interest of richer nations to give economic assistance to the poorer ones.

Unit Review V
The Changing World:
Technology and Society

CHRONOLOGY

1945 July: The first atomic bomb is detonated in New Mexico.

August: Two atomic bombs are dropped on Japan.

1951 The UNIVAC computer is invented.

1957 October: The first Sputnik satellite is launched by the Soviet Union.

1958 NASA is created by the Space Act.

1959 Invention of the transistor.

1960 CERN (Consul Européen pour la Recherche Nucléaire) is established outside Geneva.

1961 First Soviet cosmonaut orbits earth.

1962 Telstar, the first communications satellite, is launched.

Watson and Crick receive the Nobel Prize in physiology for determining the structure of DNA.

1965 Transistors are replaced by integrated circuits on silicon chips.

1967 First human heart transplant.

1969 July: Apollo 11 lands on the moon.

1974 Discovery of a hole in the ozone layer caused by CFCs.

1975 Apollo/Soyuz Space link-up.

1976 Viking I lands on Mars.

1986 January: Challenger explosion kills seven astronauts.

April: Nuclear accident at Chernobyl.

MAJOR TERMS AND CONCEPTS

acid rain
Apollo–Soyuz Project
Dr. Christiaan Barnard (1922–)
"brain drain"
CAT scans
CFCs
Chernobyl
compact discs
Concorde
consumer society
credit-card society
Francis Crick (1916–)
DDT
end of the "baby boom"
European Council for Nuclear Research (CERN)
European Space Agency
fax machines
fossil fuels
"gadget revolution"

genetic engineering
greenhouse effect
ICBM (Intercontinental Ballistic Missile)
INF (Intermediate Nuclear Forces) Treaty (1987)
jet propulsion
magnetic resonance imaging (MRI)
Manhattan Project
marriage and divorce rate patterns in the 1960s and 1970s
microwave technology
military–industrial complex
J. Robert Oppenheimer (1904–1967)
ozone layer
Pacific Rim
personal computers
rising female employment and decline in birth rate
saccharin/cancer debate
Skylab

Spacelab
space race
Sputnik
superconductors
technocratic society
Telstar/INTELSAT/Comstar

The American Challenge, Jean-Jacques Serva-
  Schreiber
The Social Function of Science
thin film technology
travel and tourism
James Watson (1928–   )

MAJOR THEMES AND QUESTIONS

1. Discuss the effects of modern technology on patterns of work, leisure, the family, and artistic expression.

2. "Technology has proven to be a two-edged sword." Discuss the validity of this statement, citing specific references to the period 1965–1985. Include environmental issues, medical issues, as well as the "technology of repression" in your essay.

3. How has modern technology shifted the centers of world political and economic power? Discuss your answer fully.

4. How has modern technology made cultural patterns "worldwide"? To what extent is this view an exaggeration?

5. Discuss demographic patterns and the effects of modern technology on population growth, density, and movement.

6. Discuss the debate between those who argued for "pure science" and those who argued for science as a creator of social, political, and economic benefits. Pay particular attention to this debate in Great Britain and in the Soviet Union.

7. "The student revolutions of the late 1960s in France and Italy can be viewed as an expression of discontent with the materialism of the consumer society." Evaluate the validity of this statement.

SAMPLE OUTLINE

Topic: *How has modern science changed everyday life in European society?*

I. In the second half of the twentieth century, to a degree far beyond what had been true ever before, theoretical science and applied technology were united. This "joining together" was a natural continuation of developments that had begun during World War II. Some of the fields affected were the following:

  A. Medicine.

  B. Electronics.

  C. Chemistry.

II. The Space Race attracted scientists from all countries and massive spending by various governments

  A. The United States versus the Soviet Union.

B. The western European nations also competed in research and development, e.g., the SuperSonic Transport.

III. The preeminence of the computer

A. Computers were initially developed for space programs; they now are everywhere.

B. John Naisbitt, in *Megatrends*, has labeled the new age "The Information Society."

IV. Creation of the consumer or gadget society

A. A generally rising standard of living in Europe.

B. Buying on credit became widespread in Europe after World War II; this was a significant social change.

C. Middle-class families purchased ever increasing numbers of household appliances and other consumer products.

D. Leisure time, both standardized and commercialized, became a major concern.

V. The effects of modern science and technology have been criticized

A. Air and water pollution; the greenhouse effect.

B. The ozone layer.

C. Nuclear dangers: e.g., Chernobyl.

D. Computers can and have been used by totalitarian societies to store information on their own citizens.

SHORT READING LIST

Rachel Carson, *The Silent Spring* (1962). This is a classic work that many believe began the modern criticism of the effects scientific "advances" on the environment.

H. Judson, *The Eighth Day of Creation* (1979)

David Landes, *The Unbound Prometheus: Technological Change and Industrial Development In Western Europe from 1750 to the Present* (1969). Landes' point of view favors technological change; he might be considered an optimist.

Alvin Toffler, *Future Shock* (1970). This work was a bestseller when it came out. Toffler argues that technology is at the root of many contemporary problems.

A. Touraine, *The May Movement* (1971). This is a description of the "events of May" in France by a sympathetic observer.

J. Ziman, *The Force of Knowledge: The Scientific Dimension of Society* (1976). Ziman, a physicist himself, calls into question the relationship between modern science and society.

Unit Review W
The Demise of the Soviet Union

CHRONOLOGY

1985 March: Mikhail Gorbachev succeeds Konstantin Chernenko and becomes the youngest leader of the Communist Party since Stalin.

April: Gorbachev declares a moratorium on deployment of medium-range missiles and urges the United States to do the same.

May: Gorbachev announces new economic plans that will include *perestroika* and *glasnost*. He also will allow discussion of social ills without fear of repression.

November: Ronald Reagan seeks to open new discussions with the Soviet Union. He abandons the philosophy of the "evil empire."

1986 February: Gorbachev calls for major economic reforms, which will include autonomy for regional managers and institution of quality control.

June: Plans are made to remove government censorship.

October: A summit meeting is held between Reagan and Gorbachev. It is considered nonproductive.

1987 June: Multiple candidates run for public office in the Soviet Union for the first time.

November: Boris Yeltsin is dismissed as Moscow party leader by the Politburo.

December: Reagan and Gorbachev sign a treaty that will eliminate medium-range nuclear weapons.

1988 May: Moscow summit is held. Gorbachev complains about missed opportunities.

June: Gorbachev asks for, and is granted, more power as president. Estonia elects a non-Communist political group. Tension increases in the Baltic countries.

December: An earthquake in Armenia cuts short a summit in New York between Gorbachev, Reagan, and president-elect George Bush.

1989 March: In the first-ever free elections in the Soviet Union, the Communist Party suffers humiliating defeats but manages to stay in power.

December: The Communist Party in Lithuania breaks with Moscow. Gorbachev vows reprisals. At the Malta summit Gorbachev and Bush agree to work to reduce conventional and strategic arms.

1990 February: Over major resistance from the "hard-liners," Gorbachev asks for, and receives, the right to push through a plan to end the Communist Party's constitutional monopoly of power.

March: Pro-democracy groups achieve major gains in Russia, Ukraine, and Byelorussia. Lithuania declares its annexation by the Soviet Union in 1940 null and void. Latvia follows suit.

May: Yeltsin wins the presidency of the Russian Republic, the largest and most populous of the Soviet Union's republics.

October: Gorbachev wins the Nobel Peace Prize.

December: Foreign Minister Shevardnadze, once closely aligned with Gorbachev, resigns. He states that reactionaries are pushing the country toward dictatorship.

1991 December: Gorbachev, after being arrested while on vacation in August, tries to restore the Union. He fails and resigns. The Soviet Union ceases to exist.

MAJOR TERMS AND CONCEPTS

Afghanistan	Malta summit
archconservative	Marxist/Leninist
Armenia	modernization
autonomy	Moscow summit
Boris Yeltsin	multi-party, multi-candidate
Byelorussia	nationalistic
Communist Party	nuclear
constitutional monopoly	obsolete
conventional weapons	perestroika
dogma	Politburo
democracy	reactionaries
deprivation	restructuring
Edvard Shevardnadze	Ronald Reagan
Estonia	Russian Republic
"evil empire"	socialism
"hard-liners"	Soviet Union
Iceland summit	star wars
inflation rate	strategic arms
isolation	summit
Latvia	Ukraine
Lithuania	Warsaw pact

MAJOR THEMES AND QUESTIONS

1. Discuss the effects of *perestroika* and *glasnost* on the politics of the Soviet Union.

2. Why did socialism fail to keep the Soviet Union and its allies competitive with the economies of the "free world"? Discuss your answer fully.

3. "The restructuring of the Soviet Union was the beginning of the end for communism." Discuss the validity of this statement.

4. "Had the Soviet Union granted autonomy to its Baltic satellites, the Union might still exist." Is this hypothesis correct? Discuss your answer fully.

5. How and where did Gorbachev make a major political mistake? Justify your answer fully.

6. Under a free market system, profit and labor are linked together. How does socialism handle the economy and the ideas of profit and labor? Pay particular attention to the Soviet Union.

7. Was the Soviet Union ready for Mikhail Gorbachev? Discuss your answer fully.

SAMPLE OUTLINE

Topic: *In what ways did the attempts to "modernize" the Soviet Union eventually lead to the collapse and end of the Union itself?*

I. **Since the birth of the Soviet Union and its adoption of a socialistic economy, the leaders of the USSR perceived a "state-managed" economy that would eventually destroy capitalism. In theory, the people owned and controlled the land and the means of production. In fact, they had no control of anything, and their needs were not being met.**

   A. The Soviet Union was falling behind in the manufacturing of consumer goods. The populace preferred the necessities of life over tanks and missiles.

   B. More and more, the modern world exposed the inequities between those who belonged to the Communist Party and the peasant-worker with no party affiliation.

   C. Censorship and propaganda were becoming more and more repressive to a people suffering economic deprivation.

II. **Gorbachev came to believe that the Union could still dominate if there were a restructuring of the old system started by Lenin and reinforced by Stalin.**

   A. He tried to turn the people's attention away from their economic troubles by directing it to their political roots.

   B. He asked the populace to forget its isolationism and political paranoia and to embrace the West.

III. **Gorbachev underestimated the currents of nationalism that existed in Eastern Europe.**

   A. There was an angry confrontation with the Baltic Republics, who threatened to break away from the Union.

   B. The collapse of the Berlin Wall marked the end of a divided Germany.

IV. **In a final effort to maintain control, Gorbachev put into effect ideas that would end Communist Party control.**

   A. Liberalization of the press.

   B. Multi-party and multi-candidate elections.

   C. Release of political prisoners.

   D. Lifting of restrictions on travel.

V. **The hard-line Soviet conservatives had to act to retain their bureaucracy or they would lose everything.**

   A. Gorbachev was seized in a coup.

   B. Yeltsin intervened and rescued Gorbachev, but then seized the reins of government.

   C. Yeltsin finally ended the existing governmental structure.

SHORT READING LIST

Current History, October 1990, pages 305-329, World Affairs Journal.

Current History, October 1991, pages 305-328, World Affairs Journal.

Foreign Affairs, Summer 1991, pages 77-97.

A. Hewett and V. Winston, ed., *Milestones in Glasnost and Perestroika* (two volumes). Brookings Institution, Washington, D.C. (1991).

New York Times Index.

Reader's Guide to Periodical Literature.

Test 1
ANSWER SHEET
Multiple Choice

1 (A) (B) (C) (D) (E)   21 (A) (B) (C) (D) (E)   41 (A) (B) (C) (D) (E)   61 (A) (B) (C) (D) (E)

2 (A) (B) (C) (D) (E)   22 (A) (B) (C) (D) (E)   42 (A) (B) (C) (D) (E)   62 (A) (B) (C) (D) (E)

3 (A) (B) (C) (D) (E)   23 (A) (B) (C) (D) (E)   43 (A) (B) (C) (D) (E)   63 (A) (B) (C) (D) (E)

4 (A) (B) (C) (D) (E)   24 (A) (B) (C) (D) (E)   44 (A) (B) (C) (D) (E)   64 (A) (B) (C) (D) (E)

5 (A) (B) (C) (D) (E)   25 (A) (B) (C) (D) (E)   45 (A) (B) (C) (D) (E)   65 (A) (B) (C) (D) (E)

6 (A) (B) (C) (D) (E)   26 (A) (B) (C) (D) (E)   46 (A) (B) (C) (D) (E)   66 (A) (B) (C) (D) (E)

7 (A) (B) (C) (D) (E)   27 (A) (B) (C) (D) (E)   47 (A) (B) (C) (D) (E)   67 (A) (B) (C) (D) (E)

8 (A) (B) (C) (D) (E)   28 (A) (B) (C) (D) (E)   48 (A) (B) (C) (D) (E)   68 (A) (B) (C) (D) (E)

9 (A) (B) (C) (D) (E)   29 (A) (B) (C) (D) (E)   49 (A) (B) (C) (D) (E)   69 (A) (B) (C) (D) (E)

10 (A) (B) (C) (D) (E)   30 (A) (B) (C) (D) (E)   50 (A) (B) (C) (D) (E)   70 (A) (B) (C) (D) (E)

11 (A) (B) (C) (D) (E)   31 (A) (B) (C) (D) (E)   51 (A) (B) (C) (D) (E)   71 (A) (B) (C) (D) (E)

12 (A) (B) (C) (D) (E)   32 (A) (B) (C) (D) (E)   52 (A) (B) (C) (D) (E)   72 (A) (B) (C) (D) (E)

13 (A) (B) (C) (D) (E)   33 (A) (B) (C) (D) (E)   53 (A) (B) (C) (D) (E)   73 (A) (B) (C) (D) (E)

14 (A) (B) (C) (D) (E)   34 (A) (B) (C) (D) (E)   54 (A) (B) (C) (D) (E)   74 (A) (B) (C) (D) (E)

15 (A) (B) (C) (D) (E)   35 (A) (B) (C) (D) (E)   55 (A) (B) (C) (D) (E)   75 (A) (B) (C) (D) (E)

16 (A) (B) (C) (D) (E)   36 (A) (B) (C) (D) (E)   56 (A) (B) (C) (D) (E)   76 (A) (B) (C) (D) (E)

17 (A) (B) (C) (D) (E)   37 (A) (B) (C) (D) (E)   57 (A) (B) (C) (D) (E)   77 (A) (B) (C) (D) (E)

18 (A) (B) (C) (D) (E)   38 (A) (B) (C) (D) (E)   58 (A) (B) (C) (D) (E)   78 (A) (B) (C) (D) (E)

19 (A) (B) (C) (D) (E)   39 (A) (B) (C) (D) (E)   59 (A) (B) (C) (D) (E)   79 (A) (B) (C) (D) (E)

20 (A) (B) (C) (D) (E)   40 (A) (B) (C) (D) (E)   60 (A) (B) (C) (D) (E)   80 (A) (B) (C) (D) (E)

Test 2
ANSWER SHEET
Multiple Choice

1 Ⓐ Ⓑ Ⓒ Ⓓ Ⓔ	21 Ⓐ Ⓑ Ⓒ Ⓓ Ⓔ	41 Ⓐ Ⓑ Ⓒ Ⓓ Ⓔ	61 Ⓐ Ⓑ Ⓒ Ⓓ Ⓔ
2 Ⓐ Ⓑ Ⓒ Ⓓ Ⓔ	22 Ⓐ Ⓑ Ⓒ Ⓓ Ⓔ	42 Ⓐ Ⓑ Ⓒ Ⓓ Ⓔ	62 Ⓐ Ⓑ Ⓒ Ⓓ Ⓔ
3 Ⓐ Ⓑ Ⓒ Ⓓ Ⓔ	23 Ⓐ Ⓑ Ⓒ Ⓓ Ⓔ	43 Ⓐ Ⓑ Ⓒ Ⓓ Ⓔ	63 Ⓐ Ⓑ Ⓒ Ⓓ Ⓔ
4 Ⓐ Ⓑ Ⓒ Ⓓ Ⓔ	24 Ⓐ Ⓑ Ⓒ Ⓓ Ⓔ	44 Ⓐ Ⓑ Ⓒ Ⓓ Ⓔ	64 Ⓐ Ⓑ Ⓒ Ⓓ Ⓔ
5 Ⓐ Ⓑ Ⓒ Ⓓ Ⓔ	25 Ⓐ Ⓑ Ⓒ Ⓓ Ⓔ	45 Ⓐ Ⓑ Ⓒ Ⓓ Ⓔ	65 Ⓐ Ⓑ Ⓒ Ⓓ Ⓔ
6 Ⓐ Ⓑ Ⓒ Ⓓ Ⓔ	26 Ⓐ Ⓑ Ⓒ Ⓓ Ⓔ	46 Ⓐ Ⓑ Ⓒ Ⓓ Ⓔ	66 Ⓐ Ⓑ Ⓒ Ⓓ Ⓔ
7 Ⓐ Ⓑ Ⓒ Ⓓ Ⓔ	27 Ⓐ Ⓑ Ⓒ Ⓓ Ⓔ	47 Ⓐ Ⓑ Ⓒ Ⓓ Ⓔ	67 Ⓐ Ⓑ Ⓒ Ⓓ Ⓔ
8 Ⓐ Ⓑ Ⓒ Ⓓ Ⓔ	28 Ⓐ Ⓑ Ⓒ Ⓓ Ⓔ	48 Ⓐ Ⓑ Ⓒ Ⓓ Ⓔ	68 Ⓐ Ⓑ Ⓒ Ⓓ Ⓔ
9 Ⓐ Ⓑ Ⓒ Ⓓ Ⓔ	29 Ⓐ Ⓑ Ⓒ Ⓓ Ⓔ	49 Ⓐ Ⓑ Ⓒ Ⓓ Ⓔ	69 Ⓐ Ⓑ Ⓒ Ⓓ Ⓔ
10 Ⓐ Ⓑ Ⓒ Ⓓ Ⓔ	30 Ⓐ Ⓑ Ⓒ Ⓓ Ⓔ	50 Ⓐ Ⓑ Ⓒ Ⓓ Ⓔ	70 Ⓐ Ⓑ Ⓒ Ⓓ Ⓔ
11 Ⓐ Ⓑ Ⓒ Ⓓ Ⓔ	31 Ⓐ Ⓑ Ⓒ Ⓓ Ⓔ	51 Ⓐ Ⓑ Ⓒ Ⓓ Ⓔ	71 Ⓐ Ⓑ Ⓒ Ⓓ Ⓔ
12 Ⓐ Ⓑ Ⓒ Ⓓ Ⓔ	32 Ⓐ Ⓑ Ⓒ Ⓓ Ⓔ	52 Ⓐ Ⓑ Ⓒ Ⓓ Ⓔ	72 Ⓐ Ⓑ Ⓒ Ⓓ Ⓔ
13 Ⓐ Ⓑ Ⓒ Ⓓ Ⓔ	33 Ⓐ Ⓑ Ⓒ Ⓓ Ⓔ	53 Ⓐ Ⓑ Ⓒ Ⓓ Ⓔ	73 Ⓐ Ⓑ Ⓒ Ⓓ Ⓔ
14 Ⓐ Ⓑ Ⓒ Ⓓ Ⓔ	34 Ⓐ Ⓑ Ⓒ Ⓓ Ⓔ	54 Ⓐ Ⓑ Ⓒ Ⓓ Ⓔ	74 Ⓐ Ⓑ Ⓒ Ⓓ Ⓔ
15 Ⓐ Ⓑ Ⓒ Ⓓ Ⓔ	35 Ⓐ Ⓑ Ⓒ Ⓓ Ⓔ	55 Ⓐ Ⓑ Ⓒ Ⓓ Ⓔ	75 Ⓐ Ⓑ Ⓒ Ⓓ Ⓔ
16 Ⓐ Ⓑ Ⓒ Ⓓ Ⓔ	36 Ⓐ Ⓑ Ⓒ Ⓓ Ⓔ	56 Ⓐ Ⓑ Ⓒ Ⓓ Ⓔ	76 Ⓐ Ⓑ Ⓒ Ⓓ Ⓔ
17 Ⓐ Ⓑ Ⓒ Ⓓ Ⓔ	37 Ⓐ Ⓑ Ⓒ Ⓓ Ⓔ	57 Ⓐ Ⓑ Ⓒ Ⓓ Ⓔ	77 Ⓐ Ⓑ Ⓒ Ⓓ Ⓔ
18 Ⓐ Ⓑ Ⓒ Ⓓ Ⓔ	38 Ⓐ Ⓑ Ⓒ Ⓓ Ⓔ	58 Ⓐ Ⓑ Ⓒ Ⓓ Ⓔ	78 Ⓐ Ⓑ Ⓒ Ⓓ Ⓔ
19 Ⓐ Ⓑ Ⓒ Ⓓ Ⓔ	39 Ⓐ Ⓑ Ⓒ Ⓓ Ⓔ	59 Ⓐ Ⓑ Ⓒ Ⓓ Ⓔ	79 Ⓐ Ⓑ Ⓒ Ⓓ Ⓔ
20 Ⓐ Ⓑ Ⓒ Ⓓ Ⓔ	40 Ⓐ Ⓑ Ⓒ Ⓓ Ⓔ	60 Ⓐ Ⓑ Ⓒ Ⓓ Ⓔ	80 Ⓐ Ⓑ Ⓒ Ⓓ Ⓔ

Test 1

Part I. Multiple Choice

Time: 55 minutes

Directions: *For each question or incomplete statement below, choose the best answer of the five suggested. Blacken the space on the answer sheet corresponding to your choice.*

1. Which of these enterprises accounted most for the wealth of the northern Italian communes at the beginning of the Renaissance?

    (A) Mining of metals
    (B) Manufacture of luxury products
    (C) Finance and banking
    (D) Overseas trade
    (E) Sale of religious artifacts and icons

2. Machiavelli's ideal prince was

    (A) Lorenzo de' Medici
    (B) Giangaleazzo Sforza
    (C) Cesare Borgia
    (D) Charles VIII
    (E) John Hawkwood

3. The Italian humanist who is generally given credit for the view that his own times were "the dawn of a new era," and an improvement over the Dark Ages was

    (A) Dante Alighieri
    (B) Lorenzo Valla
    (C) Pico della Mirandola
    (D) Baldassare Castiglione
    (E) Francesco Petrarch

4. Which of these men best exemplified the Renaissance ideal of *l'uomo universale?*

    (A) Michelangelo
    (B) Leon Batista Alberti
    (C) Aeneas Silvius
    (D) Benvenuto Cellini
    (E) Cosimo de' Medici

5. Which of these events most clearly signaled the end of Italy's reign as the leading cultural center of the Renaissance?

    (A) The Pazzi Conspiracy and the fall of the Medici bank
    (B) The invention of movable type and the printing of the Gutenberg Bible
    (C) The publication of Erasmus' *In Praise of Folly*
    (D) The invasion of France by Italy
    (E) The sack of Rome by Emperor Charles V

6. During the Renaissance, the most widely read book of manners for the wealthy was

    (A) *The Prince* by Machiavelli.
    (B) *The Book of the Courtier* by Castiglione.
    (C) *Stanze Della Giostra de Giuliano de' Medici* by Poliziano.
    (D) *The Divine Comedy* by Dante Alighieri.
    (E) *Orlando Furioso* by Ariosto.

7. One characteristic that distinguished the Italian from the Northern Renaissance was that in the north, humanists

    (A) emphasized Christian ideals and Biblical themes.
    (B) supported the middle class rather than the nobility.
    (C) condemned innovations in art.
    (D) attacked religion directly.
    (E) denied any link between painting and literature.

8. Which technical advance contributed most to Martin Luther's success in northern Europe?

   (A) Gunpowder
   (B) The printing press
   (C) Macadam
   (D) The astrolab
   (E) The telescope

9. The expulsion of the Jews from Spain in 1492 was similar to the expulsion of the Huguenots from France in that

   (A) both countries were deprived of a skilled middle class.
   (B) both were brought about at the insistence of the pope.
   (C) they were carried out in the face of the opposition of a majority of the citizens of both countries.
   (D) they were purely economic in motivation.
   (E) they were based primarily on military considerations.

10. William McNeill, in *Plaques and People* (1976), argues that the major reason for the success of the Spanish conquest of America was the

    (A) superior military organization and technology of the Spaniards.
    (B) spread of smallpox and other diseases to the indigenous people.
    (C) cruel treatment and hard work imposed on the Aztecs and other native Americans.
    (D) more healthful diet of the European invaders.
    (E) availability of modern medicines to the Europeans.

11. Which school of thought is most closely associated with the late sixteenth-century writer, Michel de Montaigne?

    (A) Religious dogmatism
    (B) Rationalism
    (C) Romanticism
    (D) Skepticism
    (E) Neoplatonism

12. In the War of the Spanish Succession, France was opposed by the Grand Alliance of

    (A) England, Spain, Prussia, and Holland.
    (B) Russia, Spain, Austria, and Prussia.
    (C) Sweden, Russia, Prussia, and Austria.
    (D) Denmark, Sweden, Austria, and Holland.
    (E) England, Prussia, Austria, and Holland.

13. When Martin Luther wrote that "the fool wants to turn the whole art of astronomy upside down," who was he calling a fool?

    (A) Pope Leo X
    (B) Nicholas Copernicus
    (C) Galileo Galilei
    (D) Ptolemy
    (E) Johannes Kepler

14. The Enlightenment in Europe was characterized by

    (A) the submission of all ideas to rational examination, a belief that social laws as well as physical laws could be discovered, and a faith in the idea of progress.
    (B) the critical evaluation of all theories, a belief that human beings are controlled by hidden drives, and a belief in the perfectibility of human society.
    (C) the rejection of traditional authorities, a firmly held belief that society's laws were undiscoverable, and a design of existence called "the Great Chain of Being."
    (D) the desire to improve society, a calling into question of traditional beliefs, and a belief in the equality of men and women.
    (E) the belief that the methods of natural science could be applied to the analysis of society, a belief in relativity and morality, and a belief in the concept that people are born with inherited talents, ideas, and understandings.

15. In *The Persian Letters* Montesquieu wrote

    (A) a "critique" of the Persian government, which in reality was a critique of his own French government.
    (B) letters to France from Persia where he had fled to escape imprisonment.
    (C) imaginary letters by Persian travelers ridiculing European customs.
    (D) letters from a French noble to Persian nobles describing the ideal government.
    (E) imaginary letters by a poor Frenchman ridiculing Persian customs.

16. "Politics, religion, philosophy, news: nothing was excluded. Her circle met daily from five to nine. There one found men of all ranks in the State, the Church, and the Court, soldiers and foreigners, and the leading writers of the day." What is being described?

    (A) The Court at Versailles presided over by Mme. de Maintenon
    (B) The Royal Academy of Sciences under the personal authority of Queen Anne
    (C) The Russian Imperial Court of Catherine the Great
    (D) The Parisian salon of Julie de Lespinasse
    (E) The Schönbrunn Palace of Maria Theresa

17. Recent research by historians investigating the enclosure movement in England has shown that

    (A) small farmers were pushed off the land.
    (B) enclosures actually created the conditions for the improvement of agriculture.
    (C) enclosures contributed to British emigration to the New World.
    (D) large landowners controlled the Parliament that passed enclosure legislation.
    (E) many enclosures were made by mutual consent, not by act of Parliament.

18. Which of these men was NOT an inventor during the early Industrial Revolution in England?

    (A) Richard Arkwright
    (B) Samuel Crompton
    (C) James Hargreaves
    (D) John Kay
    (E) Robert Owen

19. "The ordinary means therefore to increase our wealth and treasure is by foreign trade wherein we must observe this rule; to sell more to strangers yearly than we consume of theirs in value."—Thomas Mun (1664)

    Which economic theory was Mun advocating?

    (A) Comparative advantage
    (B) Mercantilism
    (C) Free trade
    (D) Autarchy
    (E) Utopian socialism

20. In church–state relations, the eighteenth century can best be described as a period of

    (A) revived papal authority over national churches.
    (B) increasing royal control over national churches.
    (C) complete separation of church and state.
    (D) the creation of established churches.
    (E) the disestablishment of previously established churches.

21. Recent challenges to the traditional explanation of the origins of the French Revolution have centered on the fact that the

    (A) Old Regime did not correspond to social reality.
    (B) nobility and upper bourgeoisie were not necessarily pitted against each other.
    (C) clergy played a liberal role in French society.
    (D) revolution broke out all over France, not just in Paris.
    (E) lower middle class was actually more reactionary than radical.

22. The Civil Constitution of the Clergy passed by the National Assembly required

    (A) all legal marriages to be performed by a government official as well as a priest.
    (B) the clergy to take an oath of loyalty to the government.
    (C) all church lands to be surrendered to the government.
    (D) all priests to resign their posts as public school teachers and nuns to leave their positions as hospital nurses.
    (E) all bishops appointed by the pope to leave France.

23. What was the main cause of the conflict between Copernicus and the Roman Catholic Church?

    (A) Copernicus's heliocentric theory contradicted church teachings.
    (B) Copernicus's geocentric theory seemed to contradict the Bible.
    (C) Copernicus's social contract theory threatened papal supremacy.
    (D) Copernicus's religious theories denied the ability of the clergy to forgive sins.
    (E) Copernicus supported "popular religion" which the Church condemned as astrology and witchcraft.

24. Which of the following best summarizes the political consequences of Luther's split with Rome?

    (A) The Hapsburg emperor used the Reformation as a tool to consolidate power against the German princes.
    (B) Rome allied itself with the German princes to defeat Emperor Charles V.
    (C) Luther's excommunication in 1520 made it politically advantageous for the German princes to join him.
    (D) Since Luther was excommunicated in 1520, the split had very little political importance.

    (E) Europe was divided along religious lines with the western half remaining loyal to Rome and the eastern region becoming more and more allied with Protestantism.

25. Which of the following did NOT contribute to Pope Clement VII's refusal to grant Henry VIII an annulment of his marriage to Catherine of Aragon?

    (A) Spanish troops had been occupying Rome since 1522.
    (B) Henry had refused to pay the bribe Clement demanded.
    (C) Catholic doctrine had already been stretched to permit the marriage of Henry and Catherine and it could not be stretched again.
    (D) Catherine was the aunt of Emperor Charles V and he would not permit an annulment.
    (E) Recent attacks on the Church by Luther and Calvin made an annulment impossible at that time.

26. Which of the following statements concerning the Parlements of France during the reign of Louis XIV are true?

    (A) They challenged the concept of "absolute monarch" by refusing to register any edicts they considered in violation of French law.
    (B) As appointees of the king, they were dependent upon him and therefore helped efforts to centralize the power of the crown.
    (C) Since these judges were, by custom, appointed by the various local nobles, they fought against the centralizing tendencies of Louis XIV.
    (D) As the Estates General never met during Louis's reign, the Parlements had very little influence over the political and legal affairs of France.
    (E) They were little more than social clubs for well-to-do merchants.

27. Which of these statements expresses a fundamental difference between the philosophies of René Descartes and Francis Bacon?

(A) Bacon's philosophy was firmly grounded in the values of the seventeenth-century middle class; Descartes expressed aristocratic values.

(B) Descartes believed in the value of deductive reasoning and was therefore less bound to observation than Bacon and his theory of inductive reasoning.

(C) Because Bacon refuted the concept of inductive logic, his theories were limited by traditional Christian doctrine; Descartes rejected traditional Christian doctrine and avoided any such conflict.

(D) Descartes's philosophy left no room for the consideration of the existence of God or a Supreme Being; Bacon's philosophy was grounded in the supernatural.

(E) Descartes and Bacon differed primarily on the question of government's right to impose values upon a society that did not share the same views of morality.

28. Which of these statements is LEAST true in explaining why Great Britain was able to avoid the revolutionary violence that convulsed other European countries during the eighteenth and nineteenth centuries?

(A) The Irish Question was used by the Crown to divert working-class attention away from protesting their own miserable situation.

(B) Mass acceptance by the middle-class leaders of Methodist and other evangelical doctrines guided people away from revolutionary movements.

(C) The succession to the throne of relatively weak monarchs combined with strong Parliamentary leadership resulted in the growth of a more democratically ruled society.

(D) Repressive measures by the government, the Riot Act, and the quartering of the army throughout the country prevented revolutionary groups from organizing effectively.

(E) The large empire offered an "escape" for the most discontented among the English.

Questions 29 and 30 are based on the following document:

Article II. His Majesty the Emperor of China agrees that British subjects . . . shall be allowed to reside . . . without molestation or restraint at the cities and towns of Canton, Amoy, Foochow-fu, Ningpo, and Shanghai. . . .

29. The paragraph was part of the

(A) Open Door Policy, 1898.
(B) Treaty of Portsmouth.
(C) Chinese Exclusion Act.
(D) Treaty of Nanking.
(E) Peking Agreements.

30. As a result of the above agreement

(A) British subjects were accorded the same rights in China as had been received by other westerners.

(B) British subjects lost the right to reside anywhere in China.

(C) British subjects were allowed into China; Chinese subjects were not allowed into Britain.

(D) British subjects were allowed to continue selling opium in China.

(E) British subjects agreed to stop selling opium to Chinese subjects.

31. Which of these was an immediate result of early inventions in the cotton textile industry?

(A) Wages of weavers fell sharply.
(B) Cotton goods became cheaper and more available.
(C) Agricultural workers were thrown out of work.
(D) Factories sprang up all over London.
(E) Women lost their traditional role as spinners.

32. Which of these is LEAST important in explaining why other European countries lagged behind Britain in industrializing?

    (A) Political upheavals, including the French Revolution, caused inflation and a climate of economic uncertainty.
    (B) Warfare disrupted trade between Britain and the continent.
    (C) British goods were produced more cheaply than could be done on the continent.
    (D) Technology had become too complex and too expensive for European small entrepreneurs.
    (E) European agriculture had not undergone the same improvements as had British agriculture.

33. "At the bar of world opinion I charge the English middle classes with mass murder, wholesale robbery, and all the other crimes in the calendar."

    The author of the above statement was

    (A) Adam Smith
    (B) Thomas Malthus
    (C) John Stuart Mill
    (D) David Ricardo
    (E) Karl Marx

34. The Quadruple Alliance at the Congress of Vienna was made up of

    (A) France, Great Britain, Prussia, Austria-Hungary.
    (B) Russia, Prussia, France, Great Britain.
    (C) Austria-Hungary, France, Prussia, Turkey.
    (D) Austria-Hungary, Prussia, Russia, Great Britain.
    (E) Austria-Hungary, France, Russia, Prussia.

35. Ricardo's Iron Law of Wages stated that

    (A) a minimum wage would make workers lazy and indolent.
    (B) if wages went up, poor people would have more children and thereby reduce their standard of living.
    (C) since wealth was based on the value of labor, wage earners should receive the largest portion of a business's profits.
    (D) higher wages would always lead to inflation.
    (E) the entrepreneur's profit only represented his actual wage.

36. Which of these French artists is most closely associated with the Romantic movement?

    (A) Ingres
    (B) Courbet
    (C) Delacroix
    (D) David
    (E) Degas

37. By the end of the nineteenth century, major European cities had all of the following improvements EXCEPT

    (A) mass public transportation.
    (B) public health facilities.
    (C) electrification of public spaces.
    (D) elimination of overcrowded and slum areas.
    (E) improved water supplies.

38. As industrialization increased in the late nineteenth century

    (A) more and more families were employed together in the factories.
    (B) sex division of labor became more rigid.
    (C) increasing numbers of middle-class women found unskilled and semiskilled work outside the home.
    (D) opportunities for better paying and management jobs for married women rapidly increased.
    (E) gender-related job titles disappeared.

39. Science! True daughter of Old Time thou
    art!
    Who alterest all things with thy peering
    eyes.
    Why preyest thou thus upon the poet's
    heart,
    Vulture, whose wings are dull realities?

    The first four lines of Edgar Allan Poe's
    Sonnet—To Science express

    (A) the Positivist triumph of science.
    (B) the Romantic antipathy to science.
    (C) the Enlightenment mixture of science
    and faith.
    (D) Scientific Socialism.
    (E) Neo-Scholasticism.

40. Count Camillo Cavour hoped to unify Italy
    by means of

    (A) popular revolts against foreign
    rulers.
    (B) a military alliance with France against
    Austria.
    (C) a democratic plebiscite in all Italian-
    speaking areas.
    (D) conquest of the Papal States and the
    Kingdom of Naples.
    (E) a military alliance with Prussia against
    France.

41. In order to prevent the spread of socialism
    in Germany, Otto von Bismarck did all of
    the following EXCEPT

    (A) censor socialist newspapers, pam-
    phlets, and journals.
    (B) limit socialist gatherings.
    (C) create national health, accident, and
    retirement pension funds.
    (D) abolish unions.
    (E) outlaw the Social Democratic Party.

42. Emile Zola wrote "J'Accuse" in defense of

    (A) the military high command.
    (B) French miners on strike in the north.
    (C) radicals who had assassinated Czar
    Alexander III.
    (D) Captain Alfred Dreyfus.
    (E) struggling modern artists.

43. The most serious internal problem faced by
    the Austro-Hungarian Empire between
    1850 and 1914 was the question of

    (A) orderly succession to the throne.
    (B) political emancipation of the serfs.
    (C) women's rights.
    (D) subject nationalities.
    (E) terrorist attempts to overthrow the
    Crown.

44. Between 1869 and 1914, Egypt was crucial
    to the British Empire because

    (A) it had replaced the United States as
    Britain's major source of raw cotton.
    (B) Britain received more than 50 percent
    of its oil from the Middle East.
    (C) the Suez Canal was considered Britain's
    "life line."
    (D) the greatest part of manpower for the
    British Imperial forces was recruited in
    Egypt.
    (E) nearly 30 percent of all British over-
    seas investments were in Egypt.

45. In arguing for the positive effects of her
    imperialist rule in India, Britain could point
    to all of the following EXCEPT

    (A) a competent Civil Service that gener-
    ally served well in India.
    (B) an increase in education including
    instruction in English.
    (C) development of the Indian infra-
    structure.
    (D) control of hostilities among diverse
    Indian religious groups.
    (E) eradication of discrimination based on
    caste.

46. The Three Emperors' League (1873) con-
    sisted of

    (A) Germany, Austria-Hungary, Russia.
    (B) Germany, Austria-Hungary, the
    Ottoman Empire.
    (C) Germany, Austria-Hungary, Italy.
    (D) Germany, Japan, Italy.
    (E) Russia, Austria-Hungary, Italy.

DROPPING THE PILOT.

(Punch, 1890)

47. The pilot in the cartoon is

(A) Otto von Bismarck.
(B) Kaiser Wilhelm I.
(C) Admiral von Tirpitz.
(D) Emperor Franz Josef.
(E) Edward, Prince of Wales.

48. Admiral von Tirpitz argued that Germany's building a large navy

(A) would waste precious resources that could be spent on social welfare programs.
(B) would cause Great Britain to engage in a naval arms race.
(C) was a legitimate activity for a major world power.
(D) was not necessary since Germany had only a very limited empire.
(E) was necessary to meet the increasing challenge of Japanese dominance in Asia.

49. Which of the following had the LEAST influence on Austria-Hungary's decision to go to war in 1914?

(A) Germany's unconditional support
(B) Austria-Hungary's desire to punish Slavic nationalists
(C) Austria-Hungary's belief that Britain would remain neutral
(D) Austria-Hungary's belief that it would gain territory in the Italian Tyrol
(E) Austria-Hungary's belief that the war would be limited and short

50. The Western Front of World War I was characterized by

(A) *Blitzkrieg* tactics by German tank divisions.
(B) the "Phony War" of quick surrender after half-hearted fighting.
(C) trench warfare and staggering losses to both sides.
(D) a repeat of the events of the Franco-Prussian War.
(E) French penetration deep into German territory.

51. In an effort to win World War I, Germany introduced a new weapon to modern warfare, one that violated the international rule of war, "fair warning." This new weapon was

(A) the tank.
(B) the airplane.
(C) the automatic "needle gun."
(D) poison gas.
(E) the submarine.

52. World War I helped to bring about the Russian Revolution in all of the following ways EXCEPT

(A) the incompetent Czarina was left in command of the government while the Czar was at the front with the troops.
(B) the lack of food in Petrograd led to bread riots.

(C) the aristocracy was able to increase its landholdings at the expense of the middle class.

(D) soldiers, filled with war weariness, refused to obey orders.

(E) tension between the liberal Duma and the autocratic Czar increased over proper wartime policies.

53. Which of these was NOT a slogan adopted by the Bolsheviks during the Russian Revolution?

(A) Peace, Land, Bread
(B) All Power to the Soviets
(C) Stop the War Now
(D) Peace Without Victory
(E) All Land to the Peasants

54. World War I had similar results in Russia, Germany, and Austria-Hungary in that

(A) republics replaced hereditary monarchies.
(B) communist parties came to power.
(C) all three countries were disarmed.
(D) nationalist parties were outlawed.
(E) all three countries were forced to give up their colonial empires.

55. "We shall squeeze the orange until the pips squeak." This expression of making the defeated nations pay the costs of the war was most opposed at the Versailles Peace Conference following World War I by

(A) Woodrow Wilson
(B) Vittorio Orlando
(C) Georges Clemenceau
(D) David Lloyd George
(E) Alexander Kerensky

56. The Treaty of Versailles addressed nationalism in the Balkans following World War I by

(A) the creation of Yugoslavia.
(B) the repatriation of almost 500,000 Slavic people from Austrian interment camps.

(C) the incorporation of Serbia into the Soviet Union.

(D) the creation of the Western Slavic Federation.

(E) Austria's granting "home rule" to Bosnia and Herzegovina.

57. "Departing from traditional grammar, syntax, and vocabulary; making use of foreign words, sounds, trivia, and riddles, the work blends a day in the life of a modern man with the adventures of an ancient hero."

This is a description of

(A) Albert Camus' *Caligula*
(B) Virginia Woolf's *A Room of One's Own*
(C) James Joyce's *Ulysses*
(D) Franz Kafka's *Metamorphosis*
(E) T. S. Eliot's *The Waste Land*

58. "Shocked by the extremism of this artist and those who followed him, the critics called them 'fauves'—'wild beasts.'"

The artist being referred to in the quotation is

(A) Vincent van Gogh
(B) Henri Matisse
(C) Maurice Utrillo
(D) Amedeo Modigliani
(E) Georges Braque

59. At its opening performance in 1913, Igor Stravinsky's ballet *The Rite of Spring* was greeted by the critics and the public with

(A) acclaim as the perfect expression of the "beautiful and the true" in modern music.
(B) contempt and hostility that almost caused a riot.
(C) indifference that lasted the lifetime of the composer.
(D) surprise at its similarity to classical compositions.
(E) laughter, recognizing its essential humor and satire.

60. Which of these was NOT a French argument to support its demand for heavy reparations payment from Germany following World War I?

    (A) Most of the war had been fought on French territory which had been devastated.
    (B) Germany was responsible for the war and therefore was morally and legally obligated to pay.
    (C) Had Germany won the war, she would have made France pay as in 1871.
    (D) Germany needed to be kept too weak to start another war.
    (E) Without reparations payments, the German economy would soon overtake the other capitalist nations.

61. Both the Dawes Plan (1924) and the Young Plan (1929)

    (A) allowed France to occupy German coal fields in the Ruhr district.
    (B) reduced German reparations payments.
    (C) contributed heavily to German inflation during the 1920s.
    (D) were vetoed by the United States Congress as well as the French Chamber of Deputies.
    (E) were rejected by the Weimar government.

62. All of the following were reasons workers became less radical in the late nineteenth century EXCEPT

    (A) the extension of the right to vote enabled them to win improvements through legislation.
    (B) the beneficial effects of industrialization had improved the standard of living.
    (C) the growth of unions had enabled workers to bargain with employers from stronger positions.
    (D) anti-socialist laws were used to crush radical workers' movements.
    (E) radical movements lacked a coherent ideology.

63. In 1931, Great Britain went off the gold standard because

    (A) gold from South Africa was no longer available.
    (B) it hoped to reduce the value of British currency and make its products cheaper in the world market.
    (C) France and the United States had already gone off the gold standard and Britain could not remain on it alone.
    (D) it could not collect outstanding debts in gold and hoped to collect them in paper.
    (E) the effects of Gresham's Law had caused hoarding of gold in Great Britain.

64. The European country hardest hit by unemployment during the Great Depression was

    (A) Great Britain.
    (B) France.
    (C) Germany.
    (D) Italy.
    (E) the Soviet Union.

65. Which of these is LEAST important in explaining Mussolini's rise to power in Italy?

    (A) Italian bitterness over the Versailles Peace Treaty
    (B) Spiraling inflation
    (C) Industrialists' fear of communism
    (D) Social effects of the Great Depression
    (E) Support from the middle class and the aristocracy

66. The Fascist organizations *Dopolavoro* and the *Balilla* were attempts by Mussolini to

    (A) have Italy join international humanitarian and labor movements.
    (B) control all leisure time in Italy.
    (C) raise the standard of living for youth and workers.
    (D) create a government-sponsored alternative to labor unions.
    (E) link Italian organizations with similar groups in other Fascist societies.

67. "The Nazi Party is the organized expression of the youth." The truth of this statement can be seen most clearly in the fact that

(A) after 1934, all civil servants over the age of 60 were forced to retire.
(B) in 1931, approximately 65 percent of the membership of the Nazi Party was under the age of 40.
(C) the number of purely youth organizations increased by more than 300 percent between 1933 and 1939.
(D) films and propaganda publications aimed at youth became the most important part of the mass media for the first time in Germany.
(E) the average age of first marriage went down from 26 years old to 22 years old.

68. The Nuremberg Laws (1935)

(A) increased the size of Germany's army to 2.5 million.
(B) forced German citizens living in foreign countries to return to Germany.
(C) deprived anyone with one or more Jewish grandparents of rights of German citizenship.
(D) prohibited the import or export of any materials considered necessary to a war effort.
(E) established military alliances with Italy and Japan.

69. During the Spanish Civil War (1936–1938), Fascist rebel troops fighting the Republican government were led by

(A) Francisco Franco.
(B) Primo de Rivera.
(C) José Antonio.
(D) Antonio Salazar.
(E) Alfonso XIII.

70. Which of the following is most similar in meaning to the German tactic of *Blitzkrieg*?

(A) Maginot Mentality
(B) War of Attrition
(C) Trench Warfare
(D) Phony War
(E) War of Movement

71. World War II turned against the Axis powers following their defeats at

(A) the Battle of Britain, the Miracle of Dunkirk, and Normandy.
(B) Tobruk, Leningrad, and Moscow.
(C) Monte Casino, Casablanca, and Iwo Jima.
(D) Okinawa, Sicily, and Moscow.
(E) Midway, Stalingrad, and El-Alamein.

72. After Japan's refusal to surrender, United States forces dropped a second atomic bomb on the city of

(A) Hiroshima.
(B) Tokyo.
(C) Nagasaki.
(D) Osaka.
(E) Yokohama.

73. Stalin refused Marshall Plan aid mainly because

(A) it called for on-site inspection of how the money was being spent.
(B) it was part of the Truman Doctrine and Cold War rivalry.
(C) the Soviet Union had not been damaged in the war and could afford to refuse.
(D) aid had been offered to his enemies in eastern Europe.
(E) the plan did not provide sufficient aid.

74. Along with the economic miracle of European prosperity, the major trend in European economic development in the past 25 years has been

   (A) increasing economic integration and interdependence.
   (B) creation of high tariff barriers and economic independence.
   (C) continued reliance on colonial empires as suppliers of raw materials and as markets.
   (D) increasing reliance on financial aid from the United States.
   (E) stagflation, period depressions, and high unemployment.

75. The policy of the first postwar French government towards its colonies in Asia was

   (A) to grant immediate independence.
   (B) to attempt to hold on to them even at the cost of war.
   (C) to appoint a bilateral commission to study the possibility of independence at some future date.
   (D) to grant Home Rule within the confines of the French Union.
   (E) to resign over the question of colonial empire.

76. Since the end of World War II, the percentage of peasants who make up European society has

   (A) remained surprisingly stable.
   (B) gradually increased.
   (C) declined by over 50 percent.
   (D) completely disappeared.
   (E) increased rapidly.

77. European demographic patterns since the 1960s indicate that

   (A) a new "population explosion" has begun.

   (B) family size has decreased.
   (C) more than one-third of first children are being born to women who are past the age of thirty.
   (D) women have been extending the age at which they conceive their last child.
   (E) motherhood has begun to occupy approximately the same percentage of a woman's life as it did at the beginning of the twentieth century.

78. Which of these was not part of the appeasement policy of the 1930s?

   (A) The vote in the Oxford Union, 1933: "That this House will under no circumstances fight for king and country."
   (B) The Anglo-German naval agreement of June 1935
   (C) French reaction to German remilitarization of the Rhineland, March 1936
   (D) The Munich Conference, September 1938
   (E) The Stresa Front of April 1935

79. What was the main significance of Willy Brandt's election as Chancellor of West Germany in 1969?

   (A) The German people seemed to be returning former Nazis to positions of power.
   (B) West Germany was turning towards the east.
   (C) West Germany was about to enter a position of isolation from European politics.
   (D) Overtures to West Germany from eastern bloc nations would be rejected.
   (E) It became the so-called bankers election, which succeeded in gaining control of the Chancellorship and a majority in the Reichstag.

80. British colonel T. E. Lawrence rose to almost mythical fame during World War I because of his

    (A) exploits of daring and courage in the Battle of Passchendaele.
    (B) leadership of the Arabs against Turkey in 1917.
    (C) ability to exhort the British troops to hold out at the Battle of the Marne, 1914.
    (D) becoming the first air ace.
    (E) development of camouflage techniques for British warships.

STOP

This is the end of the multiple choice section of this test.

If time remains, you may check your work on this section only.

TEST 1
Multiple Choice Answer Key

1. D	17. E	33. E	49. C	65. D
2. C	18. E	34. D	50. C	66. B
3. E	19. B	35. B	51. E	67. B
4. B	20. B	36. C	52. C	68. C
5. E	21. B	37. D	53. D	69. A
6. B	22. B	38. B	54. A	70. E
7. A	23. A	39. B	55. A	71. E
8. B	24. C	40. B	56. A	72. C
9. A	25. B	41. D	57. C	73. B
10. B	26. A	42. D	58. B	74. A
11. D	27. B	43. D	59. B	75. B
12. E	28. A	44. C	60. E	76. C
13. B	29. D	45. E	61. B	77. B
14. A	30. D	46. A	62. D	78. E
15. C	31. B	47. A	63. B	79. B
16. D	32. E	48. C	64. C	80. B

TEST 1—EXPLANATORY ANSWERS

1. **(D)** The northern Italian city-states, Venice, Genoa, and Milan, in particular, were leaders in commerce in the early Renaissance. These city-states benefited from the geographical accident of lying on the crossroads between Europe and the East. The Fourth Crusade saw many Europeans crossing to Constantinople and bringing wealth to the northern Italian city-states.

2. **(C)** Cesare Borgia was presented as Machiavelli's ideal ruler in *The Prince* (1517). Borgia was the son of Pope Alexander VI and ruthlessly consolidated power in the Papal States through his own personal dynamism and the use of military force.

3. **(E)** Petrarch (1304–1374) stated that he was living "at the dawn of a new age." He was particularly critical of the medieval period which was, for him, a true dark age. Classical Rome represented the high point of civilization; the German invasions of the fifth and sixth centuries ushered in a period of sharp decline from which Europe was just beginning to recover.

4. **(B)** Leon Battista Alberti (1404–1474) was primarily an architect, but he was also known as a writer, mathematician, and the best athlete of his day. "Men can do all things if they will," he said.

5. **(E)** Although the French invasion in 1494 was a shock, it did not do very much harm to Italy in a material sense; Charles V's sack of Rome in 1527, on the other hand, caused much suffering in Italy.

6. **(B)** Baldassare Castiglione's (1478–1529) widely read work (1518) was a "how-to book" for those who wished to show proper behavior in society.

7. **(A)** Although Italian humanists were Christian, pagan themes influenced their works as well. Northern humanists such as Erasmus of Rotterdam, Sir Thomas More, and the French priest Jacques LeFevre d'Etaples, shared a belief in the basic goodness of people. They tried to apply methods of humanism to the problems of society and religion.

8. **(B)** Johann Gutenberg's Bible was printed using movable type in 1455, and demonstrated the possibilities of making the written word widely available. Luther's German translation of the Bible appeared in 1523, making religious thought and learning even more accessible.

9. **(A)** Ferdinand and Isabella decreed the expulsion of the Jews from Spain in 1492. Over 80 percent of the approximately 200,000 members of the Jewish community left. French Calvinists, called Huguenots, fled France after Louis XIV revoked the Edict of Nantes in 1685. In both countries, people with different beliefs were considered politically dangerous.

10. **(B)** McNeill argues that Europeans had natural immunities to the diseases they passed on to the indigenous population of the New World. Date of publication—1976.

11. **(D)** Michel de Montaigne (1553–1592) developed a new literary form, the essay, in which he expressed his skeptic's view of life. At the end of the 1500s, many Christians began to wonder if any religion at all was absolutely true—or even if such an absolute could ever be attained. It was better, they believed, to withhold one's judgment. Indeed, they argued, no creed was worth years of civil war.

12. **(E)** The Grand Alliance was formed in 1701. The nations of the Grand Alliance held that they were joining together in order to prevent France from becoming all-powerful in Europe. With Philip of Anjou (Louis's nephew) on the throne of Spain, the Pyrenées might "not exist," in Louis's words. Added to Bourbon control would be the wealthy Spanish Netherlands and a vast overseas empire.

13. **(B)** Luther criticized Copernicus as a "fool [who] will turn the whole science of astronomy upside down." If Copernicus was right, i.e., it is the earth rather than the sun that moves, then the Biblical story of Joshua's commanding the sun not to set cannot be true. Since the Bible must be true, Copernicus must be wrong.

14. **(A)** The general world view of the Enlightenment period was one of progress. Natural laws could be discovered and society ameliorated through education.

15. **(C)** *The Persian Letters* (1721) were a brilliant satire of European manners and customs.

16. **(D)** Paris set the style for Europe during the Enlightenment in many aspects of life. The social gatherings known as salons attracted the best thinkers and talkers of the age. Members of various social groups—the nobility and the high bourgeoisie, men and women—could meet as nowhere else. Life at the Court of Versailles, for example, was bound by rules which circumscribed behavior and conversation.

17. **(E)** Enclosure of land in England had been going on for a hundred years before 1760. It was after that date that acts of Parliament replaced private arrangements. The negative view of the enclosure movement, although still popular, has come under recent challenge.

18. **(E)** Robert Owen (1771–1858), a wealthy cotton manufacturer, is perhaps best known as a utopian socialist. He founded several cooperative communities.

19. **(B)** Mercantile theory insisted on a favorable balance of trade in order to bring gold into a country. Jean-Baptiste Colbert (1619–1683), a chief minister to Louis XIV, argued for France's not buying anything from other countries.

20. **(B)** Austria, although not the only nation in which the ruler gained further control over the territorial church, was perhaps the most successful in this regard. Both Maria Theresa and Joseph II asserted their royal authority very strongly.

21. **(B)** Some historians who have recently reinvestigated the origins of the French Revolution have challenged earlier theses. These revisionists have argued that all three estates were not monolithic blocs; that they contained many internal divisions; and that there was a community of interests among members of different estates. The revisionist argument challenges the long-held view that the French Revolution was brought about by a dissatisfied bourgeoisie out to destroy feudal privileges.

22. **(B)** The Civil Constitution of July 1790 required Catholic priests to swear allegiance to the revolutionary government. Priests who refused to take the oath were called "nonjuring clergy." Most priests refused to swear and became enemies of the Revolution.

23. **(A)** The heliocentric theory apparently contradicted the Bible and Catholic and Protestant leaders both agreed that Copernicus's views contradicted accepted religious thought. The strength of religious thought was so great during Copernicus's time that, for the most part, the heliocentric theory was disregarded.

24. **(C)** Even the condemnation of Luther by the Diet of Worms was not enforced because the German princes found it useful to support Luther and gain control of the wealth of the Catholic Church. In his *Appeal to the Christian Nobility of the German Nation* (1520), Luther urged the German rulers to confiscate Church property. The rulers welcomed Luther's calling on their patriotic duties.

25. **(B)** There is no evidence that Pope Clement demanded a payment or that Henry refused to give one.

26. **(A)** The Parlement of Paris retained the right to "register" royal decrees. For example, when Fleury, the finance minister, instituted the *vingtième* (a 5-percent income tax), the Parlement refused to register it.

27. **(B)** Bacon's inductive reasoning called for starting with empirical research; Descartes' deductive reasoning called for beginning with self-evident principles.

28. **(A)** While the other points listed—the growing influence of certain evangelical doctrines, strong Parliamentary leadership, and new opportunities throughout the British empire—all contributed to the prevention of revolutionary violence in England, the Irish Question addressed very different issues. Ireland was politically joined to Great Britain by the 1801 Act of Union. Appalling social conditions suffered by the majority of the Irish, resulting from the famine of the 1840s and the severely limited tenant rights of the Irish peasantry, encouraged the development of a strong Nationalist movement, taken up by the Land League (agrarian reform) and the Home Rule movement (repeal of the Act of Union and self-government for Ireland).

29. **(D)** The Treaty of Nanking (1842) ended the Opium Wars, gave Britain control of Hong Kong, opened four additional cities to trade, and forced China to pay an indemnity of $100 million.

30. **(D)** The opium trade expanded and Hong Kong became a major trading center.

31. **(B)** In the mid-nineteenth century, for the first time, cotton goods became widely available to people of all classes. With the increased demand, weavers' pay rose dramatically.

32. **(E)** Although England led in agricultural improvement, there was progress in agriculture—and the population increase which accompanied it—throughout Europe.

33. **(E)** Karl Marx (1818–1883) fled the continent for England after the failure of various revolutions in 1848. Marx had argued that the bourgeoisie inevitably exploited the proletariat. The "crimes" of the Industrial Revolution—working conditions, low wages, slums—could be laid at the door of the middle class.

34. **(D)** The Quadruple Alliance was formed at the international Congress of Vienna, held in 1814–1815 to discuss the reconstruction of Europe after the Napoleanic Wars. The Quadruple Alliance was made up of the victorious powers.

35. **(B)** David Ricardo (1772–1823) argued that wages would always be just high enough to keep workers from starvation. If wages were raised above that level, population would increase and force them back down.

36. **(C)** Eugène Delacroix (1798–1863) painted perhaps the most well-known Romantic painting, *Liberty Leading the People* (1831). Jean-Auguste-Dominique Ingres (1781–1867) was, despite some innovations, a Classicist; the story of art in the first half of the nineteenth century can be told, in

many respects, as a battle between Delacroix and Ingres. Gustave Courbet (1819–1877) was the great Realist of the nineteenth century. His paintings *The Stone Breakers* (1849) and *The Burial at Ornans* (1849) both shocked and fascinated the French public. Jacques Louis David (1748–1825) was a leading Neo-Classicist in the period of the French Revolution and Napoleon; Edgar Degas (1834–1917) was a leader of the Impressionist school.

37. **(D)** Although some of the worst slum areas had been erased and housing had been improved, London still was, according to the census of 1901, more than nine percent overcrowded. Other large cities had even worse conditions.

38. **(B)** Industrialization made less prevalent the previous pattern of husband and wife working together in the cottage. Only in a few areas, such as "mom-and-pop" stores, did the old pattern survive. Only in poor families did married women work outside the home.

39. **(B)** Edgar Allan Poe (1809–1849) wrote this poem in 1829. The view that science had "created a monster" had been popularized by Mary Shelley (1797–1851) in her novel *Frankenstein* (1818). Wordsworth (1770–1850), too, had written that technology and the Industrial Revolution had stolen humanity's ability to appreciate the beauties of nature ("The World is Too Much With Us"). Critics such as John Ruskin added their voices to the anti-industrial spirit.

40. **(B)** Count Cavour (1810–1861), prime minister of Piedmont-Sardinia, was a practical and realistic political man. His ambition was to unite Italy with King Victor Emmanuel as its leader. He knew the Italian states, divided as they were, could not rid themselves of Austrian domination without help from a strong ally. He was willing to trade Nice and Savoy to France in return for her military assistance against Austria. In 1854, Cavour entered Piedmont into the Crimean War on the side of France and Britain in order to tie his country and France closer together. In the summer of 1858, Cavour managed to get Napoleon III's promise to help Piedmont in a war against Austria.

41. **(D)** Bismarck viewed socialism as a threat to the monarchy and to the nation; therefore, he did all he could to destroy the Socialist movement in Germany. One of the issues that divided Bismarck from the new emperor, Wilhelm II, was the question of whether to renew the law outlawing the Social Democratic Party. German unions received political rights in 1869 and, although harassed, were not abolished. By the outbreak of World War I, Germany was the most unionized country on the continent.

42. **(D)** The Dreyfus Affair of 1898–1899 divided France into two bitterly opposed camps. Emile Zola's article forced the government to reopen the case. There have been many studies of *L'Affaire*, as the French refer to the Dreyfus case. Alfred Dreyfus, a captain in the French Army, was accused of acting as a spy for the Germans. The evidence against him was fabricated, yet he was convicted. Dreyfus was Jewish and anti-Semitism was a major factor in the case. In addition, the reputation of the French Army was on trial. Nationalists and anti-Semitic elements joined together to exert pressure on the government. Liberals and radicals, the most famous of them being Emile Zola, led the fight for a fair trial and for finding Dreyfus innocent. After his conviction, Dreyfus was exiled to the French penal colony on Devil's Island. Only years later was the verdict overturned. The significance of the case is that it revealed deep divisions inside the Third Republic.

43. **(D)** Hungarian nationalism was an important factor in the savagely crushed revolution of 1848. After the defeat of Austria by Prussia in 1866, the so-called Dual Monarchy, creating the Austro-Hungarian Empire, was set up. But the emotional and explosive issue was not resolved. Germans, Czechs, Poles, and other Slavs within the Dual Monarchy were all divided on matters of language and other nationalist concerns.

44. **(C)** Since 1858, India had been ruled directly by the British government. It had become "the crown jewel" of the British empire and much of British foreign policy centered on protecting the route to India. After 1869, the year the Suez Canal opened for maritime traffic, the British sought to secure it under their protection. Moves by the British in Egypt and the Sudan during the decades after 1870, though harmful to relations with France, were seen as necessary for the security of the Canal.

45. **(E)** The Hindu caste system originated in status of occupation, priests belonging to one caste, merchants to another, soldiers to a third, and so on all the way down the line to the Untouchables, or outcastes. The Indian Constitution, promulgated after independence in 1947, barred discrimination based on a person's caste. The government has found the law difficult to enforce and the cruel treatment of members of low castes is still reported in the press.

46. **(A)** This alliance was designed to counteract radical movements and preserve the conservative social order in the three countries.

47. **(A)** The new German Kaiser Wilhelm II dismissed Bismarck in 1890. Wilhelm was interested in asserting a more personal control over the government. In addition, he did not understand or agree with several of Bismarck's policies. Some historians see Bismarck's dismissal as an unsettling factor in European politics, a factor that contributed to the outbreak of World War I.

48. **(C)** Admiral von Tirpitz believed that world powers had the right to have large navies. Kaiser Wilhelm, influenced by Alfred Thayer Mahan's book on the role of sea power in the world's history, agreed. Germany's naval-building program had the predictable effect of causing Britain to increase its spending on armaments, despite David Lloyd George's argument that such spending was a waste of the "People's budget."

49. **(C)** Austria's plans depended on what Germany would do, not Britain. Austria knew that Serbia would turn to Russia for support in any war between Austria and Serbia. The German kaiser, Wilhelm II, had decided to give Austria his full support. With this "blank check" in hand, Austria issued the ultimatum to Serbia on July 25, 1914. On July 28, Austria declared war on Serbia.

50. **(C)** Created after the first Battle of the Marne in September 1914, the Western Front was a long line of trenches stretching from Belgium to Switzerland. The German Schlieffen Plan called for a quick victory against France before Russia would be fully mobilized and force Germany to face enemies on the east and the west at the same time. When German troops entered Belgium on the way to Paris, Britain entered the war on France's side. Russia was able to mobilize much faster than the six weeks German planning anticipated. As a result of these two events, Germany had to weaken her forces in the west to face Russian troops in East Prussia and had to face a stronger combination against the German armies in the west. The Battle of the Marne, 40 miles from Paris, prevented Germany from achieving the quick victory she had hoped for.

51. **(E)** The Germans decided that they would be able to starve Britain, an island nation that imported food and other supplies, by means of their new weapon—the *Unterseeboot* or submarine. When ships carrying United States citizens were sunk, Germany agreed to end submarine warfare. Later in the war, however, Germany returned to her use of the U-boat and soon after, the United States entered the war on the Allied side.

52. **(C)** The Bolsheviks (communists) adopted the slogan "Peace, Bread, and Land." The aristocrats had not increased their holdings during the war. The Kulaks had been able to amass large holdings after the emancipation of the serfs in 1861 and were resented by the peasants.

53. **(D)** "Peace Without Victory" was a phrase used by President Woodrow Wilson.

54. **(A)** The Romanov, Hapsburg, and Hohenzollern dynasties were all replaced by republican forms of government. In Russia, the events of 1917 led to the Bolshevik Revolution and the creation of the Soviet Union; in Austria, separate and independent republics were established in Austria, Hungary, and Czechoslovakia; after a period of unrest and revolution in 1918, the Weimar Republic was established in Germany.

55. **(A)** Wilson's reasonable peace policies were spelled out in his Fourteen Points. Clemenceau, Lloyd George, and Orlando all sought gains at the expense of the defeated nations.

56. **(A)** The Balkans had been divided into several small states, some independent, some controlled by Austria, and others under Turkish domination. Slavic nationalism in states controlled by Austria made the area a powder keg. Although there were differences among them, the Slavic people in the Balkans shared linguistic, religious, and other cultural commonalities. Serbia wished to play the part in a southern Slavic nation that Piedmont had played in the Italian *Risorgimento* and that Prussia had played in Germany's unification.

57. **(C)** James Joyce (1882–1941), the Irish writer, was most noted for his "stream of consciousness" style. His novel *Ulysses* was published in 1922 and caused a stir in the literary, publishing, and legal communities.

58. **(B)** Art critic Louis Vauxcelles gave Henri Matisse (1869–1954) and the other Fauves (Georges Roualt, for example) this name pejoratively after the 1905 show of their work.

59. **(B)** Igor Stravinsky (1882–1971) brought to his music many of the same ideas that were current in the visual arts in the early 1900s. Sergei Diaghilev's Ballet Russes premiered the work in Paris in 1913. In many ways, the new music paralleled the work of the Cubists and the Fauves. Henri Matisse and the others of his circle seemed to eliminate recognizable objects from their canvasses; line, form, and color were ends in themselves. Pablo Picasso and Georges Braque began the movement known as Cubism in 1907. They were greeted with the same scorn by the establishment of the art world that Stravinsky met from the music world.

60. **(E)** France did not make this argument; Britain, furthermore, argued that a healthy German economy was essential for the economic well-being of all European nations.

61. **(B)** Both plans reduced German reparations payments and included loans from the United States to Germany. By the end of the 1920s, Germany's economy was 50 percent greater than it had been just before the outbreak of World War I.

62. **(D)** Although several governments passed antisocialist laws, notably Germany and Russia, the movements went underground, not out of existence. They surfaced periodically as part of other political and social developments.

63. **(B)** When Britain went off the gold standard in 1931, its banknotes were no longer convertible into gold. This had the immediate effect of reducing the value of the British pound. Foreign currency was therefore worth more British pounds and British goods could be sold abroad more cheaply. Britain's advantage was, however, very shortlived.

64. **(C)** In 1932, unemployment in Germany was over 5.5 million; in Italy, slightly over 1 million; in France, slightly over 300,000; and in Britain, less than 100,000. By 1938, the Nazi government had reduced unemployment to less than 500,000, whereas in the other countries mentioned the figures had remained relatively constant.

65. **(D)** Mussolini's March on Rome took place in October 1922. The Great Depression began seven years later. Mussolini's Fascists (the Black Shirts) had done much to create the chaos that was plaguing Italy. Political life had apparently degenerated into street fighting between the Fascists and the Left (Socialists and Communists). Mussolini's supporters threatened the king and demanded that he appoint Mussolini prime minister. Rather than call out the army and possibly ignite a civil war, Victor Emmanuel III invited Mussolini to form a cabinet. The Fascists claimed that their seizure of power was strictly within the Italian Constitution.

66. **(B)** *Dopolavoro* (After Work) and the *Balilla* (the Fascist Youth Organization) were attempts made by the Fascist government to control leisure time in Italy. They were relatively unsuccessful in "Fascitizing" Italian society. The two organizations developed educational and recreational programs for their members. Sports contests, film and radio programs, and vacation "colonies" were among the more popular programs. The organizations never had enough funds to carry out the ambitious programs they had planned, but many of their activities were well received by the Italian people, although not totally in the spirit the government had intended.

67. **(B)** Four out of ten members of the Nazi party were under 30 years of age. Gregor Strasser, a Nazi party leader before 1933 had strongly emphasized the new Germany was to be for young people. "Make way, you old ones" was the slogan he used at party rallies. In 1933, Hitler was only 44 years old (about the same age as John F. Kennedy when he became president).

68. **(C)** Among the other restrictions enacted in the Nuremberg Laws, Jews were not permitted to teach, to act on stage or in films, to work in hospitals or banks, or to employ non-Jews. Jews were not allowed to fly the German flag and were forced to wear a yellow Star of David.

69. **(A)** Franco's troops, who called themselves the Nationalists, were assisted by Fascists from Italy and Nazis from Germany. The Soviet Union sent some assistance to the legitimate Republican government, but its forces were divided among several left-wing factions who seemed to be fighting each other as much as the Fascists.

70. **(E)** German tactics may be considered to have been the complete opposite of the Soviet Union's—strike fast and get to the main objective rather than to gain and make secure small increments of territory. New weapons and formations (the Panzer divisions) were suited to this strategy. In many ways, German military strategy was based on correcting what they considered to be the mistakes of World War I, i.e., trench warfare.

71. **(E)** At Midway, the Japanese fleet was defeated in June 1942; at El-Alamein, the British under Montgomery defeated the Germans led by Rommel in October 1942; at Stalingrad, the Germans surrendered in January 1943.

72. **(C)** On August 9, 1945, three days after the dropping of the first atomic bomb on Hiroshima, the United States dropped a second on the city of Nagasaki. At least 40,000 people were killed by this second bomb.

73. **(B)** The European Recovery Program (ERP, commonly referred to as the Marshall Plan, June 1947) was originally offered to all European countries that had suffered wartime damage. Stalin refused the aid not only for the Soviet Union but for all of eastern Europe under his control.

74. **(A)** The Common Market (the European Community) and Eurotom (joint atomic research) were both formed in 1957 by the same six nations: Belgium, France, West Germany, Italy, Luxembourg, and the Netherlands. Tariff barriers among the members were reduced and, as a result, trade increased. Other countries joined later on: Great Britain, Ireland, Denmark, and Greece.

75. **(B)** From the end of World War II until 1954, the French fought a bitter war in an attempt to hold onto her colony in Indochina; the conflict ended in France's withdrawal and the division of the country into North and South Vietnam. A leading cause of the demise of the Fourth Republic and the birth of the Fifth Republic (with a powerful president rather than a weak premier) was over the dissolution of French control in North Africa. Many French "colons" believed that de Gaulle had abandoned them; a dissident faction in the French army formed the Secret Army Organization and tried to carry on a war against the Algerians and the French government. The overwhelming majority of the French people supported de Gaulle and wished to see the conflict ended. Ahmed Ben Bella became the first president of Algeria in 1962 when the country was granted independence.

76. **(C)** Among the striking social changes in Europe after World War II was the flight from the countryside. Urban areas grew at the expense of the rural parts of Europe. At the same time, the percentage of workers in industrial enterprises also declined. Where did all these people find employment? In white collar and service occupations.

77. **(B)** Since the 1960s, the birthrate in Europe has declined. Whereas in past times, the major portion of a woman's life was spent giving birth to and raising children, modern women live longer and so devote a smaller percentage of their lifespan to child rearing.

78. **(E)** When Hitler showed intentions of rearming, Britain, France, and Italy met at the Italian town of Stresa (April 1935) and issued a joint statement condemning Hitler's moves. They agreed to work together to prevent Hitler from making aggressive advances in the Rhineland and Austria. Britain, however, soon backed out of the agreement and signed a separate naval treaty with Hitler.

79. **(B)** The one-time-Socialist mayor of Berlin, Willy Brandt (1913—), as Chancellor of West Germany, began a policy of reconciliation with eastern Europe. In late 1970, for example, he traveled to Poland and signed a treaty of friendship. He also helped foster better relations with the Soviet Union and East Germany.

80. **(B)** Colonel T. E. Lawrence, Lawrence of Arabia, stirred Arab nationalists to revolt against their Turkish masters in the early days of 1917. This was intended to aid the Allied war effort against the Central Powers.

Test 2

Directions: *For each question or incomplete statement below, choose the best answer of the five suggested. Blacken the space on the answer sheet corresponding to your choice.*

1. Which word or phrase best defines or describes the *signoria* of Renaissance Italy?

   (A) Oligarchies
   (B) Despotisms
   (C) Democracies
   (D) Theocracies
   (E) Utopian communities

2. Which was NOT true of Italian city-states during the Renaissance?

   (A) Their governments promoted the movement for Italian unification.
   (B) Their ruling elite shared a nostalgia for Roman antiquity.
   (C) The upper classes demonstrated a "worldly" outlook.
   (D) They undertook massive building programs to demonstrate their wealth and to provide employment for workers.
   (E) Only a small percentage of inhabitants enjoyed political rights.

3. Renaissance humanists believed that their most important accomplishment was

   (A) progress in physics and chemistry.
   (B) advances in mathematics and medicine.
   (C) creation of a new Italian language.
   (D) correction of patristic literature and biblical scholarship.
   (E) creation of beautiful, modern Latin poetry.

4. Humanism was based on the belief that

   (A) human nature was most vividly revealed in the Greek and Roman classics.
   (B) ethical human beings had to share their wealth with those less fortunate.
   (C) human beings ranked higher than the angels in God's plan for the universe.
   (D) history has never been an accurate guide for the present.
   (E) the world was a contemptible place and was destructive to the human spirit.

5. "Thus all artists are under a great and permanent obligation to Michelangelo, seeing that he broke the bonds and chains that had previously confined them to the creation of traditional forms." Vasari, *Lives of the Artists* (1550)

   Vasari was expressing the contemporary view that

   (A) by the early Renaissance, traditional art forms had become dated.
   (B) artists should be honored as geniuses who create beautiful new works.
   (C) all honest work, including oil painting, was a "holy calling."
   (D) great art brought fame to the artist, his patron, and his city-state.
   (E) only during the Renaissance had truly beautiful art been created.

6. In which area did the status of women rise and opportunities for them increase most during the Italian Renaissance?

   (A) Types of occupations held
   (B) Influence on society's values
   (C) Ownership of property
   (D) Access to education
   (E) Political power

7. In the early years of the sixteenth century, calls for reform of the Roman Catholic Church centered LEAST on

   (A) immorality of priests.
   (B) absenteeism among the clergy.
   (C) doctrinal errors.
   (D) clerical pluralism.
   (E) clerical ignorance.

8. Luther's teachings included

   (A) infallibility of church councils, salvation by faith alone, and authority of the Bible and traditional church teachings.
   (B) infallibility of church councils, salvation by faith and good works, and exclusive authority of the Bible.
   (C) salvation by faith alone, equal merit of all vocations, and exclusive authority of the Bible.
   (D) salvation by faith and good works, equal merit of all vocations, and exclusive authority of the Bible.
   (E) infallibility of church councils, equal merit of all vocations, and salvation by faith alone.

9. As a result of the Peace of Augsburg (1555),

   (A) religious freedom was recognized in Europe.
   (B) religious toleration was permitted in the territories of nations that signed it.
   (C) religious dissidents had to convert or emigrate.
   (D) rulers had to convert to the religion of the majority of the inhabitants.
   (E) religious leaders were permitted to become civil servants.

10. The immediate cause of the Protestant Reformation in England was

    (A) the visit of Martin Luther to Henry VIII.
    (B) the Pilgrimage of Grace.
    (C) the confiscation of the English monasteries.
    (D) the divorce of Catherine of Aragon.
    (E) the attempted invasion by Spain.

11. Which of the following provided the strongest threat to the absolute authority of seventeenth-century monarchs?

    (A) National assemblies, including Parliaments and Estates General
    (B) Standing armies and their military leadership
    (C) Ecclesiastical authorities
    (D) The bureaucracy of civil servants and career officials
    (E) "Underground" opponents such as Levellers, Diggers, and religious sects

12. Colbert did all of the following to promote the French economy EXCEPT

    (A) build a large merchant fleet.
    (B) build new roads and canals.
    (C) enact high protective tariffs.
    (D) give state support to domestic industries.
    (E) destroy the remnants of power held by the craft guilds.

13. "The thirty-six years of his reign knew only one year of peace."

    Which European ruler is being described in the quote above?

    (A) Louis XVI
    (B) George III
    (C) Peter the Great
    (D) Wilhelm II
    (E) Napoleon Bonaparte

14. What did John Locke mean by the term *tabula rasa?*

    (A) Instinctual behavior
    (B) The "blank slate" that is the human mind at birth
    (C) The "gene pool" passed from parent to child
    (D) The "unchangeable tablet" on which the largest amount of an individual's future has already been written
    (E) The hierarchy of races in the world—with Europeans occupying the highest position

15. At whose eighteenth-century court did Voltaire become "philosopher-in-residence" for a time?

    (A) Peter the Great
    (B) Frederick the Great
    (C) George II
    (D) Alphonso XII
    (E) Maria Theresa

16. Viscount Townshend's contribution to the Agricultural Revolution in England has been generally accepted as

    (A) inventing the seed drill.
    (B) introducing barbed wire.
    (C) introducing turnips as part of crop rotation.
    (D) experimenting with selective breeding of cattle.
    (E) publicizing the agricultural improvements made by others.

17. In the seventeenth and early eighteenth centuries, the typical European marriage was most often made by

    (A) two young people in their teens.
    (B) two mature people, generally in their late twenties.
    (C) a girl in her teens and a young man in his twenties.
    (D) two people in their early twenties.
    (E) a young man in his early twenties and a mature woman in her mid-thirties.

18. What did Great Britain gain from Spain when Spain was forced to relinquish the Asiento?

    (A) The Rock of Gibraltar
    (B) The east coast of Honduras
    (C) The West African slave trade
    (D) The northernmost part of Florida
    (E) Assurance that Spain would make no further claim to the British throne

19. Edward Jenner's reward for having inoculated people with his smallpox vaccine was

    (A) banishment to the Australian penal colony.
    (B) a prize of £30,000 from the British government.
    (C) a life of obscurity and disappointment.
    (D) appointment as Britain's first Royal Health Commissioner.
    (E) excommunication by the Church of England.

20. Which of the following was NOT part of the Protestant revival known as Pietism?

    (A) An appeal to the emotions of the masses of believers
    (B) A reassertion of the radical doctrine of the "priesthood of all believers"
    (C) Strong emphasis on leading good, moral lives
    (D) Enthusiastic Bible study
    (E) Doctrinal quarrels among the many self-appointed spiritual leaders

21. In the Tennis Court Oath, the Third Estate swore to

    (A) abolish the French monarchy.
    (B) confiscate land held by the Church and distribute it among the landless.
    (C) uphold the "ancient and good laws of France."
    (D) remain in session until a new Constitution was written.
    (E) abolish all feudal privileges.

22. What was the main theme of Machiavelli's *The Prince* (1517)?

    (A) The survival of the state depends on its adherence to moral principles.
    (B) The survival of the state must take precedence over moral law.
    (C) Human nature strives naturally to justice and religion.
    (D) The ruler is God's lieutenant on earth.
    (E) The pope, as vicar of Christ, has ultimate authority.

23. What was the significance of the marriage of Ferdinand of Aragon to Isabella of Castile?

    (A) It brought Spain into an alliance with the Holy Roman Empire.
    (B) It signaled the rise of the Cortes as a powerful political institution.
    (C) It united the two largest states in Spain under one kingdom.
    (D) It joined the Bourbon families of Spain and France in an alliance against England.
    (E) It effectively sealed off northern Spain from Moslem invaders.

24. What did Calvin teach about salvation?

    (A) He believed in the necessity of "good works" for the attainment of salvation.
    (B) He believed in predestination.
    (C) He believed in "salvation by faith alone."
    (D) He denied the possibility of salvation because of "original sin."
    (E) He reduced the number of sacraments from seven to three.

25. Which statement best summarizes Elizabethan foreign policy?

    (A) Containment of papal influence in France and Germany was paramount.
    (B) Temporary alliances had to be formed in order to maintain the balance of power on the continent.

    (C) Alliance with the Hapsburg Empire was necessary in the pursuit of economic advantages.
    (D) Neutrality towards the Ottoman Empire helped to secure trade with India and the East.
    (E) Renewal of ancient claims on Normandy, Brittany, and Calais were instigated by the need for a male heir.

26. Which of the following best explains the seventeenth-century theory of mercantilism?

    (A) Wealth is generated by the working class and must be returned to them either by indirect benefits or direct ownership of the means of production.
    (B) Wealth is measured by hard currency and the state must obtain as much of that currency as possible through maintaining a favorable balance of trade.
    (C) In order to assure a fair distribution of national wealth the government must nationalize major industries.
    (D) Governments, as much as possible, should have no commercial contacts with other nations.
    (E) The government, as much as possible, should limit involvement with business enterprise.

27. What was the political significance of the Treaty of Utrecht (1713)?

    (A) French expansionist policies were effectively ended.
    (B) The Hapsburg Empire was finally checked in its drive to dominate Europe.
    (C) The supremacy of the British navy was acknowledged.
    (D) The Holy Roman Empire was dissolved.
    (E) The Dutch were recognized as masters in Belgium.

Questions 28 and 29 are based on the following quotation:

"The state of monarchy is the supremest thing upon earth: for kings are not only God's lieutenants upon earth and sit upon God's throne, but even by God himself they are called gods. . . . "

28. The author of the statement believed most strongly in

(A) natural rights.
(B) divine right of kings.
(C) theocracy.
(D) popular sovereignty.
(E) constitutional monarchy.

29. The author of the statement was

(A) John Locke.
(B) James I.
(C) John Calvin.
(D) Jean Jacques Rousseau.
(E) Baron Montesquieu.

30. *Assignats* were

(A) paper currency issued by the National Assembly.
(B) parcels of land confiscated from the nobility and sold to the bourgeoisie.
(C) military units to which French citizens were assigned.
(D) units of civil administration that replaced the royal generalities.
(E) seats in the National Assembly divided according to party membership.

31. Strongest support for the Committee of Public Safety came from

(A) peasants in the west of France, especially in the Vendée.
(B) upper-middle-class Parisians.
(C) Parisian sans culottes.
(D) the clergy.
(E) the Girondists.

Questions 32 and 33 are based on the following document:

'I send you this to inform you That wee the Clothworkers of Trowbridge Bradford Chippinham and Melkshom are allmost or the greatest part of Us Oute of work and Wee are fully Convinst that the gretests of the Cause is your dressing work by Machinery And Wee are determind if you follow this Practice any longer that Wee will keep som People to watch you Abought with loaded Blunderbuss or Pistols And will Certainly blow your Brains out it is no use to destroy the Factorys But put you Damd Villions to death. . . .

We are yours the Clothworkers of the afforsaid Towns, Apreil 7th 1799'

SOURCE: London Gazette, 1799, page 507. Cited in *Albion's Fatal Tree*, Hay, Linebaugh, Rule, Thompson, Winslow. New York: Pantheon Books, 1975. Reprinted with permission.

32. The clothworkers' main complaint was that

(A) traditional relationships between master and journeymen had disappeared.
(B) wages for clothworkers had dropped dramatically.
(C) unemployment in the clothing industry had skyrocketed.
(D) hours and conditions in the factories had become unbearable.
(E) they were unable to learn how to operate the new machinery.

33. The clothworkers blamed their troubles mainly on

(A) immigrants who had taken their jobs.
(B) the employers who made increasing use of machinery.
(C) themselves for being unable to adjust to new conditions.
(D) the government for allowing the introduction of machinery.
(E) the factory system.

34. G.M. Trevelyom's *British History in the 19th Century* (1922) was most closely associated with which "school" of historical scholarship?

    (A) Marxist
    (B) Freudian
    (C) Cliometrics
    (D) Whig
    (E) Annales

35. "The history of all hitherto existing society is the history of class struggles." These are the words of

    (A) Pope Pius X
    (B) Benito Mussolini
    (C) Karl Marx
    (D) Adam Smith
    (E) Maximilien Robespierre

36. As a result of the Reform Bill of 1832 Great Britain

    (A) adopted universal manhood suffrage.
    (B) eliminated most rotten boroughs and extended the franchise.
    (C) eliminated the power of the House of Lords.
    (D) adopted the program of the People's Charter.
    (E) granted women the right to vote.

37. Jeremy Bentham's Utilitarian principles included which of the following?

    (A) the greatest good for the greatest number
    (B) dialectical materialism
    (C) survival of the fittest
    (D) the "trickle down theory"
    (E) the moral economy of the poor

38. The remodeling of Paris during the Second Empire, which added grand boulevards, a central marketplace, and a new water supply, was accomplished under the direction of

    (A) Calvert Vaux
    (B) Edwin Chadwick
    (C) Henri Gervex
    (D) Georges Haussmann
    (E) Auguste Comte

39. Which of these best explains the decline in the size of middle-class families during the late nineteenth and early twentieth centuries?

    (A) a religious and moral revival
    (B) decline in the health status of women
    (C) greater availability of birth control
    (D) increasing desire to improve the family's economic position
    (E) increase of postponed marriages

40. "But if variations useful to any organic being do occur, assuredly individuals thus characterised will have the best chance of being preserved in the struggle for life; and from the strong principle of inheritance they will tend to produce offspring similarly characterised. This principle of preservation, I have called, for the sake of brevity, Natural Selection."

    The author of the quotation above was

    (A) Herbert Spencer
    (B) Charles Lyell
    (C) Jean Baptiste Lamarck
    (D) Charles Darwin
    (E) Thomas Huxley

41. Adolphe Thiers called it "the government which divides us least." He was referring to

    (A) the commune of 1871.
    (B) the Third French Republic.
    (C) the War Coalition of 1914.
    (D) the Vichy Regime of Marshall Pétain.
    (E) the Fifth Republic of Charles de Gaulle.

42. A major result of the Reform Bills of 1867 and 1884 was

    (A) creation of a strong radical, underground opposition to the government.
    (B) use of more modern political techniques.
    (C) decreased influence of the middle classes in politics.
    (D) removal of the power of the House of Lords in government.
    (E) increased power of the prime minister.

43. Karl Lueger, mayor of Vienna from 1897 to 1910, was noted for his

    (A) enthusiastic support for Freud and the Vienna school of psychology.
    (B) anti-Semitism.
    (C) urban planning and modernization of the city.
    (D) hosting international peace conferences at the Schonbrunn Palace.
    (E) transforming Vienna into the center of ultramodern art and music.

44. As a result of the Boxer Rebellion (1900)

    (A) the Manchu Dynasty was overthrown.
    (B) foreign imperialists were thrown out of China.
    (C) China suffered a severe defeat and was required to pay an indemnity.
    (D) the United States decided to sever all contacts with the Chinese government and people.
    (E) the opium trade was ended in China.

45. The "great migration" of the late nineteenth century was

    (A) the sudden movement of people from Asia to eastern Europe.
    (B) British resettlement of convicted criminals to Australia.
    (C) the huge number of poor Europeans who left their native lands for new homes abroad.

    (D) the "return to the countryside" which became official policy of the governments of Italy and Germany.
    (E) the opening up of new lands in Asiatic Russia.

46. Between 1871 and 1914, the two European countries LEAST likely to ally were

    (A) France and Great Britain.
    (B) Austria-Hungary and Russia.
    (C) Germany and Italy.
    (D) France and Germany.
    (E) Great Britain and Russia.

47. Which of these had the greatest influence on the formation of the Franco-Russian alliance of 1891?

    (A) Germany's naval armament program
    (B) Germany's financing of the Berlin-to-Baghdad Railway
    (C) The revelation of the Italian-Austro-Hungarian nonaggression treaty
    (D) The failure of Germany to renew the Reinsurance Treaty with Russia
    (E) Germany's insistence on the French cession of Alsace-Lorraine

48. In the first decade of the twentieth century, many contemporary observers predicted that a major war would begin in the Balkans since

    (A) the area had been the scene of three previous international conflicts.
    (B) Slavic people were considered "an emotional, irascible race."
    (C) it was the least modern and poorest area of Europe.
    (D) the area was the scene of intense national feelings coupled with the break-up of two crumbling empires.
    (E) the area had undergone rapid economic development yet its social and political institutions were still medieval.

49. Sidney Bradshaw Fay, in *The Origins of the World War*, argues that responsibility for the outbreak of World War I can be

    (A) assigned mostly to Germany for "the blank check."
    (B) assigned mostly to Austria-Hungary for refusing Serbia's answer to her ultimatum.
    (C) assigned mostly to Russia for calling for partial mobilization.
    (D) assigned mostly to France for her aggressive stance towards Germany.
    (E) shared just about equally among all the Great Powers of Europe.

50. Italy entered World War I on the side of the Allies because

    (A) Germany had reneged on its promise to secure colonies in Africa for Italy.
    (B) Italy feared Germany's growing military power and political ambition.
    (C) Italy hoped to avoid paying its huge debt owed to British bankers.
    (D) the Allies promised Italy territory controlled by Austria.
    (E) the Italian and British kings were first cousins.

51. In general, during World War I, the belligerents utilized their country's economic resources by

    (A) adhering strictly to laissez-faire doctrines.
    (B) using officers and soldiers to operate the factories and coal mines.
    (C) requiring the banks to grant loans and imposing huge new taxes on the population.
    (D) regimentation of the economy by government planning boards.
    (E) nationalization of all primary industries.

52. Which of these policies was adopted by the Provisional Government of Alexander Kerensky in 1917?

    (A) Redistribution of land to the peasants

    (B) A separate peace treaty with the Central Powers
    (C) The granting of civil rights and civil liberties despite the war effort
    (D) Outlawing Bolshevik and other revolutionary parties
    (E) Depriving all former army officers of their power to command and replacing them with ordinary soldiers

53. Which of these is the MOST important reason for the Bolshevik victory in November 1917?

    (A) Military aid from the Allies
    (B) Dedicated leadership able to exploit conditions
    (C) Better technology and weapons
    (D) Support from a majority of Russians
    (E) Ineffective opposition by the czar

54. France's spokesperson at the Versailles Peace Conference following World War I was

    (A) Philippe Pétain
    (B) Georges Clemenceau
    (C) Charles de Gaulle
    (D) Jean Jaurès
    (E) Marshal Ferdinand Foch

55. "If Russia 'makes converts,' it's perfectly clear
    We need for 'converting' a well-defined sphere;
    If Germany's 'mission' hold meetings for prayer,
    So Christian a work 'tis our duty to share.
    Incidentally, too, there is cash to be made;
    There's naught like religion to stimulate Trade."

    Sir Wilfred Lawson and France Corruthers Gould, *Cartoons in Rhyme and Line* (1905).

    The area of the world under discussion is

    (A) China
    (B) Africa
    (C) India
    (D) South America
    (E) Australia

56. The scientists Werner Heisenberg, Albert Einstein, Marie Curie, and Max Planck were alike in that they all

(A) confirmed the validity of the Newtonian synthesis.
(B) challenged long-held beliefs in physics.
(C) sought to dissociate pure from applied sciences.
(D) argued against the military use of science.
(E) were forced to leave their native countries because of their religion.

57. Walter Gropius and Ludwig Mies van der Rohe were both leading members of which of the following schools of art?

(A) Futurism
(B) Bauhaus
(C) Art Deco
(D) Art Nouveau
(E) Cubism

58. The Italian artists Marinetti, Severini, and Balla were all

(A) Cubists.
(B) Abstract Expressionists.
(C) Futurists.
(D) Dadaists.
(E) Minimalists.

59. During the 1920s and 1930s, the most important director of Soviet epic films was

(A) Sergei Prokofiev
(B) Sergei Eisenstein
(C) Vladimir Nabokov
(D) Leni Riefenstahl
(E) Dimitri Shostakovich

60. John Maynard Keynes, in *Economic Consequences of the Peace* (1919), argued that

(A) Germany should be converted into a mainly agricultural country.
(B) former German colonies should be used to absorb Europe's surplus population.

(C) only if Germany was forced to make heavy reparations payments could Europe's economy hope to recover.
(D) munitions dealers had been the major cause of the war; therefore, armaments industries must be nationalized.
(E) Europe could recover economically if Germany were permitted to forego payments of reparations.

61. The Spirit of Locarno indicated growing

(A) tension between democratic and totalitarian governments during the 1920s.
(B) disappointment in the failure of the League of Nations.
(C) isolation among European powers.
(D) stability in international relations.
(E) nationalist unrest and outbreaks of revolutions during the 1920s.

62. Lenin's New Economic Policy was a major departure at the time because

(A) it put heavy industry temporarily into the hands of private businesspeople.
(B) it halted the land reform policies designed to give peasants more autonomy over crop production.
(C) it repudiated the concept of world revolution in favor of foreign investments to develop Russian industry.
(D) it concentrated Russian resources away from agricultural growth in favor of rapid industrialization.
(E) it allowed limited private enterprise for both farmers and merchants.

63. The Popular Front in France was a combination of

(A) Fascists, Nationalists, and Conservatives.
(B) Socialists and Liberals.
(C) Socialists, Radicals, and Communists.
(D) Liberals and Communists.
(E) Fascists, Socialists, and Radicals.

64. A major distinction between traditional authoritarian governments and totalitarian regimes is their different

   (A) uses of police and secret police forces.
   (B) degrees of mass participation.
   (C) attitudes toward religion.
   (D) beliefs in a strong military and an assertive foreign policy.
   (E) willingness to accept opposition parties.

65. Forced collectivization of the farms in the Soviet Union led to

   (A) a rapid increase of agricultural output.
   (B) economic disaster as peasants protested their treatment.
   (C) a gradual shift from an agricultural based economy to an industrial state.
   (D) the Soviet Union's ability to export grain for the first time in Russian history.
   (E) a significant rise in the Soviet standard of living during the 1930s.

66. During the Stalinist period, the improved position of women in Soviet society can be seen from the fact that

   (A) nearly 80 percent of university professors were women.
   (B) approximately three-quarters of the nation's doctors were women.
   (C) divorce was outlawed.
   (D) women were given the right to vote.
   (E) the number of "women's magazines" increased by nearly 300 percent.

67. Mussolini's Lateran Agreement was similar to Napoleon's Concordat in that they both were

   (A) attempts to get papal support for their regimes.
   (B) expressions of increased religious feeling.
   (C) symbolic of the homogeneity of their respective nations.
   (D) designed to eliminate any "foreign" elements in society.
   (E) forced on the pope by military aggression.

68. Which was a major weakness of the Weimar political system that facilitated the Nazi rise to power?

   (A) Proportional representation which gave even minor parties several seats in the Reichstag
   (B) The large property qualifications for holding office
   (C) The many overrepresented "rotten boroughs" similar to those in Britain in the late eighteenth and early nineteenth centuries
   (D) The lack of strong majority parties and reliance on coalition governments
   (E) The absence of an educated electorate

69. In order to meet the problem of German unemployment, the Nazi government

   (A) forced all workers over the age of 60 to leave active employment.
   (B) established high tariffs and export restrictions.
   (C) created a program of public works and military spending.
   (D) forced all women to leave work in factories and schools.
   (E) forced all Jews to leave their jobs.

70. The important decision made by leading German officials at the Grosse Wannsee conference was

   (A) to develop an atomic bomb.
   (B) to begin implementation of the "Final Solution" to the Jewish Question.
   (C) to invade the Soviet Union.
   (D) to begin day-time air raids over Great Britain.
   (E) to back up Japan's declaration of war on the United States.

71. The French idea of a Civilizing Mission as a rationale for imperialism was most similar to

   (A) Dollar Diplomacy
   (B) The White Man's Burden
   (C) A Place in the Sun
   (D) Social Darwinism
   (E) Might Makes Right

72. At the Yalta Conference, February 1945, the Big Three—the United States, Great Britain, and the Soviet Union—agreed to

   (A) "free elections" in eastern Europe and the Soviet declaration of war on Japan.
   (B) creation of a United Nations Organization.
   (C) no separate peace treaties with any of the Axis Powers.
   (D) self-determination for countries previously occupied by Fascist powers.
   (E) restoration of legitimate rulers to positions of leadership in their enemy-occupied countries.

73. The North Atlantic Treaty Organization was formed in response to

   (A) the Soviet formation of the Warsaw Pact.
   (B) the events surrounding the Berlin Blockade.
   (C) Soviet detonation of its first nuclear device.
   (D) the communist victory in the civil war in China.
   (E) Soviet refusal of Marshall Plan assistance for all of eastern Europe.

74. The policy of the postwar Labour government on British colonialism in India was

   (A) to refuse to "preside over the dismemberment of the British empire," i.e., to either hold on to the colony or to resign from power.
   (B) to grant independence as rapidly as possible.
   (C) to issue limited Home Rule based on the Irish model.
   (D) to appoint a bilateral commission to study the feasibility of future independence.
   (E) to provoke armed conflict between Hindus and Muslims as an excuse to remain in control.

75. The French Algerian War (1954–1962), which ended in the withdrawal of France from Algeria, was resolved by

   (A) the defeat of the Secret Army Organization.
   (B) the assassination of Ahmed Ben Bella.
   (C) President Charles de Gaulle with the support of the French voters.
   (D) the invasion of Algeria by the Arab League.
   (E) intervention by the United Nations Security Council.

76. During the 1960s, a major observation made in the book *The American Challenge* that disturbed Europeans was the

   (A) increasing cooperation between the United States and the Soviet Union.
   (B) support the United States was giving to independence movements in colonial Africa and Asia.
   (C) the "brain drain" of European scientists to the United States.
   (D) the "invasion" of Europe by affluent tourists from the United States.
   (E) dissemination of American culture into traditional European centers via Hollywood and Motown.

77. All of the following were outcomes of the transformation of Europe into a "consumer society" following World War II EXCEPT

   (A) the decline of employment opportunities in domestic service.
   (B) the growth of "installment buying" and use of credit.
   (C) the increased percentage of family income spent on staple foods.
   (D) the increasing electrification of rural areas.
   (E) the increased mobility of working-class people.

78. The growing emancipation of women has had all of the following effects EXCEPT

    (A) delayed marriage.
    (B) more married women working outside the home.
    (C) increased incidence of divorce.
    (D) more structured relationships between men and women.
    (E) falling birthrates.

79. Which of these has NOT been cited as a reason for the claim that the Treaty of Versailles led to the outbreak of World War II?

    (A) The Allies refused to acknowledge Italy's contribution to victory in World War I.
    (B) Many territories were separated from Germany in which the population was German-speaking.
    (C) The general European disarmament created a League of Nations unable to enforce its decisions.

(D) The security of Germany's reparations payments contributed to a European economic depression and the rise of fascism.
(E) The treaty was too harsh to be enforced permanently or even on a long-term basis.

80. Which of the following was accomplished by the Treaty of Brest-Litovsk?

    (A) The Soviet Union gained control of Poland and the Baltic states.
    (B) Italy was promised control of Trieste and Trent in return for "defecting" from the Triple Alliance.
    (C) The treaty fulfilled the Bolshevik promise of immediate peace.
    (D) The Soviet government was given $400 million in direct aid.
    (E) Turkey lost its strategic hold over the Dardanelles.

STOP

This is the end of the multiple choice section of this test.

If time remains, you may check your work on this section only.

TEST 2
Multiple Choice Answer Key

1. B	17. B	33. B	49. E	65. B
2. A	18. C	34. D	50. D	66. B
3. E	19. B	35. C	51. D	67. A
4. A	20. E	36. B	52. C	68. D
5. B	21. D	37. A	53. B	69. C
6. D	22. B	38. D	54. B	70. B
7. C	23. C	39. D	55. A	71. B
8. C	24. B	40. D	56. B	72. A
9. C	25. B	41. B	57. B	73. B
10. D	26. B	42. B	58. C	74. B
11. A	27. A	43. B	59. B	75. C
12. E	28. B	44. C	60. E	76. C
13. C	29. B	45. C	61. D	77. C
14. B	30. A	46. D	62. E	78. D
15. B	31. C	47. D	63. C	79. C
16. C	32. C	48. D	64. B	80. C

TEST 2—EXPLANATORY ANSWERS

1. **(B)** The term *signoria* referred to despotisms best exemplified by the Borgia family whose use of patronage and nepotism extended their rule not only throughout Florence but also to the papacy during the rule of Pope Alexander VI. John Addington Symonds's classic nineteenth-century study of Renaissance Italy contains one volume entitled *The Age of the Despots*.

2. **(A)** With one brief exception, that being Alfonso the Magnificent (1435–1458), king of Aragon and Sicily, and his resistance to French rule in Naples, the Italian city-states opposed all attempts at unification. They often combined to prevent any single state from becoming too powerful.

3. **(E)** The modern Latin poetry of the humanists emulated that of classical Rome; medieval Latin was considered degenerate. Writers such as Petrarch and Boccaccio, despite their examinations of human pleasures of the flesh, lived not among the common people but among the upper class. Similarly, the literature of the humanists also reflected their decidedly educated, privileged backgrounds.

4. **(A)** Humanists constantly studied the ancient writers as a guide to human nature. Even historical studies were often intermingled with myths from ancient Rome. Giovanni Villani (1280–1348), in his work *Florentine Chronicle*, included the story of the Tower of Babel.

5. **(B)** Artists received high praise and significant material rewards from wealthy patrons. Michelangelo, for example, was often called "divine."

6. **(D)** Although women gained no actual political power, or any significant legal status (save the right to own and inherit property, a right they already had) during the Renaissance, their access to education increased. Young upper-class ladies were able to receive the same education in the classics as young men. For upper-class women, the Italian Renaissance represented a reduction in property rights, political power and sexual equality.

7. **(C)** In the early years of the sixteenth century, calls to reform the Catholic Church stressed practices, not doctrine. Cardinal Jimenez in Spain, Lefever d'Etaples in France, and John Colet in England were three such reformers.

209

8. **(C)** Luther disagreed with Catholic doctrine on these three issues: salvation by faith and good works, the superiority of the religious vocation, and the authority of the Bible and of canon.

9. **(C)** Charles V officially recognized Lutheranism when he signed the Peace of Augsburg in 1713. Each prince within the Holy Roman Empire was permitted to determine whether his territory would be Lutheran or Catholic. Those who did not follow that faith had to convert or leave.

10. **(D)** Seeking a male heir, Henry VIII wanted to marry his mistress Anne Boleyn. He first needed a divorce from Catherine of Aragon, which Pope Clement VII refused to grant. The refusal can be explained not only by the fact that Catherine was the aunt of Charles V, the Holy Roman Emperor whose troops occupied Rome, but also to the increasing accusations of the corruption of the papacy. As a result, Henry defied the authority of the pope and proclaimed himself head of the church in England.

11. **(A)** Because these assemblies, the Parlements, provided a focal point around which opposition to royal authority could gather, absolute monarchs stopped summoning them—or at least tried to do so. The best example of this would be the Parlement of Paris, which saw itself as the only opposition to royal prerogative.

12. **(E)** Colbert's (1619–1683) policies were designed to further the advance of trade in accordance with the ideals of mercantilism. In this case, his expansion of the merchant fleet, building of roads and canals, and advocation of tariffs would be consistent. His strengthening of the authority of the craft guilds, which were a restrictive force in trade abroad, were contrary to such a mercantilist policy.

13. **(C)** Peter the Great (1672–1725; ruled from 1689) engaged Russia in almost constant warfare. The Great Northern War against Sweden (1700–1721) was only one of his many wars and resulted in the acquisition of Estonia and part of Latvia and Finland.

14. **(B)** In the *Essay Concerning Human Understanding* (1690), John Locke posited the concept of the tabula rasa; he believed that the environment shapes all human knowledge and ideas, i.e., all knowledge comes from experience.

15. **(B)** Frederick II, "the Great," of Prussia (1712–1786; ruled from 1740) invited Voltaire (1694–1778) to come to his court in Berlin. Voltaire accepted and stayed for three years. Some say that Voltaire left because he got tired of praising Frederick's poetry, which he believed was inferior.

16. **(C)** "Turnip Townshend," as he was called, learned about using turnips and clover for crop rotation (the practice of dividing the field into quarters and planting one quarter with the above-mentioned crops in order to replenish nitrogen) while he was his country's representative in Holland.

17. **(B)** The typical age at first marriage was 27. William Laslett points out, in *The World We Have Lost* (1980, second edition) that the image of the teenage lovers Romeo and Juliet is a false one.

18. **(C)** Britain gained the right of Asiento (the monopoly given to British traders to sell African slaves to the Spanish colonies in America). The right was under the terms of the Treaty of Utrecht (1713), ending the War of the Spanish Succession.

19. **(B)** Edward Jenner (1749–1829) spent 18 years amassing data on the possibility of using cowpox as a vaccine against smallpox. He performed his first vaccination in 1796. This was a much safer method of disease prevention than variolation, which used smallpox itself as the preventive. The royal family, including the very young Victoria, was vaccinated and Jenner was rewarded in his own lifetime.

20. **(E)** The Protestant revival of the late seventeenth century, which produced the Methodist religion, founded by John Wesley (1703–1791), was formed as a response to the perceived aristocratic tendencies of the Anglican Church of England. The revival began in Germany and emphasized a living faith filled with human emotion rather than one that emphasized doctrinal points.

21. **(D)** June 20, 1789. The Third Estate (after June 17, the National Assembly), having been locked out of its meeting place, adjourned to the nearby indoor tennis court rather than allow itself to be divided into separate assemblies along class lines which would have favored the First and Second Estates (the clergy and the nobility). The Third Estate decided not to disband.

22. **(B)** The effective ruler, according to Machiavelli, follows the precept that "the ends justify the means." Machiavelli advises the ruler to be both "a lion and a fox." Put in plain terms, this means that a ruler must be utterly pragmatic with the final goal of maintaining his rule at any cost.

23. **(C)** The wedding of Ferdinand and Isabella, in 1469, brought together the two most important Spanish states, Castile and Aragon. Spain may be considered unified, at least in terms of the modern concept of the cultural and political nation-state, from that date on. Previously, Spain had been two relatively autonomous kingdoms connected by culture and occasional political necessity.

24. **(B)** Calvin had written that "predestination," the concept that those who are destined to achieve eternal salvation have already been predetermined by God, "is the eternal decree of God."

25. **(B)** Elizabeth hesitated a long time before joining the Netherlands in their fight against Spain. To prevent Spain from becoming too powerful, she finally did assist the Dutch. This alliance was fleeting, and was based more upon Elizabeth's desire to maintain a balance of power on the Continent than any policy of permanent alliances.

26. **(B)** According to mercantile theory, a country's status was determined by the amount of gold (and to a lesser extent, silver) it had in its treasury. Possession of colonies and a favorable balance of trade were both factors in bringing in hard currency.

27. **(A)** Although France remained quite strong as a world power, the Grand Alliance of Great Britain, Russia, and Austria defeated Napoleon at Leipzig (October 1813) and was able to check France's expansionist ambitions, ultimately defeating Napoleon completely at Waterloo, 1815.

28. **(B)** The divine right theory ruled that kings received their authority directly from God and were his representatives on earth.

29. **(B)** James I (1566–1625) ascended to the throne of England at the death of Elizabeth I in 1603. He had ruled Scotland as James VI and began the Stuart reign in England. He brought with him his belief in the divine right of monarchs. Elizabeth also seemed to hold this belief but because of the financial state of the crown and her own precarious claim to the throne early in her reign, she made certain never to act upon this belief as James did. This statement was made in 1609.

30. **(A)** *Assignats* were supposedly backed by land and would therefore not depreciate; very shortly, however, they suffered the fate of most fiat money, becoming less and less valuable.

31. **(C)** The sans culottes were the popular force behind the Jacobins; they were a heterogeneous group identified more by their dress and speech patterns than by either income or education. A. Sobul (a French Marxist historian) believes that they were used by the upper middle class as shock troops against the aristocracy and then destroyed when the bourgeoisie had achieved its goals.

32. **(C)** This letter can be seen as part of the Luddite (named after their mythical leader "General Ludd" or "King Ludd") reaction to the new factories that were being opened in the west of England. The Luddite movement itself was as much a response to the decline in exports as a result of the blockades of 1810–1811 as it was a movement against mechanization of the factory.

33. **(B)** According to E. P. Thompson in *Making of the English Working Class*, threats were made against both the factory owners and the shearmen who worked for them. The net result was, in the short term, some slowdown in mechanization, but it was ultimately not very effective against the growth of industrialization.

34. **(D)** The Whig school has been associated with the concept of "inevitable" progress. Whig historians have pointed out that measures such as the Reform Bills of 1832 and 1867 were examples of the inevitable march of democratic progress. Critics of Whig history describe the school as being too accepting of whatever happened as good and minimizing the problems associated with the events being considered.

35. **(C)** These are the opening lines of Karl Marx's *Communist Manifesto* published in 1848. As 1848 was a revolutionary year throughout Europe (a fact Alexis de Toqueville had predicted a few years earlier), Marx's allusion to a "spectre haunting Europe" was most appropriate.

36. **(B)** With the Whig Party in power, this reform act extended voting rights to middle-class industrialists. In addition, rotten boroughs—those which had lost population but not their representation in Parliament—lost either one or both of their M.P.s.

37. **(A)** Jeremy Bentham (1748–1832) wrote that public problems could be solved scientifically and rationally. His ideas greatly influenced John Stuart Mill (1806–1873), the great advocate of political liberalism during the Age of Romanticism.

38. **(D)** Baron Georges Haussmann was Napoleon III's prefect (1851–1870) in charge of Paris. Under his administration, Paris changed into a new city. Haussmann's changes were not without controversy and opposition. Haussmann was accused of enriching his friends, making rents too high for ordinary people, and designing the wide boulevards so as to make revolutions less possible.

39. **(D)** Between the 1860s and the 1920s, the average number of children in a British family decreased from six to two. The most important reason was the desire to improve the family's economic and social status. Children were no longer seen as an economic asset; in fact, they were viewed as a definite obstacle to "getting ahead."

40. **(D)** Charles Darwin (1809–1882) was unquestionably the most important of all nineteenth-century writers on evolution. His work *On the Origin of the Species by the Means of Natural Selection* was published in 1859. Herbert Spencer (1820–1903) applied Darwin's ideas to human society and coined the phrase "survival of the fittest."

41. **(B)** Adolf Thiers, President of the Third Republic (1851–1870) in France, was referring to opposition from the right (monarchists) and from the left (radicals and others who remained adherents to the Commune). Thiers led an attack upon the Commune in 1871 and brutally crushed the "Communards."

42. **(B)** After 1867, political parties became more modern. Old techniques for winning elections (i.e., the traditional Tory appeal to the landed gentry of agricultural protectionism) were seen to be inadequate; they were replaced by championing (or at least appearing to champion, as Disraeli would discover in 1868) causes such as enfranchisement of the working class and labor reform measures. To the surprise of their "betters," the new voters behaved quite responsibly and took their voting rights seriously.

43. **(B)** Dr. Karl Lueger was mayor of Vienna from 1897 to 1910. He appealed to the lower middle class which believed its position in society was deteriorating. Lueger pointed to the Jews as bearers of ultramodern and alien ideas.

44. **(C)** The Boxer Rebellion (1900–1901) began with an attack upon Christian missionaries in northern China. Two hundred were killed; several thousand Chinese converts to Christianity were also killed. The combined western forces (United States, France, Germany, and England) inflicted on China a severe defeat; China was forced to pay a very large indemnity.

45. **(C)** Between 1870 and 1910, emigration of Europeans increased fairly steadily. In Italy, where poverty was endemic in the rural south, emigration affected almost every village. In Germany, on the other hand, where industrialization provided economic opportunities, emigration declined after 1880.

46. **(D)** Although there were attempts at rapprochements, especially during the presidency of Jules Ferry, the wounds that remained from the war of 1870–1871 were too great to permit an alliance between these two countries.

47. **(D)** After Bismarck's dismissal, Wilhelm refused to renew the Reinsurance Treaty with Russia. It did not make sense to Wilhelm to be allies with both Austria and Russia who had rival claims in the Balkans. Russia, therefore, saw Germany as a menace on its borders and sought an alliance with France.

48. **(D)** Both the Ottoman and Austrian empires were believed to be in serious decay. Both had extreme troubles with subject nationalities.

49. **(E)** In 1930, Sydney Fay, in his work *The Origins of the First World War*, wrote that " . . . all the European countries, in a greater or lesser degree, were responsible."

50. **(D)** At the outbreak of war, Italy abandoned her allies in the Triple Alliance and declared her neutrality. About a year later, having been promised the spoils of war carved out of territory held by Austria, Italy entered the war on the side of the Allies.

51. **(D)** Nationally unified governments established planning boards to fight a "total war." Price controls, rationing, and other methods of regimenting the economy were imposed by the belligerents.

52. **(C)** The short-lived Provisional Government granted civil liberties and civil rights very quickly. These reforms included freedom of speech (at least compared to the previous regime); the return and release of many exiles; planned elections by universal manhood suffrage; and land redistribution to the peasants—benefiting Lenin and the Bolshevik Party as well as the rest of the population at large.

53. **(B)** Lenin believed that even in an agrarian society a revolution could succeed if it were made by a highly disciplined party led by ruthless revolutionaries. After his return to Russia in April 1917, he refused to cooperate at all with the Provisional Government.

54. **(B)** Great Britain was represented by David Lloyd George, the United States by Woodrow Wilson, Italy by Vittorio Orlando, and France by Georges Clemenceau.

55. **(A)** The area of the world in which Russia, Germany, and Britain all had spheres of influence was China.

56. **(B)** All these scientists not only challenged long held views but replaced the fixed, orderly Newtonian system with "uncertainty."

57. **(B)** Walter Gropius (1883–1969) and Ludwig Mies van der Rohe (1886–1969) were two directors of the Bauhaus, one of the main centers of instruction for modern art and architecture, founded in Germany in 1919.

58. **(C)** Futurism was mainly an Italian movement, active between 1909 and 1914. Their manifesto decried all forms of conservatism and ridiculed critics. They saw violence as a method of emotional expression and purification. Some became associated with the Fascist government after 1922.

59. **(B)** Sergei Eisenstein (1898–1948) created many epic films for the Soviet government. According to Soviet philosophy, art was intended to serve the state.

60. **(E)** Keynes's book had great influence in Britain, where it would become the bible for the concept of direct government involvement in the economy and therefore, indirectly, the Welfare State, and in the United States (i.e., Roosevelt's New Deal program). He argued that a healthy German economy would benefit all European nations.

61. **(D)** The 1925 Locarno Agreements settled boundary disputes between Germany and France, and Poland and Czechoslovakia, among other questions.

62. **(E)** Lenin introduced his New Economic Policy (NEP) in 1921 in an attempt to bolster agriculture and industry. Factories were not operating, farms were not producing food fast enough and starvation was spreading. This was the result of severe drought, the "war on communism" from outside forces, the ravages of World War I, terror brought on by the civil war itself, and Lenin's miscalculation on the state of Russian industry. Heavy industry, however, remained in the hands of the state.

63. **(C)** The Popular Front won the election of 1936. The Socialist Party Leader, Léon Blum headed the new government. The effects of this political change were felt both internally in the passing of pro-union legislation, and externally as Stalin, through the Comintern, allowed communist parties throughout Europe to support Social Democratic movements he once claimed were greater threats to communism than the capitalists.

64. **(B)** The Nazi revolution involved the masses. Rallies, media, and all institutions in the state were designed to include the largest number of people as participants—at least passive—in the regime. In Italy too, organizations to control leisure time were set up. This was a change from the absolutist regimes of the seventeenth century (e.g., Louis XVI, "I am the state"), which ran independently and were unconcerned with the population at large.

65. **(B)** Peasants burned crops, killed livestock, and destroyed farm implements to protest forced collectivization (the taking over of previously private farmland by the state). By 1932, 60 percent of the Russian peasants had been "collectivized"; between 1932 and 1938, more than 90 percent of the peasantry had been transferred onto collective farms. Starvation killed millions of Russians between 1929 and 1932.

66. **(B)** Opportunities for women in professions increased dramatically under Stalin. By 1950, 75 percent of the doctors in the Soviet Union were women.

67. **(A)** The Lateran Treaty of 1929 gave official recognition to Catholicism as the state religion in Italy. The Vatican was recognized as an independent state. In return, the Holy See gave its support to the Fascist regime. As with Napoleon's Concordat, friction between the Church and State was not ended by these agreements.

68. **(D)** In the five elections for the Reichstag held between 1928 and 1933, no one party was able to achieve a majority. Coalition governments seemed unable to take strong measures to deal with the growing economic problems affecting Germany.

69. **(C)** Public works projects begun by Hitler, which put millions of Germans to work, included the construction of the new highway system (*Autobahns*), sports stadiums, and public housing. In addition, after 1936, Germany began a program of rearmament.

70. **(B)** Hitler began his program of genocide in 1941 when Jews from all over Europe came under his power. The Final Solution was the murder of every Jewish person, including very young children, in Europe. Historians still debate whether this program originally included actual genocide or only the planned enslavement of the Jewish people.

71. **(B)** Rudyard Kipling (1865–1936) first used the term, "the white man's burden" in his poem of the same name. The French considered their civilizing mission a "sacred duty." A modern debate on imperialism concerns the supposed failure of the liberal middle class to prevent imperialism as they were supposed advocates of free trade.

72. **(A)** In return for a promise of pro-Soviet governments established in eastern Europe, whereby elections would be held but dominated by Moscow-approved communist parties, Stalin agreed to enter the war against Japan within three months of victory in Europe. Japan's surrender came before Soviet troops were engaged.

73. **(B)** The Soviet Union began a blockade of Berlin in 1948. For 324 days, airplanes from the United States and other nations flew in supplies to the people of Berlin until the Soviets ended the blockade.

74. **(B)** The Labour Government had decided to withdraw from India as soon as possible; the major obstacle to decolonization was the question of whether there should be a separate Muslim state. In 1948, the British withdrew from Palestine, Burma, and Sri Lanka (Ceylon, at the time).

75. **(C)** General de Gaulle was elected first president of the Fifth Republic and given strong powers by the French voters. He used those powers to grant Algeria its independence in 1963.

76. **(C)** *The American Challenge* (1967) was the title of a book by the French author Jean-Jaques Servan-Screiber. The "brain drain" was causing Europe to fall behind the United States. Europe needed to spend more on research and development, he argued.

77. **(C)** Between 1850 and 1950, the percentage of family income the average European spent on food dropped from over 60 percent to less than 40 percent. The decline of employment opportunities in domestic service, the electrification of the rural areas, the increased mobilization of the working class, and the increase of installment credit are all true of Europe after World War II.

78. **(D)** As women have become more independent and less rigidly confined to traditional roles, relationships between the sexes have become less structured.

79. **(C)** Europe, as Germany complained, did not disarm following World War I. In addition, Article X of the League Charter provided a mechanism for the enforcement of its decisions. The League of Nations was also associated with a western European ascendancy that no longer was linked to the new political and social realities of central and eastern Europe (the exclusion of Germany until 1926 and Russia until 1934 helped discredit the League).

80. **(C)** The Bolsheviks signed the costly separate peace with Germany in March 1918 and Russia withdrew from World War I. Germany was then able to shift her troops from the eastern to the western front.